Standing at Lemhi Pass

Andrea + Stephen
Happy Trails
Scott

Standing at Lemhi Pass
Archetypal Stories for the End of Life and Other Challenging Times

Scott Janssen

ISBN-13: 978-1543067620
ISBN-10: 154306762X

Thus, storytelling – from wherever it comes – forms a layer in the foundation of the world; and glinting in it we can see the trace elements of every tribe on earth.

Frank Delaney

Introduction

As Teddy Roosevelt rushed into his New York City apartment in February of 1884, the twenty-four-year-old politician had no idea that his world was about to shatter. He'd hurried home from Albany after receiving an urgent telegram that things were not well. His wife Alice had just given birth to their first child and was near death in one room. His mother was dying in another. His mother died first. Her once powerful vitality snuffed out like a spent candle. Alice hung on for a few more hours. The deaths left Roosevelt reeling and in shock. The personal journal he'd kept for so long came to an abrupt end that day with a final somber entry, "The light has gone out of my life."

Roosevelt was not one to sit still in his grief. After the funerals he left his infant daughter in the care of his sister and plunged back into his work as a state Assemblyman, attempting to outrun his pain. When he found it impossible to outrun something he was carrying in his heart, he left politics altogether, retreating into the rugged Bad Lands of North Dakota for the rigors and distractions of running a western cattle ranch. He worked to exhaustion, went on long solitary rides and wrote a memorial to his wife. He found that the melancholy sound of doves cooing in the scrubby cottonwoods expressed "more than any other sound in nature the sadness of gentle, hopeless, never-ending grief." Eventually sadness loosened its grip amidst the vast, uncluttered landscape.

Though it's common to remember Roosevelt storming San Juan Hill or pontificating from his bully pulpit, it is in the times of his grief – and there were many – that he is most human. The death of a loved one can send tremors to the core of our being, casting doubt on the future and raising questions about who we are and what's important. It reminds us of life's fragility and the need to tend to what matters most.

It is in his struggle to heal that Roosevelt's status as an exalted historical figure dissolves and he becomes someone with whom we can empathize and relate. In telling this part of his story we may find wisdom, solace, and strength. In its most elemental form history is an exploration of the human story and a reflection on how people have made sense of things and dealt with the uncertainty of the times in which they have lived. At its most inspiring, it is a reflection on how people have withstood, even thrived, during times of crisis. What could be more relevant to people living the final weeks or months of their lives, or to their loved ones?

History is full of stories illustrating the ways others, even those who lived long ago, have dealt with the same kinds of challenges we all face at one time or another. Reflecting on their lives connects us with those who have walked similar paths and borne similar burdens. In remembering history, we find insights as well as cautionary tales. We may even feel the silent accompaniment of those who emerge as kindred spirits to inspire or comfort.

Stories – whether from history or other sources – have forever been repositories for deep and enduring truths. In many societies storytellers have been healers, history-keepers and sacred figures whose tales bridge the divide between the earthly and unseen realms. Diverse cultures have used narratives in the form of myths, songs, poems, oral histories, dream visions and folktales as essential building blocks for personal and communal identity.

In a sense, stories are a bridge into the inner world of our psyches. Even the simplest stories can contain profound wisdom and archetypal truths which can be conveyed in familiar images and language. As we follow the trials of heroes and protagonists we may, as Joseph Campbell put it, discover our own inner hero as we face difficult challenges, changes and losses.

At the end of life, there can be great value in hearing and telling stories. Sometimes these are simply stories patients tell themselves or confidantes about the lives they have lived. Those of us working with the elderly or serving those who are terminally ill have long recognized and encouraged this impulse toward life review.

There is also value in offering stories to those who are dying and their caregivers. A good story can help us see and assimilate truths about our life and circumstances from a comfortable distance, at a safe pace. We are free to identify with central characters and events yet remain separated by time and context. From the days we were children stories have engaged the creative power of our imaginations and helped us visualize new ways of being. This creative power remains with us until our final breath and can be unlocked by the sharing of stories.

For someone with little energy, facing long days in a hospital bed, a story can come as a pleasant respite during which one can simply close one's eyes and listen. Some stories serve by distracting or entertaining. Others do far more, enhancing perspective, altering troubling thoughts and beliefs, loosening painful emotions, fostering connection. In his book *101 Healing Stories: Using Metaphors in Therapy*, psychologist George Burns contends that offering the right story to someone who is suffering may evoke positive emotions, inspire, encourage personal growth and provide new metaphors and ways of understanding which become a fulcrum for healing and positive change.

Though stories can come from virtually anywhere, the focus of this book is on how they can be found in American history; a realization which came to me years ago while working with a sixty-eight-year-old woman who was dying of bone cancer.

Rose was ferociously independent and had refused to accept help from her daughter Tamara because she was convinced that doing so would make her a "useless burden." For months she fought the steady momentum of her illness but when she became weak and unsteady on her feet, she had no choice. Tamara had moved into her apartment and, as Rose put it, "started changing my damn diapers."

Though self-conscious and at times resentful, Rose found that surrendering arduous tasks and responsibilities conserved energy she'd been using dressing herself and managing medications. She now used this energy to have conversations with family and friends. On one visit she was reflecting on the paradox of how her emaciated body had become weak and uncooperative but her spirit – which she felt in her connection with God, her courage and the love she had for Tamara – had grown stronger.

She searched for words and images to describe this paradox but couldn't find any with enough richness and texture to satisfy her. As she spoke, I remembered an anecdote about the bus boycott in Montgomery, Alabama, in the 1950s, when African American citizens protesting the racial segregation of public transportation refused to ride the city's buses. It was one of the seminal events of the civil rights movement. Rose had often spoken about attending civil rights marches in the 1960s and I wondered if the story might offer a metaphor of her experience.

I told her about an elderly woman weary from many months of walking to work rather than taking the bus. Fatigue showed in her bent frame and slow gait. At one of the rallies after a long day, Martin Luther King, Jr. spoke to her. Acknowledging her fidelity and commitment to their cause, he told her there would be no reproach if she started riding the buses again. When she told him she would keep walking he asked if she was tired. She responded, "My feet are tired but my soul is rested."

Rose smiled softly. She knew the story but hadn't thought about its metaphorical quality. She repeated the phrase as though it had sacred power. For a few minutes we talked about the woman's fatigue and the ardors of walking to work every day. Beneath the old woman's exhaustion was a core of unpretentious strength and what Rose called "spirit peace." The story underscored some of the emerging truths of Rose's experience: her life had innate value and inner strength was more substantive than physical strength.

Weeks later, during my last visit, Rose slept as Tamara and I spoke at her bedside. Her respirations were shallow and blood pressure weak. Tamara knew she was dying. We talked about Rose's life and the ups and downs of their relationship. As I prepared to leave, Rose opened her eyes and looked at us.

"Want some water Mama?" Tamara asked. Rose didn't respond.

"Uncle Shawn came by while you were sleeping. He'll be back tonight." When Rose smiled Tamara filled her in on some of the neighborhood gossip. Rose looked at her quietly, too weak to speak.

When Tamara reached the end of her update, Rose closed her eyes as if preparing to return to the deep transitional sleep that often comes when someone is near death. Before she did, I asked her a final question.

"Rose, is there anything you want Tamara to know before you go back to sleep?"

She opened her eyes and looked at her daughter. In a whisper, she said, "My feet are tired." Then she looked at me.

"But my soul is rested," I whispered. As she drifted back to sleep, she smiled again. The story had remained with her, illuminating and affirming her journey.

Rose's story is representative of the chapters that follow. Each introduces a family dealing with terminal illness and identifies places they found themselves getting stuck. In each of these 'stuck places' a story is offered from American history as an analogy or metaphor intended to broadened perspective on the situation. As with Rose whose involvement in the civil rights movement made it likely the story about Montgomery would be one with which she would identify, these stories were chosen not simply because they contain a specific theme or meaning, but because there is something likely to resonate with a particular person or family.

4

The chapters are arranged into five parts: Finding Meaning; Facing the Past; Staying Connected; Letting Go; and Moving On. Details have been changed in the interests of privacy and a few of the stories are composites.

In the process of distilling the complex, often enigmatic stuff of history into short narratives, my focus has been on finding a thread which speaks in a meaningful way to a particular situation but also contains universal truths about the human experience. While writing this book I've had the advantage of supplementing these stories, originally drawn from memory, with enough fact-checking to offer what I hope are reliable accounts. Historical interpretation, as with life, is a fluid and changeable process, large enough to accommodate many, often discordant, viewpoints. Whatever my limitations as a historian, I have always tried to draw interpretations that are true in a deeper sense in that they illuminate places within and beyond our immediate field of vision that might otherwise have remained in shadow. When direct quotes from historical accounts are used I have modernized spelling, punctuation and grammar in the interests of narrative flow.

Throughout this book themes emerge such as the inextinguishable power of human resilience, the omnipresence of paradox and a common longing for love and connection. In the end, the main theme is simple: Life is a journey and we are all imperfect travelers doing the best we can. Along the way there will be hard times that leave us afraid and confused, perhaps filled with sadness or anger. At such times, we endure and grow stronger if we hold fast to our most compassionate personal and transcendent truths, honoring and supporting those we love. It is my hope that this blending of stories will offer the reader insight for his or her travels. During difficult times, or simply times when we pause to reflect on how we are living our lives and what it means to be human, may one of these stories alight and give comfort.

Section One
Invincible Summer
Finding Meaning

*In the midst of winter, I finally learned that
there was in me an invincible summer.*

Albert Camus

The diagnosis of a potentially fatal illness turns our lives upside down. Suddenly the future seems fraught with uncertainty. Familiar roles, routines, plans we have made, are thrown into flux. Intense thoughts and emotions stir like heavy winds knocking us off balance. Profound questions arise, sometimes at the center of our awareness, sometimes along the periphery. Why is this happening? How can I find strength for the way ahead? What is most important right now? How can I find peace? What is death? What will happen to my loved ones when I'm gone?

For some, these thoughts and feelings are unwelcome visitors insinuating themselves into previously orderly lives and wreaking havoc. Many try avoiding them or pretending nothing has changed. Others plunge into the currents searching for peace, perspective, forgiveness, hoping to use what time remains wisely.

Whatever our response, unsettling thoughts and emotional pain are likely to ebb and flow alongside joy, hope, laughter and love. We may label those things that distress us as negative and try to suppress or minimize them but, like love and hope, they are a part of our path. Often the harder we try to escape our sadness the more powerful and adaptable it becomes. These things are not our enemies and it can take more energy to avoid painful thoughts and emotions than it does to make peace with them.

Some are surprised to find that their vulnerability can become an avenue toward important insights, greater self-compassion and an increased sense of connection. However difficult the circumstances, opportunities for growth and meaning always abound, manifesting perhaps in deeper empathy for the suffering of another or an enhanced appreciation for simple moments of closeness, love or beauty. The lessons we learn at such times can be transformative. In fact, they can endure beyond death bringing comfort to those who grieve. The stories in this section underscore this theme.

Chapter One
Child of the Sun
Growth Within Suffering

After Robert's back surgery, his doctor told him to stay off his feet while he recuperated. He may as well have instructed him to float through the air or dance on the head of a pin. It was hard for him to sit still under the best of circumstances and these were among the worst. Weeks earlier, he'd injured his back while working as a security guard at a local shopping mall. Money was tight so, in addition to his job as a police officer, he'd been working there part-time.

The timing couldn't have been worse. His wife, Sandy, had developed a repetitive motion injury in one of her wrists and had temporarily left her job as a medical transcriptionist. Robert would be out of commission for several weeks and was getting the run around about his workman's compensation claim. They were both in pain and the bills were piling up. As if this weren't enough, Robert's mother, Tess, had been diagnosed with lung cancer and moved in with them when the rest home where she'd been living said they could no longer meet her increased needs. He and his wife had searched for another facility with a higher level of care but they were unable to afford the cost.

Robert was an energetic, muscular man whose kindness was often camouflaged by mercurial sarcasm and a style of black-and-white thinking that quickly divided the world and its inhabitants into simple, inflexible categories – good versus bad, strong versus weak, sane versus insane. Back pain and regular doses of tramadol hadn't muted his bustling energy. At times, as he lay on the couch trying to stay still, he seemed like a pressurized barrel about to fly apart.

As for his mother, he was quick to inform me that cancer was the least of her worries. In fact, she seemed unperturbed by her diagnosis, insisting that her physician had been tricked by "the mist." As far as she was concerned, she was perfectly healthy. When I asked Robert what Tess meant by the mist he rolled his eyes and threw his hands up, "Mom has schizophrenia," he said, as though it wasn't worth talking about. "She's always lost in the mist."

Schizophrenia is a complex mental illness about which Robert had become an informal expert. Although it affects people differently, the disease has some common features. In Tess's case these included delusions, compulsive behaviors, hallucinations and illogical thought processes. Although antipsychotic medication had helped her maintain a delicate balance she, as I was to find out, occasionally felt threatened by the concerns of her inner world.

For as long as Robert could remember his and Tess's lives had been punctuated by times of crisis. As a child he'd been afraid to make friends lest they find out something was wrong with his mother. His father had expected him to be secretive about family matters, soothe his mother when she became anxious, and accept without question her odd demands and compulsive personal rituals. "She had a ritual for everything," he remembered. "One when she got out of bed, another before she went to sleep and probably twenty more throughout the day." Without siblings to divide the weight of his parent's complex demands, Robert's early life had been stressful and confusing.

His mother had expected him to accept beliefs and behaviors even a child could see were bizarre. If he didn't comply with her requests her reactions could be dramatic. "She might have thought I was under the influence of the devil," he recalled, "or that my body had been taken over by evil spirits." Even as a child he worried that if he went along with her he'd become lost in an alternate world of delusion from which there would be no escape. On the other hand, if he didn't comply, things might escalate quickly into chaos. His solution had been to placate Tess by appearing to go along with her while inwardly giving little or no credibility to her words or behavior.

When his father died from a heart attack when Robert was only seventeen it was a crushing loss. His father had been like a lighthouse guarding treacherous reefs and shoals. "Whenever things got out of control I'd look up and see Dad, steady and solid." At the time, Robert had been visualizing ways to leave home and start a new life. Suddenly he'd become solely responsible for looking after his mother.

Tess's grief had been so all-consuming that Robert had put his own aside. Her already disorganized thoughts became a cacophony of jumbled suspicions and bizarre speculation. Where was her husband? Who had kidnapped him? Why wouldn't anybody tell her the truth? She couldn't comprehend that he was dead. When she began retreating into the root cellar for hours on end, Robert was at his wits end. "She was convinced Dad was hiding down there in a secret chamber and she could communicate with him telepathically."

Robert's father had driven home the need to protect Tess from the scrutiny of others (in fact, she hadn't yet been diagnosed with schizophrenia) but for a young man confronted with such complicated responsibilities it had been overwhelming. He agonized over whether to seek help, knowing that doing so violated a fundamental family rule. Finally, after much anguish and self-criticism, he called the sheriff.

Though fearful of his mother's response and of losing control of what happened to her, he'd been relieved to shed the lonely burden of their family secret. Looking back, he saw this as a turning point. "I just shut myself down till I was numb to her," he said. "I decided Mom was crazy and I needed to treat her that way from there on out. I just stopped taking anything she said seriously or letting her make her own decisions about anything important. I was the sane one, she was crazy."

It was a decision that had ossified into a cold personal truth as, in the ensuing years, his mother had bounced between family care homes and psychiatric hospitals. In fact, Robert became so detached that each new crisis became a bland routine in which he was more observer than participant. Amid the well-ordered halls of the state psychiatric hospital, he stopped thinking of Tess as his mother struggling with schizophrenia and began thinking of her as a schizophrenic who happened to be his mother. Her illness defined everything.

Viewing her life as a bundle of symptoms clustered around a mental illness had taken pressure off of him to fix things. It was something he couldn't control and for which he was not responsible. He no longer second-guessed himself or wondered if he had done something that had triggered his mother's behavior, no longer had to walk the fine line of taking seriously what he called her "crazy talk" without getting drawn into a surreal world of unreality. Instead, he could detach himself and respond with the coolness of a stranger. Taking his mother seriously in any way, he believed, would only "encourage her and get you into trouble."

While this perspective had protected him from the emotional gyrations that had haunted his youth, he'd lost something as well. Beneath the clatter of Tess's alternate world was an enduring flame of love, creativity and humanity – the essence of who she really was. Despite her delusions and hallucinations, she was kind and generous, filled with compassion for those who suffered. For Robert, this dimension of his mother's life had disappeared beneath the perplexing shadow-world of her schizophrenia.

Though Tess needed help with daily tasks she was able to move around the house with the help of a walker. She was congenial and liked to laugh. Her round face was effervescent and expressive and she fidgeted constantly as she talked. Initially, she was cautious about answering questions, asking several times if the hospital had sent me to bring her back. Despite her suspicions, she was soon at ease and came to relish the opportunity to talk about her life.

She seemed unfazed by the events around her, in part because Robert and Sandy had insulated her in a blanket of routine and predictability. She didn't know money was tight or the extent of Robert's physical pain. She seemed unaware that her moving in had turned her son's life upside down. She flatly rejected any notion that she had cancer. Her days were alive, however, with drama of another sort.

Once comfortable with my visits, she drew a vivid and textured picture of her extraordinary inner world. She said she received messages regularly from the voice of a spirit she called the King. Faces appeared on the walls of her room and she was convinced her caged songbird was a feathery friend through which she communicated with higher beings.

She believed the people of the world belonged to a single family that was lost in the mist – an imperceptible haze of negative energy separating each person from his or her most advanced state of spiritual development. In her mind, a great cosmic war was being fought between forces that wished to strengthen the mist and those that wanted to see it disappear. She believed she was an important ally of the King who was leading the fight against the mist.

Although her world was full of what most would regard as strange sensations and enigmatic ways of thinking, in its center was an oasis of latent sanity. She had a warm, genuine desire to help others. "Every time I make someone laugh," she said, "the mist gets a little bit weaker."

I encouraged Robert to join Tess and me during our visits but he preferred to speak privately. His interactions with her were minimal and revolved around practicalities like what she wanted for lunch and when it was time to take her medications. His primary concern was making sure she was comfortable for whatever time she had left. It was one area, at least, over which he had some control.

My visits developed a pattern. I'd spend time with Tess, getting a sense of how things were going and assessing for any concerns then Robert and I would talk. As was the case with his mother, he was initially reluctant to share much but, maybe because he had so much time on his hands, he soon began using the time to reflect on his current circumstances. A tough-guy cop, he told me his fellow officers called him Conquistador, a nickname given by a friend from Central America who worked in the motor pool. The conquistadors were tough, battle-hardened men who, in the sixteenth century, conquered much of the Americas for the Spanish Empire. He was proud of the nickname. It captured how he saw himself and how he wanted to be seen by others.

He admitted, however, that the back pain was getting to him and he wasn't feeling much like a conqueror. He was starting to worry he might not be able to return to his job. He was losing his temper with Sandy and, somewhat self-consciously, confessed he was sliding into "the blues."

Over the next weeks he began losing interest in things and started gaining weight. His considerable energy slackened beneath the gravity of burdensome thoughts and it was harder to see beyond the unhappiness of his immediate experience. The categories into which he'd divided the world – strong versus weak, sane versus insane – began to lose their meaning. He no longer felt strong, and, as his depression intensified, he wondered whether he was sane. This suffering became the solvent into which his timeworn categories dissolved, leaving him confused and disoriented. He felt "useless" and worried that he was a burden to his wife who "has to take care of me and Mom even though she's hurting too."

With Sandy's encouragement, he spoke to his doctor and agreed to try an anti-depressant. It was a big step. Not just because of his stalwart intention to do things without asking for help, but because his mother's hit-or-miss experiences with psychotropic medications had given him an intense distrust of all drugs. He found, however, that although it was no panacea for his emotional pain, the medicine gave him a reserve of energy with which to deal with things more constructively.

One visit Robert surprised me by asking if he could join Tess and I. "I guess I just want to see how she's doing with all that's going on," he said, fidgeting nervously as I helped him up from the couch. I asked about his change of heart and he told me he'd been thinking about many things lately, including the fact that Tess would not be around much longer. Chronic back pain had taken much away, but it had given him time to think about things that were important. And depression – something which he'd previously associated with mental weakness – was giving him a new compassion for Tess's battle with mental illness.

After some initial awkwardness he and Tess settled into a playfully oppositional style of sharing memories and reflecting on their lives together. Neither was willing to surrender his or her version of events, but each indulged the other in his or her recollections. From then on, our visits were spent jointly. When she could, Sandy sat with us and offered her perspective as they sifted through the complex strata of shared experiences. These visits became a time when they could talk openly, acknowledge the challenges and affirm the strength of their enduring bond.

Slowly, Robert's staunch refusal to let Tess's delusions go unchallenged relaxed. He learned to suspend his impulses to correct her and instead, tentatively, entered his mother's world – exploring its unique dimensions without attempting to orient her to his version of reality. In doing so, he rediscovered the wellspring of kindness and love beneath the hallucinations and delusions.

One day he and I were standing on the front porch at the end of a visit. He recalled that when he was a kid, no matter how chaotic things had gotten his mother had always found ways to let him know that she loved him.

"I'd forgotten about that until the other day."

"What reminded you?" I asked.

He wasn't sure, but such spontaneous memories were happening more frequently. He had opened his heart and allowed himself to be vulnerable. By doing so, it seemed, lost memories were able to float up from the depths of forgotten experience and deliver important messages about his connection with his mother.

"What does the part of you that has stored these memories know about your mother that the rest of you had forgotten?" I asked.

He swallowed hard, "She has such a big heart."

As Tess's condition deteriorated she slept more and had less stamina for conversation, often becoming short of breath. Robert, on the other hand, began to feel less pain and was able to move around more freely. Although he continued to contend with psychological pain, it was less enveloping. He cut down on his pain medication, hoping to restore even more of his energy.

13

Inwardly, he was wrestling with an embryonic realization. Something inside him was different but he wasn't sure what. He knew this intuitively though he wasn't sure he liked it. His formerly rigid views about his mother, himself, and the world no longer seemed to work. Things, it seemed, were more multifaceted and no longer fit into the neatly crafted mental boxes that had always been so convenient and reassuring. It was as though he had been washed up on some strange land far from familiar paths or landmarks, uncertain of his bearings.

"When I hurt my back," he said, "it got me thinking about what it's like to have things happen to you that you can't control. Thinking about how hard life can be."

He saw parallels between his struggles and Tess's – a pervasive sense of vulnerability, losing control and seeing one's life unexpectedly career off course. He'd felt the eruption of powerful emotions and labored with the irrational thoughts that sometimes accompanied them (something he'd previously viewed with judgment when such things had thrown his mother off balance). He'd also learned what it meant to rely on medications to feel better and how it felt to sit on the sidelines as others engaged in activities no longer available to him, simple things like having lunch with a friend or driving to the store. He now understood what it was like to have a quiet, inexplicable feeling of otherness, of being in some way different.

He was awed by the realization that while Tess had struggled nearly all of her life with such challenges, they had nearly driven him "off the deep end" in only a few months. His suffering was giving him an animated compassion and sensitivity to the challenges of his mother's life, enhancing appreciation of her resilience and strength.

Though grateful to have a deeper understanding, he was also scared. "It's like I don't know who I am anymore." Old assumptions and beliefs were breaking down and new ones were as yet unformed. Robert's early life had been awash in chaos and uncertainty. To survive he'd carved out a few unbending rules around which he could find stability. One of these rules was that people didn't change. Now, he knew this wasn't true because *he* was changing, shedding old beliefs much like a snake sheds worn-out skin when it's time to grow. Unfortunately, he had no language for what was happening, no stories or images to serve as mileposts as he made his way into unexplored, potentially frightening territory.

Remembering the pride he took in his nickname, I asked if he'd ever heard of Cabeza de Vaca. He laughed and asked if this was one of

Tess's secret messengers. I told him that he was a conquistador of the most tenacious sort. In 1528 Cabeza de Vaca was one of the few survivors of an ill-fated quest for riches in the wilds of Florida. He had endured eight years of unimaginable suffering. By the time it was over he had discarded many fixed ideas about who he was and how the world worked. In the crucible of his backbreaking hardship, he'd found deeper, more fundamental truths than he'd ever imagined.

*

In April 1528, a one-eyed, red-bearded Spaniard named Panfillo de Navarez led three ships carrying some four hundred men into a harbor along the Gulf Coast of Florida near present-day Tampa. His second in command was Alvar Nunez Cabeza de Vaca, a leathery soldier also serving as the expedition's treasurer. It was Cabeza de Vaca's job to keep track of the gold they expected to find when they cut their way through towering forests and cane-filled swamps in search of glory and gold. They saw themselves as strong and noble and they viewed the native inhabitants with disdain. For these Spaniards the world held no subtlety and their beliefs were as inflexible as Castilian steel. They were conquerors. As Cabeza de Vaca gazed out on the coast of Florida he could not have conceived how his suffering during the next several years would shatter these simplistic notions and transform him.

Navarez divided his force. Sending his ships up the coast, he and Cabeza de Vaca marched inland with three hundred conquerors intent on plunder. As they slashed their way through the forest their treatment of Native Americans was brutal. Cabeza de Vaca and his companions considered them to be savages and were no more sensitive to their pain or grief than they would have been to that of a pack mule.

When the conquistadors discovered small amounts of gold their greed was enflamed to a fever pitch. As the clattering band of heavily armed soldiers headed north in search of more, native tribes avoided them as though they were a swarm of bees. The terrain was difficult. Fallen trees, marshes and thickets seemed to block every step. The heat and humidity, combined with lugging heavy weapons and supplies, taxed their strength. Soon the meager rations of biscuits and bacon were depleted and some of the men were reduced to eating palmettos. By the time they reached the land of the Apalachee there were many who, according to Cabeza de Vaca, "besides great fatigue and hunger, had sores on their backs from carrying their weapons in addition to the other things they had to carry."

The Apalachee had no gold but they had plenty of arrows. Beating a hasty retreat amid a flurry of skirmishes, the demoralized soldiers found their way back to the Gulf Coast where they dropped from exhaustion. Their ships were gone. Many were sick and no longer able to work. Some, like Cabeza de Vaca, had been injured. Fifty were dead. The rest were starving. The expedition that had once boldly entered the forest with dreams of conquest and riches was now struggling to survive.

Those who could work set about building barges from fallen pine trees. Though they had no tools and little chance of surviving anything but the most placid seas, they saw no choice but to try sailing for Spanish settlements in Mexico. Six weeks later, they dragged five crude rafts into the Gulf of Mexico. The vessels each held about fifty men and, according to Cabeza de Vaca, were "caulked with palmetto fiber, and we tarred them with a kind of tarry pitch made...from pine trees; and from the same palmetto fiber and the tails and manes of the horses we made cords and rigging, and sails out of our shirts, and from the juniper trees that grew there we made the oars that we believed we needed."

Several weeks later, only two of these waterlogged vessels carrying a handful of woeful survivors washed ashore on a small island they dubbed the Isle of Ill-Fortune (present-day Galveston, Texas). Most, including Cabeza de Vaca, collapsed on the beach so tired that they couldn't move. When they were found by a group of Karankawa Indians, the forlorn party must have looked like some melancholic drift of jetsam splashed up by frigid waters indifferent to their suffering.

Had circumstances been reversed, the Spaniards likely would have been unmoved by the Karankawa's plight but the Indians were sympathetic and eager to help. They brought food and, seeing that the naked, emaciated conquistadors were freezing in the chill November wind, built fires to warm them. Despite these acts of compassion, most of the men who washed ashore died. When an illness swept through the Indian's community and killed half of them, they blamed the Spanish and their kindness turned to wrath. Those few Spaniards remaining were quickly enslaved.

For Cabeza de Vaca it was an inconceivable link in a growing chain of doleful events. He had arrived as a conqueror, favored by God and harbinger of the most powerful nation on earth. Like his companions, he had been aspiring to ascend the social hierarchy through glorious conquest. Once he and his fellow Spaniards had debated whether

Indians were even human, now he was in bondage to them. Any assumptions he had held about himself or his future not already obliterated by months of punishing hardship must have been whisked away like salty spray dispersed in a winter gale.

Cabeza de Vaca was separated from his friends and his life became a monotone of privation and anguish. Reduced to the sad anonymity of a slave, he subsisted on thin seasonal fare such as berries, cacti, fish and nuts. At times, he was immersed in water for so long digging for edible roots that the mere touch of a twig or blade of grass was enough to lacerate his skin. He endured humiliation, ill-treatment and unrelenting hunger. Assailed by a skin-sizzling sun, plagued by bloodthirsty mosquitoes and nearly freezing in the cold of winter, his former life must have seemed like a surreal hallucination. Finally, unable to bear it any longer, he escaped to the mainland of Texas.

Here he learned that as an outsider with no tribal affiliation he posed little threat to neighboring tribes and could travel in peace. So he became a trader, carrying goods such as shells, snails and beads from the coast, exchanging them further inland for pelts, dyes, flint and ornaments. "Everywhere I went," he said, "they gave me good treatment and food on account of my merchandise."

Although his circumstances had improved, they were far from desirable. Hunger was constant as was danger from harsh storms, cold nights, predatory animals and withering heat. He also had to contend with the psychological suffering of being separated from his home and family, adrift in a strange land, uncertain of survival, strangely alone.

Somehow he reunited with the three other survivors of Navarez's fatal debacle and the four decided to try to make their way overland to Mexico. They must have cast a bizarre, otherworldly shadow as they traveled together speaking in a strange tongue, communicating with Indians through hand signs and fragments of native dialect. Coming from a land behind the eastern horizon and belonging to no tribe, their scraggly beards and unfamiliar skin pigmentation branded them with an inescapable otherness.

Word spread that these outlandish strangers had supernatural powers and could cure the sick and injured. When Indians began arriving seeking help, the surprised Spaniards offered prayers, genuflected a few times and blew on each petitioner in his or her turn. Amazingly, Cabeza de Vaca reports that time and again Indians from diverse tribes found relief from their afflictions after these simple ministrations.

As they traveled from one village to another, great crowds of people began following them in a long human caravan. Celebrations were held everywhere they went. Grateful Indians showered them with whatever gifts they could offer which the Spaniards distributed among their followers.

Cabeza de Vaca had come as a warrior, intent on pillaging this New World and subjugating its people. After descending into the humiliations of slavery and losing everything that had been the bedrock of his identity, the Indians hailed him as a healer and bringer of peace. The befuddled Spaniard had ceased being a conqueror and had been transformed by his suffering into what the Indians called a "child of the sun," a holy man capable of penetrating the veil of the heavens.

In the course of his travels, Cabeza de Vaca gained affection for the Indians, learning their languages and customs, adopting their clothing, mannerisms and tattoos. He admired their capacity for generosity, love and friendship. He shed rigid ideas rooted in ignorance and separation. He now saw in his Indian companions their full and irreducible humanity, convinced that the natives should be treated not with arrogance and disdain but with kindness and friendship.

Without calendars or clocks to measure the passage of time, his life unfolded with the phases of the moon and the movement of the seasons. Amid the vast Texas space, Cabeza de Vaca must have wondered if he would ever again set foot in Spain. Whenever he and his companions came upon a new tribe they carefully gathered information about what lay ahead and whether there were others who looked Spanish. When they could, they moved west and south toward Mexico. Ultimately, they traversed some six thousand rugged miles.

When they crossed the Rio Grande into present-day Mexico they saw signs of Spanish soldiers out searching for slaves to dig in silver and gold mines to the south. Villages and fields lay destroyed. Indians were harder to find since, as Cabeza de Vaca put it, "all the people were hidden in the woods, fleeing so that the Christians would not kill or make slaves of them." Despite his newfound abhorrence for slavery, he was eager to find his countrymen. Traveling with a few Indian friends, he moved ahead of the main party.

In March 1536, he spotted a small group of Spanish soldiers. They mistook him for an Indian and would have attacked but when he spoke their native tongue they were stunned to realize he was Spanish. They were "thunderstruck," Cabeza de Vaca recalled. "They went on staring at me for a long space of time, so astonished that they could neither speak to me nor manage to ask me anything."

By then he had been changed in ways he could not yet fathom. Years of indescribable hardship had fashioned him into a different person. He was no longer completely Spanish nor was he Indian. He was of both worlds.

If he harbored any hopes that his kinsman would hear his message of friendship and respect for the Indians these were quickly dispelled. The mist of brutality and greed that had once blinded him continued to occlude the vision of his countrymen. Instead of seeing the native peoples as potential allies, they saw only slaves. Cabeza de Vaca tried to protect his friends from the violence of such men, but, in the end, he could not.

When the slavers told the Indian's that they had come from the same distant land as the four healers, the Indians knew better. They said the Spaniards were lying. According to Cabeza de Vaca they pointed out the obvious differences between the children of the sun and the Spaniard slave hunters:

> we cured the sick and they killed the healthy; and that we came naked and barefoot and they well dressed and on horses and with lances; and that we did not covet anything, rather we returned everything that they gave us and were left with nothing, and the only aim of the others was to steal everything they found, and they never gave anything to anyone.

The Indians knew instantly what it would take Cabeza de Vaca years to understand, he was forevermore to be a child of the sun living in a land encumbered by mist and darkness.

*

Sometimes it is during the times when our pain – whether physical, emotional or psychological – is most acute that we discover who we are and who we may become. In Robert's case, it opened him up as if cutting furrows into the ground of his existence and planting seeds bearing the promise of deeper insight and sensitivity.

He appreciated the parallels between Cabeza de Vaca's story and his own: the way myopic beliefs can break down beneath the weight of new experience, how suffering can season us with the potential for empathy, and that while facing great hardship there are opportunities for expressions of love, kindness and connection. He also appreciated that this was a tough, tenacious man, like himself, who had learned that true strength has more to do with one's heart than the ability to act forcefully.

"If I hadn't been knocked on my backside," Robert mused, "I'd never have understood or appreciated Mom the way I do now." In the final analysis, he reckoned, "if going through all this stress with my back and being outta work and fighting depression has helped me see things more clearly, as far as I'm concerned it's a pretty good deal."

As his recovery progressed, he assisted Tess whenever he could. Things he'd once done perfunctorily, like getting her an extra blanket or a spoonful of ice cream, became important gestures of love. "I can't change that she's dying," he said, "but I can sit with her and read her a story. I want to do little things like that."

Robert's patience was tested when his mother's paranoia intensified. It was impossible to avoid the fact that she was deteriorating and rather than attributing this to her illness she was convinced some malignant force was trying to kill her. When breathing became difficult, she grew anxious. She insisted her windows be sealed with masking tape and refused to take morphine, convinced the doctor wanted to poison her. When Robert tried coaxing her into taking medications she clamped her jaws in defiance.

Weeks earlier, he would have gotten angry and tried forcing her to take them. The result would have been another battle of wills and mutual resentment. This time, he didn't argue. Instead of demanding Tess orient to his world, he entered hers.

When she told him the morphine was poison he asked what he could do to help. When she gave him cryptic instructions about finding the King he assured her that he understood, left the room, put some food coloring in the morphine and returned saying the King had advised that the medicine was now safe. It felt awkward at first. It flew in the face of his longstanding belief about the need to fix firm personal boundaries when it came to his mother's inner world, but compassion had emerged as a higher value than being right.

Instead of resisting or correcting, he simply accompanied her. To his surprise, he found he could do so without losing his perspective. By standing beside her as a loving son instead of in front of her as the sane one, he was even able to get her to take an increased dose of her anxiety medication.

As Tess's condition worsened, Robert's grief was complicated by her schizophrenia. She appeared to have no knowledge that she was going to die. It was not a matter of avoiding something she preferred not think about, no mere repression or denial. She truly did not equate her physical decline with terminal disease. Robert was faced with the challenge of knowing his mother would soon be gone and wanting to find a way to say goodbye, while at the same time being limited by Tess's lack of comprehension and her anxiety about death.

He decided to take every opportunity to let his mother know he loved her and to reassure her that he would be by her side. He tried his best to stay in the moment. When he lost his cool or lashed out in frustration, as often happened, he practiced allowing himself to be imperfect and vowed to do better the next time his buttons were pushed. A month earlier he had longed to return to work, now he wanted to spend as much time with his mother as possible. "I don't even know if I want to keep on being a cop anymore," he said with visible anxiety, "but I'll deal with that identity crisis after Mom is gone."

Doubts about being a police officer fused with other questions about his role as a son, husband, as well as existential questions about meaning and identity. As with many who find ways to transcend self-limiting ideas and restrictive worldviews, Robert was disoriented. The familiar world, what psychologists sometimes call the assumptive world, had been shattered and he had yet to develop a sense of what lay ahead.

He might not have been surprised to learn that Cabeza de Vaca had a similar experience. Though he'd attempted to fit back into the world of his fellow Spaniards he was forever changed. After his wanderings in North America, he no longer fit neatly into this old world. His suffering had unearthed deeper insights and sensitivity than were known to the unreflective men around him focused on competition and power. It had made him a soldier for peace in a land of warriors bent on violent conquest.

Cabeza de Vaca never forgot about his Indians friends and, although his moral courage sometimes failed when pressured to conform, he continued to share his vision of how we all might live. "For the rest of his life," according to David Duncan, "Cabeza de Vaca would try to convince his fellow Spaniards that the best way to conquer Native Americans was to be firm, but also to show kindness and respect – a notion other Spaniards dismissed as the Quixotic impulse of a man who had gone native far too long."

For Robert, the challenge laid ahead of integrating a new vision, a new sense of self, into a world with practical demands, fixed expectations and pressures. Tess slipped into a coma a few days before she died. Almost simultaneously Robert's back pain intensified. Rather than increase his medications and retire to his bedroom, he decided to use just enough medicine to mute his discomfort without causing too much sleepiness. He settled down on the couch in his mother's room next to her hospital bed and watched over her until she died.

I didn't see him again until after the funeral. He told me Tess had woken up out of her coma in the pre-dawn hours of the day she died. For a few minutes, he said, she "looked at me and we talked just as clear as a bell. She told me she loved me and said she knew it'd been hard on me all these years and she was sorry. Then she said she had to go."

He likened that moment to his mother "coming out of a fog at the last minute and telling me straight from the heart that she loved me and she wasn't afraid anymore."

"It's kinda funny," he said, as we rocked in battered wicker chairs on the front porch, "All my life what I saw when I looked at my Mom was her mental illness. Now that she's gone it doesn't really seem important."

Chapter Two
Days of Forty-Nine
Mindfulness and Gratitude

Lizzie liked the facts. The facts were, at thirty-three, with a husband and two young children she had a brain tumor that would probably kill her within a matter of months. It was likely she would become disoriented and need help with the most basic tasks. She knew the path would be difficult. Her deepest fear was that there would come a time when she wouldn't recognize her husband, Ray, or her kids, Tad (five) and Dana (four). She was haunted by fears that when the children were grown they would have no memory of her or how much she had loved them.

After aggressive medical treatment failed to stop her disease she'd begun giving away possessions with sentimental value, carefully matching each object with the person she believed would most appreciate it. An autographed photograph of Elvis Presley had gone to her sister-in-law, her collection of seashells to a nephew and the necklace she'd gotten hiking across Ireland went to a friend who had always admired its luminosity and delicate metalwork. Though some accused her of being morbid or defeatist, she found it comforting to find homes for things Ray and the kids might not want and which she didn't want winding up in the trash.

As special keepsakes for her children, she had come up with a creative idea. She bought an old tape recorder and box of cassette tapes. Several times a day she sat with the recorder and talked about her life. She spoke in detail about when her children were born, how she and Ray met, things that made her laugh and things that made her sad. Woven throughout were her hopes for Tad and Dana, encouragement for when times were tough and expressions of unconditional love.

She had even coaxed Ray into participating. He answered questions as she interviewed him or played guitar as they sang the folk ballads they loved. Now and then, she simply recorded Dana and Tad playing in the family room – wrestling with their father, arguing about video games or pretending to be astronauts.

She made copies of each recording and placed one in a box for Tad, another for Dana. She called these her "treasure chests." When the tapes were nearly gone she made separate cassettes for each child, putting each in its proper box. Then, she put a handmade card on top, wrapped the packages tightly and put her tape recorder away. She instructed Ray to keep them safe until Dana was eighteen, at which time he was to deliver them to the children. Secretly, she had made a treasure chest for Ray and given it to his mother for safekeeping.

By the time she finished the project Lizzie was having difficulty remembering words and losing her short-term memory. She braced for more changes. The next weeks were difficult as she and Ray tried to keep things as normal as possible for Tad and Dana. Despite their efforts to insulate the children, they couldn't hide what was happening. The kids knew things were not normal but joined their parents in pretending otherwise.

Prior to her diagnosis, Lizzie had been an excellent athlete. She was still physically strong and able to do most things for herself but needed increasingly frequent prompts from Ray to remember things like how to get her jacket on and where to put the dirty dishes. Conversations were difficult to follow and, at times, seemed to move so fast she couldn't keep up with them. She was having a harder time tracking things.

Her strength was still evident the morning we met. Her handshake was firm and she easily restrained their affable collie, Maxwell, as she opened the door. Lizzie was cheerful and at ease discussing her illness but whenever the conversation focused on her for more than a few minutes she deflected it toward Ray or the children. Ray was exhausted. He'd rearranged his work schedule so he could be home during the day but wasn't getting much sleep. "Even when I'm in bed," he admitted, "I don't sleep much." His days were filled with caring for Tad and Dana, working from home and keeping an eye over Lizzie's shoulder.

A year earlier, Ray and Lizzie had assumed they were at the beginning of their lives together. It was painful absorbing the realization that they were actually near the end. When talking about their relationship they had learned to compress the beginning, middle and end of the story into a mere ten years. A story that began with a chance meeting at a nearby botanical garden, the middle was somewhere around the time Tad was born. Now they were talking openly about living in the closing chapter, which Lizzie predicted would be over before her thirty-fourth birthday.

Her parents lived nearby. When I met them it was clear they were having a difficult time. "Parents aren't supposed to bury their children," her mother said, choking back a swell of emotion, "They're supposed to carry on *our* memory not the other way around." It was inconceivable that she would outlive her daughter and be left to speak of her in the lonely intonations of past tense. "I fought in the Korean War," her father said. "I saw bodies floating dead in the Yalu River till it looked like a river of blood. This is worse."

Lizzie was declining more quickly than her cheerful personality and firm handshake suggested. She was losing coordination and having increasing episodes of confusion. I would have to introduce myself each visit since she had no memory of the one before. Each time she was weaker, less focused. Although Ray was able to take a leave of absence, taking care of Lizzie and the kids was almost more than he could manage.

As her physical needs increased she became acutely anxious and occasionally woke up screaming at night, afraid that people were in the room trying to hurt her. Dana and Tad withdrew, nervous about their mother's behavior and fearful of upsetting her. Her worst fear, it seemed, was coming true.

"I'm worried about the kids." Ray admitted one day as we sat in the living room watching them draw pictures with colored pencils.

As if responding to his cue, Tad looked up and asked, "What should I draw next?"

"Why don't you and Dana draw pictures of your family?" I suggested.

They set themselves to the task. Tad was done quickly. Like the racecars he was fond of drawing, he liked to finish first. He showed us a picture in which he and Dana were very small, standing together in a corner of the page. In the middle was a large green lizard with a face drawn on its belly. Ray was dwarfed next to the creature and was holding its hand. I asked where his mother was.

"That's her in the monster's tummy," he said.

"How'd she get in there?"

"He swallowed her."

"Why'd he do that?"

"Because he's bad and he likes to make people cry."

"Why does he like to make people cry?"

"Because he's real mean and no one likes him."

"What's the monster's name?"

"Cancer-Man."

"What's going to happen to your Mom?"

Tad shifted his gaze to his feet and grew quiet. He looked up transiently at his father as if seeking permission to answer. Ray nodded gently and told him it was okay. Finally Tad said, "He's going to kill her."

It's common for parents to try to protect their children by avoiding direct conversation or discouraging questions about illness and death. Many find it hard to explain what is happening and resort to bland, potentially confusing euphemisms like "Mommy is going to be going on a long trip." Sometimes, in attempts to reassure children, parents even portray death as a happy experience by over-emphasizing that someone has "gone to heaven" or "become an angel." Such explanations though offered with the best intentions can confuse children and leave them to sort things out on their own.

When Ray and I spoke openly about what was happening with Tad and Dana it was clear they were more aware of what was going on than he had realized. In the absence of honest information, though, they had come to some troubling conclusions. Tad, for example, was afraid he had caused Lizzie's disease by being "bad." Dana was worried that Ray was going to "catch" cancer and that she and her brother would be left alone. Once the subject was out in the open, Ray's sensitivity and ability to speak in ways his children could understand opened the channels of communication.

Shortly after this talk Lizzie began sleeping most of the time and staying in bed around-the-clock. As Ray and I sat at the kitchen table one morning, his face was suffused with sadness. All signs suggested she was nearing the end. With his head down in his left palm he said, "It feels like ninety-five percent of my life with Lizzie right now is pure hell."

Watching her struggle, feeling powerless to change the fact that she was "slowly fading away" had worn him down. If he could have traded places with her he would have done it, if there were a treatment with even a remote chance of curing her he would have sought it however expensive or far away. But he had fantasized about such things enough to know they were pipe dreams.

Hearing Lizzie shouting, he bolted from the table to check on her. When he came back he was smiling. He laughed, shook his head as if surprised and said, "You know what? Ninety-five percent may be hell but that other five percent is pure joy. And it's all worth it for a single one of those moments."

"It looks like you just had one," I smiled.

"I did."

"Is it something you're comfortable sharing?"

"It's hard to put in words," he said. "Sometimes it's just a feeling, like a minute ago when she started singing a lullaby the way she used to. It reminded me..." His voice trailed off as though disappearing down a gently cresting bluff.

"Reminded you...?"

"Reminded me of when we brought Tad home after he was born."

As the challenges of terminal illness accumulate and nerves wear thin, it is easy to lose sight of such moments as Ray was describing. They can be fleeting. Unless we watch closely for their arrival we may miss them. As our conversation turned to these moments Ray began mentally sifting them from recent days. There were moments of closeness and small expressions of affection that, in spite of all the challenges, arrived every day without fail. They were, he thought, "like finding a treasure buried under a mountain of crap."

While we were talking about ways he could hone his sensitivity to these moments and create opportunities for them to arise, he had an idea. He remembered the tape recorder Lizzie had put away months earlier and jumped to his feet. After some searching, he dug it out from under a pillow on a shelf in a hall closet. He brought it to the kitchen table, tested it, and found that it worked perfectly. "Those tapes aren't quite finished," he said, smiling broadly. "I'm going to catch some of those moments if I have to tape ten hours of hell to do it."

I asked what he had in mind. He explained that he was going to record their interactions whenever he was with her. "Then when I catch one of those moments," he said, "I'll transfer it to another tape."

"What will you do with it?" I asked.

"I don't know. Maybe I'll hide it away and just know it's there."

Remembering his and Lizzie's love of historical ballads, I asked if he had ever heard a ballad called, "The Days of Forty-Nine." He had. I asked if he knew what it was about.

"The California gold rush," he said, not sure where this was going.

"I wonder Ray, if maybe there's a story there that gets at what you're talking about."

I explained that during the gold rush in the late 1840s people came from all over the globe looking for shiny nuggets. Ninety-five percent found more hell than gold. Some of the lucky ones got rich, others left with a small cache of treasure extracted from months of hardship and sacrifice. I offered to tell him the story and he agreed.

"One of the things Lizzie always loved about ballads," he said, "was all the stories."

*

By 1848 John Sutter had built a thriving empire in the present-day state of California. His large estate boasted a ranch, fort and blacksmith shop. He had herds of cattle and sheep, agricultural fields and an orchard. Although his success had been dependent on his professed allegiance to Mexico, when California had recently been ceded to the United States Sutter had shifted with the prevailing winds. He was not picky about alliances as long as they were good for business.

Americans had already been trickling in along the Oregon-California Trail and Sutter figured when more arrived they would need beef and leather from his ranch, supplies from his store and timber from the sawmill he planned to build. He'd already sent his foremen, James Marshal, to a bend of the American River to construct the mill. What lumber Sutter didn't use he planned to float down the river and sell in San Francisco, a small town of about eight hundred, known for little more than its cowhide, tallow and its role as a supplier for Yankee whalers.

On January 24 Marshal was inspecting a mill race his men were digging when his eye was caught by the glint of flecks of gold. Despite Sutter's attempts to keep Marshal's discovery secret, when word got out most of the inhabitants of San Francisco packed up and headed to the American River, eager to strike it rich. As news traveled, others followed suit. Walter Colton, who was living in Monterey, recalled that "the blacksmith dropped his hammer, the carpenter his plane, the mason his trowel, the farmer his sickle, the baker his loaf, and the tapster his bottle. All were off to the mines."

News took longer to reach the eastern states, at first arriving as rumors and suspiciously unbelievable anecdotes. President Polk confirmed these accounts to the nation in December in his message to Congress, claiming that fortunes of "extraordinary character" were there for the taking.

His words inspired tens of thousands of Americans to head west. Men (and some women) who would otherwise never have thought of leaving their friends and families came down with "gold fever." They would join thousands more coming from places like Mexico, South America, Hawaii, and Australia. So many people would come to California in the next year that they would be known collectively as "Forty-Niners."

Polk hadn't warned them about the hardships involved getting to the far-flung gold fields or the fact that by the time they arrived, finding gold would be far more difficult than simply reaching into a river and pocketing a few nuggets. For those on the eastern seaboard there were three ways to get to "the diggings." The easiest was by ship around Cape Horn and onto San Francisco but this could take six months and was expensive. A second option was to travel by ship to Panama, cross the Isthmus and hop a ship to California. This was quicker but one had to contend with the cholera and yellow fever epidemics raging through Panama. Most preferred to keep their feet on the ground and go overland.

The first challenge of the overland route was simply getting to one of the "jumping off" towns on the Missouri River that marked the beginning of the western trails such as Independence or Saint Joseph. These towns were on the fringe of the frontier and reaching them wasn't easy. By April 1849, about thirty thousand gold-seekers had jammed themselves into these towns with more arriving every day. They scrambled to buy wagons, gather supplies and form themselves into traveling groups known as companies. They broke in teams of oxen or mules, dashed off letters to family and poured over maps and travel guides trying to decide their precise route. Some would head down the Santa Fe Trail then go west; others would take the trail recently blazed by the Mormons on their exodus to Salt Lake City. Most followed the Oregon-California Trail.

It was mid-April before the wagon trains could safely head out. The trick was to leave late enough in the season that there would be enough grass to provide forage for livestock but early enough to ensure they wouldn't get trapped in the Sierra Nevada during winter. Just two years earlier this is what had happened to the Donner party and the results were well known. Trapped by mountains and heavy snow, more than half of the eighty-seven men, women, and children, died of starvation. There were whispers that some had resorted to cannibalism.

Many would-be Forty-Niners never made it beyond Independence or Saint Joseph, dying of the cholera that raged along the rivers and trails that year. Once underway, this scourge would dog them all the way to the Rockies, killing thousands.

When the first companies rolled onto the prairie many wagons sank into a quagmire churned up on grassland drenched from rain and melting snow. Wagons broke axles and cracked wheels as teams of oxen strained under the heavy burdens. To move ahead, many had to lighten their loads and things were hastily thrown onto the prairie and left behind.

The agonies of sloughing through mud and rain, going without sleep, managing unruly oxen and the ever-present specter of accidents and disease caused some to turn around and head home before reaching Fort Kearney near the Platte River in present-day Nebraska. Those who continued began a three-hundred-forty mile stretch along the Platte to Fort Laramie where rain and mud were replaced by withering heat and lung-choking, eye-irritating dust clouds tilled up by wagon wheels and oxen.

Cholera continued to kill and hastily dug graves became a common sight along the trail. One prospector wrote that it "would make your heart ache to see how some of the companies buried their dead. I have visited graves where the person was not buried more than twenty inches deep and found them dug up by wolves and their flesh eaten off and their bones scattered to bleach upon the plains."

There were plentiful sources of frustration – the rigors and monotony of trail life, slow pace of advance, disagreements within companies and separation from loved ones. Animals died from overwork till the corpses of mules, oxen and cattle punctuated every part of the trail. The Platte coughed up great swarms of mosquitoes which one letter-writer described as "abundant and unmerciful." River crossings could be deadly. At one crossing it was reported that nearly thirty people drowned that year. Even shallow rivers could be dangerous, especially for those inexperienced at driving teams and livestock. Wagons could be ferried but oxen, mules, horses and cattle were usually driven into the water.

By the time the gold-seekers left Laramie and began the trek into the Rockies the path was strewn with discarded supplies, abandoned wagons and shallow graves. For those that hadn't turned back or been killed by cholera, infections or accidents, the Rockies marked the hardest part of the journey. Rivers flowed across the Forty-Niner's path as though intentionally laid out to frustrate them. In some places steep grades or stretches of desert fought them for every step.

Shortly after crossing South Pass the trail began splitting and companies had to make choices based on little or no reliable information. Should they take Sublette's Cut-off or the Mormon Trail? What about Hudspeth's Cut-off? Lassen's Cut-off? Carson's Cut-off? By then supplies were often dangerously low and some companies faced starvation. After weeks on a diet with little variety many showed symptoms of scurvy. Making matters worse, a potentially fatal disease known as "mountain fever" was added to the list of woes besetting the weary Forty-Niners.

In addition to physical challenges and dangers, there were psychological and emotional ones. Privacy was nonexistent. Tempers were tested. Conflict and disagreement were common. The men were separated from loved ones, packed together day after day with others eager to be at the end of their journey. At night they slept on the ground or wooden wagon planks. Many must have wondered if they would ever see their wives or children again. Would a handful of letters sent hurriedly from the trail have to stand as the only reminder to a child whose father had died in a distant land?

Exhausted by the desolate heat and alkali sands of the Blackrock desert or the menacing spires of the Sierras, spirits flagged and sometimes failed. More wagons were abandoned, battered beyond repair or too difficult to pull forward. Some men left their companies and headed out on foot taking nothing but backpacks. Companies disbanded, leaving every man for himself. With winter descending and many in danger of freezing to death, the army's fledgling Pacific Division sent out rescue parties trying to bring in stragglers.

Many downplayed the hardships in their letters, wanting to protect wives and children from worry. Others, like Andrew Orvis, had no qualms about describing the rigors of his ordeal. He wrote his wife that, "you will shed tears when you come to know how much I have suffered and the hardships I have encountered. If it had not been for you and the children to think of, I should certainly have given up and died."

Despite the difficulties of the overland journey, most who set out onto the prairie in April and May made it to California still optimistic they'd strike it rich. Some ninety thousand were magnetized to the goldfields that year, joining thousands who had arrived the year before. By then, the surface gold that had once been so plentiful was gone. There was still gold left, but it was much more difficult to get and there were many more people digging for it. Rather than simply dipping a pan into the water men now had to dig through tons of earth and divert streams and rivers. Dreams of instant riches disappeared like fragile gossamer threads blown away by a gust of cold air.

Nearly every foot of riverbed from the Feather River to the Mariposa had crews of miners parked on it. Prices for supplies were exorbitant. Most miners worked in groups. The labor was intense and strenuous. Dams needed to be built, rivers channeled, earth shoveled. The work required lifting, sifting, hauling, smashing and pulling, often while standing in ice-cold water or balancing on piles of slippery rock.

Miners crammed into tents and hastily built shelters. Accidents were common, so were illnesses like dysentery, scurvy and pneumonia. Alonzo Delano wrote in his journal that many went to the diggings "without tents, many without blankets to shield them from the cold night air, living on pork and hard bread…Hundreds have been stricken down by disease; many died, while others have been unfitted for work for the rest of the season."

After months of back-breaking toil, paying outrageous prices and possibly succumbing to the temptations of towns like San Francisco or Sacramento, the average prospector had little if any gold to show for his efforts. Although some had indeed struck it rich, most were lucky to return home with a few flakes or nuggets stashed away. The days and nights spent on the trail and in the diggings often boiled down to a few precious flecks drawn from an otherwise stingy earth. For every nugget found there was a week spent straining across rivers or through prairie mud. For each golden rock, sweat had been lost bent over with dysentery or the aches of relentless labor.

Some, of course, went home bitter and disappointed, but many, like William Swain, returned with a small pouch of another kind of gold. The kind no cardsharp, whiskey dealer or grasping merchant could touch. Gold that had been chipped away from the rock and sifted from the sand of difficult experience and days spent prospecting in a river larger than the American or the Sacramento: the river of one's life.

In a letter to his brother from the goldfields, Swain wrote that he would not choose to "traverse the same route under the same circumstances, even were a princely fortune the sure reward. But were I to be unfortunate in all my business here and arrive at home at last without one cent, I should be ever glad that I have taken the trip to California. It has learnt me to have confidence in myself, has disciplined my impetuous disposition and has learnt me to think and act for myself and to look upon men and things in a true light."

*

When we are engaged in difficult tasks or laboring in rivers of sadness, grief, and uncertainty, it can be hard to remember that alongside the rough gravel and swirling detritus of the riverbed there are nuggets of gold. These take many forms. Perhaps it is something important that we learn about ourselves or others. Maybe it's an enhanced awareness of our resilience and capacity for sacrifice or a gentler acceptance of our limitations. Some gold may appear as moments during which we find reassurance, peace, or happiness amid the churning waters. Maybe it's a moment holding a hand or looking into another's eyes with love. All of these become, in a metaphorical sense, part of our own personal cache of treasure. When our labors are over, or even as they continue, if we have been attentive to this gold we may look back and be glad to have prospected so well despite the suffering endured.

I only saw Ray one more time before Lizzie died. On that visit he said he was "finding some gold dust down in the diggings." He'd bought a voice activated recorder so he could leave it on a bedside table in Lizzie's room. At night he sifted out moments he wanted to save and recorded them onto a single tape. He estimated that over the course of a day he probably got three or four minutes of gold. In the process, he learned to pay close attention to these moments and appreciate them more deeply. Even when sadness and frustration arrived, as they often did, he didn't lose his bearings and was able to stay focused.

I asked if there were themes emerging from his gold sifting. He said there were two things: songs and laughter. It was when she laughed and sang that Ray could feel her spirit and their connection. "You never know when she is going to do either or even why she does it," he said, "but when she does, I can see her come out briefly from behind her illness."

Armed with his recorder and deepened awareness, Ray rarely missed even a fleck of Lizzie's spirit as it sparkled beneath her confusion. And the same was true of the time he spent with Dana and Tad. Once he stopped trying to insulate them from what was happening and allowed them to ask questions and express feelings openly, he was able to support them better.

When the kids understood that Lizzie wasn't mad at them and her seemingly strange words and behaviors were due to the illness, they were more at ease going into her room. Although Lizzie was sleeping most of the day, Ray and the kids set aside a special time every afternoon when they all sat in her room and, even if she was asleep, told her about their day, read her stories or sang songs she liked. "What started as special time for the kids," Ray said, "turned into a special time for me too." Focusing on the golden moments buried in life's silt and grit had changed everything.

Ray and I talked about his clarity in fostering and being mindful of these transient expressions of love and happiness. I commented that not only would it positively alter and enhance the way his family used Lizzie's remaining time, it would alter the stories they told themselves when they looked back.

Such was the case with William Swain as he looked back. His participation in the gold rush, despite the fact that he returned flat broke, became one of the most important and formative experiences of his life. As years passed and memories became stories, he didn't gloss over the suffering of those days but he affirmed that the journey had been well worth it. The experience, he told his family, had deepened his self-confidence and made him more discerning about his companions. The inexpressible joy he had felt when reunited with loved ones had reminded him of the wealth he'd always possessed but had at times failed to appreciate.

Lizzie died peacefully in her home. About two months after her funeral, Ray was surprised when his mother stopped by with a box full of tapes for him. Initially, Lizzie had asked that it be delivered on the first anniversary of her death. On reflection she had decided that a "mother's intuition" would be a better guide and she had asked Ray's mother to listen to hers. On hearing Lizzie speak directly to him, her voice strong, mind clear, Ray was ambivalent about his mother's timing. The experience brought forth waves of sadness and grief, but also joy and love. He soon found comfort in her words of encouragement, especially as they related to his new role as a single father. Ray realized he had been given a treasure of inestimable value.

Chapter Three
Navigating the Strait
Persistence

"We can't get around this." Bev said, frustrated. Ike threw up his hands, exasperated. They had grown apart, wanted to feel close again, but felt stuck.

"Maybe," Ike suggested, "if you'd learned to relax we wouldn't always get like this."

Bev's perception that he was blaming her for the impasse set off another wave of angry criticism and hurt feelings. We'd explored this pattern before, the way a word, facial expression or voice tone could quickly lead to an argument that neither wanted but which neither knew how to avoid. They understood some of the ways they pushed each other's buttons. We'd discussed strategies for changing these interactions but they kept happening anyway.

They had been married forty-four years, raised seven children and had several grandchildren. For most of their lives they had also taken care of Bev's brother, Dean, who was born with Cerebral Palsy. Dean, though now receiving hospice care, had lived well beyond the most optimistic guesses of his doctors.

Much of Bev's life revolved around her brother's needs and comfort. She frequently sacrificed her own well-being while attending to his – neglecting her elevated blood pressure, chronic arthritis and need for sleep. Although Dean wasn't able to speak, Bev seemed to know intuitively what he needed and how to reassure him.

Initially, my visits had been short. Bev had been reluctant to discuss her internal experience, preferring more general topics of conversation. If Ike wasn't already working at his automobile shop he usually found a reason to go there shortly after I arrived. They described themselves as simple country folks who kept their thoughts and feelings to themselves. At first, Bev rarely spoke about herself, her marriage or the details of her frightening childhood. It was over. There was no point bringing it up. Besides, it was nobody else's business.

Over time, however, she came to appreciate the opportunity to discuss what it was like caring for Dean, as well as her anxiety about his impending death. In doing so, she made several references to their early years. It was impossible, she said, "to understand why I protect him and baby him the way I do, unless you know what we went through."

Memories began tumbling out. As is typical with psychological trauma, keeping them buried had not mitigated their intensity. When Bev began exploring these childhood years she was surprised at the power of the emotions they evoked. "It feels," she said, "like it just happened yesterday."

Vivid memories of her father came flooding back. He had been a violent man, full of rage and he'd made her life nearly unbearable. Physically abusive, he regularly assaulted Bev and her mother, Geraldine. On one occasion he choked Bev so violently she had lost consciousness.

He drank heavily, his most savage abuse coming when he was drunk. She remembered listening for clues to what might be in store when he came through the door each night. "I could always tell when he was drunk by the way the dogs acted. If they were quiet when he got out of the truck I knew we were in trouble, if they barked we were probably going to be okay that night."

At the age of eleven she stole a box of rat poison from a hardware store, intending to put it in her father's food. For weeks she agonized over whether to kill him before finally deciding to pour it out.

"Sometimes I think I shoulda done it," she said coldly.

"Why didn't you?"

"Maybe I was scared I'd wind up like him."

"How did you want to be instead?"

"I wanted to be the opposite of everything he was."

Geraldine had tried to protect Bev by distracting her husband's rage and directing it toward herself but he knew he could hurt her more by attacking Bev. "There were times," Bev recalled, "the more she tried to protect me the more glee he got in coming after me." She and her mother had shared lives under a siege invisible to neighbors who thought, or chose to believe, "we were just one big happy family." Every day she had walked on tenterhooks hoping to avoid an explosion, knowing no amount of accommodation or compliance could guarantee safety.

Dean had not been a target of his attacks. Her father had treated him, Bev said, "like a useless piece of furniture to be put away and forgotten about." Bev helped with his care, often looking after Dean when her mother was recovering from an attack.

When her father was killed in a bar fight when Bev was seventeen she was relieved. Now, years later, whenever she talked about him her voice vibrated with rage, her respirations increased and her hands shook. I asked why she thought it had remained so fresh.

"Where do you want me to start?" she quipped.

"What comes to mind first?"

She looked annoyed. "What comes to mind first is how that bastard stole twenty years of my mother's life and stomped on them. He made her life hell and she was stuck there. And he made me feel ashamed I couldn't protect her."

"How has his violence affected the rest of your life?"

She started to speak then stopped, catching the thought before it was spoken then said, "It's impossible for me to trust people or feel like I can rely on them."

"Even Ike?"

"Yeah," she admitted.

"What stops you from trusting him?"

Sweat appeared on her forehead and her face flushed. When someone is carrying this kind of post-traumatic injury the nervous system can react quickly to painful memories or stimuli associated with the traumatic event as though that event were occurring in the present. When working with people in these situations it's important not to push too hard. I guided her through a quick breathing exercise and gently asked her to feel her feet on the floor. When her nervous system calmed, Bev changed the subject.

She and Ike had met when he was on leave from the army. Bev had been taken by his good manners and cheerful attitude. Unlike many of the young men with whom she interacted, she felt safe with him. A year later, after he returned from the army and landed a job as a mechanic, they were engaged. "I was scared," she said. "Mama had gotten stuck marrying a man who seemed like a decent fellow at the time. But I just had a feeling Ike was different."

Her instincts had been well-founded. In the first years of their marriage they'd done nearly everything together. For example, every Saturday they would borrow a neighbor's trailer, load up their rowboat and head for a nearby lake and spend the day paddling and talking. When their first child was born they brought him along too.

They'd only been married three years when Geraldine had a stroke that left her unable to walk without assistance. She and Dean moved in. By then, Bev was pregnant with their second child and they were

37

scrambling to pay the bills. Overnight they had new responsibilities pulling them in different directions. By the time Geraldine died several years later there were six children and Dean's needs had increased along with the expense of his medical care.

In addition to caring for Dean and the kids, they ran a farm raising hay for livestock. Ike worked evenings at an auto shop and picked up side jobs fixing farm machinery. Bev stayed busy at home from early morning until late at night. "There were days," she recalled, "when between the kids and Dean and the farm I didn't have time to eat." By the time Ike returned from work and the evening chores were done, there was no time for anything other than catching a few hours of sleep before they got up and did it all over again.

Pulled into separate spheres, Bev and Ike began living what they referred to as parallel lives. With little time to reflect on what was happening and constant demands to distract them, the distance grew. Years passed, Ike's shop expanded and the situation got worse. It was as though they were living on different coasts of the same broad ocean. By the time the last of their children left home, Bev and Ike were like strangers, their separation wielding the weight of a long-standing habit.

Rather than face the problem, they ignored it. "I guess," Bev admitted, "we were scared to look at what was going on." She made Dean the center of her attention, telling herself she was the only one who knew how to take care of him. Ike poured his energies into work, telling himself he needed to keep an eye on the business or things would fall apart. Along with separation came feelings of resentment and of being unappreciated. Arguments became more common and there was tension whenever they were in the same room.

Now, two things were converging that had heightened the tension – Dean was dying and Ike was nearing retirement. Responsibilities that had provided a buffer and a distraction from their relational problems would be soon gone. In light of these twin specters of death and retirement, Bev and Ike were filled with an awareness that they were getting older. Silently, each had been taking stock of their lives and reflecting on their mortality.

Such thoughts are common when caring for someone with a terminal illness. Questions about the meaning of life and death are normal. Caregivers may even experience the lingering tides of earlier grief as memories of others who have died return to their minds. In Ike's case this was particularly true. When he was a teenager a younger sister had died after a short struggle with influenza. As Dean fought a respiratory infection, his lungs filling with fluid, Ike began reliving days long before when his sister had endured similar symptoms. "I watched Mama take care of her," he said, "just like I'm watching Bev take care of her brother. It tore me up then and it's tearing me up now."

Bev was having equally serious thoughts. She knew big changes lay ahead and worried that she might be left to grieve Dean's death with little support from Ike. It was even possible she would find herself in a relationship, though not abusive, as seemingly constricting and inescapable as her mother's had been.

Motivated by private reflections, Ike began staying for my visits. He and Bev started talking. They'd spent a lot of time and energy finding ways to avoid communicating openly so the first few conversations were hard and tempers had flared.

They loved each other, but, in many ways, they no longer knew each other. Without Dean, the children, or the repair shop to hold their attention they would have to find a way to get reacquainted. Swallowing hard, trusting in their mutual commitment and, as importantly, shared sense of humor, they struggled to reconnect. They wanted to understand each other and to be more forgiving of each other's foibles (real and perceived). They missed talking and laughing, but the defenses they had developed were formidable. Anger, blame and misunderstanding continued making a muddle of things.

We focused on creating small changes in how they interacted and responded to each other, carving out ground rules and enhancing their ability to listen without reacting. Finding satisfaction in this, they began laughing more, interrupting less. As often happens in situations like these, though, the excitement of early successes gave way to difficult seas and strong headwinds. Old patterns they were trying to escape proved resilient and adaptable. Before long they once again found themselves getting angry and avoiding each other. Discouraged, they questioned whether change was worth pursuing, each blaming the other for not caring enough to follow through.

Ike started skipping my visits again. Bev wondered if the joint visits had been a mistake. Still, the idea that after Dean died she and her husband might be like strangers living in the same house haunted her. She'd spent much of her early life feeling unloved and unsafe. The thought of living the last part of her life the same way was painful and unsettling.

Fortunately, Ike's absence turned out to be temporary. When he returned, they reflected on their initial enthusiasm for navigating through difficult relational straits toward deeper closeness and their discouragement at being blown off course. It was on this visit that Ike, frustrated and feeling hopeless, had suggested that Bev "relax" and once more they had found themselves at loggerheads.

I asked them to think about something each appreciated about the other then took them through a series of questions intended to center them in this feeling of gratitude. I asked each to share a memory of when they had felt close. Bev's mind went back to a time they were out on the lake in their rowboat and a storm had come up. They laughed recounting their efforts to reach the shore, afraid they were going to capsize at any moment.

We spent some time reflecting on how they had kept their cool as the rain came down and thunder boomed, working together, encouraging one another. I wondered aloud if this might be a good analogy for their situation and asked if I could tell them a story

Bev said playfully, "Anything's better than listening to more of Ike's nonsense." Taking the humor, not the bait, Ike laughed, "You go on and tell us a story. At least one of us will listen with good manners."

*

In the winter of 1892 Joshua Slocum was down on his luck. Nearly fifty, out of work and penniless, he was unsure of his next move. Since the age of sixteen he'd worked on the water and he longed to return. After making inquiries on the Boston waterfront though, he had come up empty. With no options, he was feeling stuck. While walking on the wharves he ran into an old friend who saw Slocum's plight and offered him a ship. The *Spray*, he admitted, was in need of repairs, but if he was willing to put in the work it might once again be seaworthy.

In fact, it would take a lot of work. The vessel had been rotting in a pasture in Fairhaven and hadn't been afloat in years. Most who saw it assumed it would be hauled off as salvage, its days as an Atlantic oyster sloop long gone. Slocum, however, jumped at the chance to fix it up and get himself and the *Spray* back to sea.

For the next thirteen months he worked on the *Spray*. He felled an oak with which to rebuild the keel, hauled in pine for planks, curved saplings for ribbing and brought in spruce for a mast. He planed, sanded, scraped, bolted, caulked, sewed and tied until finally both he and the roughly thirty-six foot long vessel were ready for launch.

Slocum tried his hand at fishing and chartered the *Spray* for short passenger cruises but found little satisfaction in either line of work. By spring of 1895 he'd decided on a daring plan. He would sail alone around the world. So far as anyone knew, nobody had ever attempted a solo voyage before. Most who watched him weigh anchor that April and sail out of Boston Harbor doubted it could be done. More than a few were convinced he would never be seen again.

He had no such misgivings. Talking with a reporter, he explained that he would simply "sleep in the day time and keep the boat going at night." His first stop was his childhood home in Nova Scotia. Perhaps he realized the dangers of his impending journey and wanted to see his home once more. Maybe he wanted to start this new chapter of his life from the place of his birth. Whatever his reasons, something drew him home.

From Nova Scotia he intended to sail across the Atlantic to the Mediterranean Sea. He figured he'd sail through the Suez Canal and make his way to the Indian Ocean. Helped along by the dependable winds of the Gulf Stream, he made good time in the Atlantic. After several days he worked out a system for tying the *Spray's* rudder in a fixed position so it would sail on its own while he rested or did chores. When he arrived on the edge of the Mediterranean a month later he was in good spirits. By then he'd adjusted to the stark solitude that, initially, had left him "drifting into loneliness, an insect on a straw in the midst of the elements."

At Gibraltar, British authorities persuaded him to change his route. The Mediterranean, they said, was home to pirates and a small vessel traveling alone would be an irresistible target. He decided to heed their advice and cross the Atlantic again, this time on a southwesterly course with the goal of making his way to the Pacific by going around the tip of South America.

For anyone else sailing solo, crossing the Atlantic again would have been daunting but Slocum was a nautical jack-of-all-trades. Part oceanographer, part meteorologist, part astronomer, he could read the wind, clouds and stars. He could decode subtle messages in the surface of the water, the sounds made by sea birds or the feel of a breeze. Part mechanic, part homemaker, he could set sails, splice rope, repair hulls, sew, cook, and wash clothes. He was a one-man crew and his second voyage across the Atlantic went as well as if he had been accompanied by a full set of deck hands.

By late autumn he was approaching Cape Horn at the tip of South America where some of the world's most treacherous waters awaited. Here the Atlantic meets the Pacific creating mountainous waves, whirlpools and thundering gales of sail-tearing, rig-ripping wind, often accompanied by hail, snow or sleet. Some of the worst sailing conditions on the planet guard the transition from one ocean to another.

Having second thoughts about tackling the Cape, Slocum decided to go through the Strait of Magellan – a winding channel over three hundred miles long between the southern tip of Chile and the island of Tierra del Fuego. Though the route offered protection from the open ocean, it was no easy journey. The Strait had been making ghosts of seafarers for centuries. Making it through would require patience, persistence and a willingness to keep trying in spite of the many setbacks that would blow him off course.

In January 1896, as the *Spray* approached the Strait's entrance, the water was rough, the waves choppy. According to Slocum, the wind was "blowing a gale [that] sent feather-white spume along the coast." Once in the narrow channel, he recalled that, "long trailing kelp from sunken rocks waved forebodingly under [the *Spray's*] keel, and the wreck of a great steamship smashed on the beach abreast gave a gloomy aspect to the scene."

As soon as he entered the narrows a tremendous squall swept down with a force that threatened to push the *Spray* back into the Atlantic. For thirty hours Slocum strained to hold the rudder and adjust the sails. When the winds finally subsided, despite all of his exertions, the sloop was in nearly the same place as when the storm had started. By the time Slocum landed in Punta Arenas, a coaling station on the tip of Chile, he was exhausted.

The port captain advised him not to proceed without hiring a crew to assist in repelling the gangs of men that often preyed on smaller vessels. Slocum, however, decided to go it alone. Fortunately for him, a farseeing fellow captain gave him a bag of carpet tacks, a gift Slocum would find "worth more than all the fighting men and dogs of Tierra del Fuego."

Departing Punta Arenas, he kept his rifle and pistol loaded. He had fair winds that day and the sailing was good. Night, however, brought his first experience with the frightening squalls called williwaws. He described their awesome power as "compressed gales of wind that Boreas handed down over the hills in chunks," noting that a "full-blown williwaw will throw a ship, even without sail on, over on her beam ends." These harrowing winds pushed against him all the way to Fortescue Bay where, worn-out and glad to be alive, he dropped anchor for a much needed rest.

42

The next day he headed into gales so powerful they seemed animated with a will bent entirely on stopping him. He tried to move forward but couldn't. After only three miles, for which he exchanged a great deal of sweat, he slipped into a cove to sit out the tempest. When the gusts finally slackened, he raised sail and resumed course.

Not far from the cove, he met a threat as dire as any that nature had presented. Bearing down on the *Spray* were several canoes paddled by men from Tierra del Fuego. It was plain their intentions were hostile. He fired his rifle a couple times and they retreated back to the bay, unwilling to risk a full attack. Rather, they would wait for an opportunity to take the *Spray* by surprise.

For the next two weeks the vessel inched forward against wind, rain, sleet, large waves and strong currents. By early March, the end of the Strait was finally in view but, of course, another squall was brewing. The *Spray*, Slocum later remembered, "plunged into the Pacific Ocean at once, taking her first bath of it in the gathering storm." For a moment it looked like the feisty captain would sail clear. Visions of sailing up the Chilean coast must have flashed in his mind and lifted his spirits. But the storm that greeted him in the Pacific was too fierce to take head on. Rain fell in sheets, waves the size of tall buildings rolled with horrifying pitch tossing the *Spray* as through it were a speck of wood. Whips of lightening lashed the water's surface. The wind was so destructive Slocum had to lower sail and let the gales and water take him wherever they pleased.

It must have been a hard pill to swallow. Just as he had made it to the Pacific he was not only being pushed back, he was being pushed away from the Strait and into the Cape he had tried so hard to avoid. He had no choice as he struggled to keep from being wrecked.

For days he was pushed back. His face bled where it had been pelted by sleet and hail. His hands were raw from pulling wet ropes and he'd barely slept. The *Spray's* rigging and sails were in tatters. Making matters worse, in the midst of the storm's kaleidoscopic fury, he'd lost his bearings.

When the seas finally settled it was night and Slocum had no idea where he was. The next morning, he realized he was drifting in one of the most dangerous waterscapes any sailor could imagine. It was a place known as the Milky Way, a name that came from the countless rocks jutting just beneath the water's surface. These stony sentinels stretched like stars in a night sky, stirring up breakers, threatening hulls and churning up currents. Charles Darwin had come this way on the

Beagle and written that, "Any landsman seeing the Milky Way would have nightmares for a week."

If he could navigate this maze of rocks and waves he might be able to re-enter the Strait of Magellan through the Cockburn Channel, still preferable to trying to round South America in the open ocean. Cautiously, he found his way through the treacherous labyrinth back into the Strait. By the time he made it back to Punta Arenas he'd mended his sails and weathered another attack by Fuegians. This time they had attempted to board his vessel when he was asleep only to find that the carpet tacks scattered strategically on deck played havoc with bare feet.

It would be the middle of April before Slocum once more found his way into the Pacific. In the end, his trip through the Strait took almost as much time as his two Atlantic crossings combined. Moving forward had been slow and arduous, on some days impossible. Many times he had been blown back by winds and waves, left to retrace his earlier progress.

The transition from one ocean to another is not easy. It can be frightening sailing away from the shores of a familiar coast in search of new waters and new possibilities. It takes time, patience and a willingness to continue sailing even while being pushed back by unfriendly winds. As Slocum finally headed into the Pacific, a final wave, larger, he recalled, "than others that had threatened all day," broke over the *Spray* and seemed to "wash away old regrets."

*

On any journey there are bound to be capes and barriers that obstruct or hinder. As we attempt to find our way we may have to work hard and endure many setbacks before we finally succeed. It can be discouraging losing ground. With each setback, however, we may grow wiser and more familiar with the way ahead.

Sometimes these obstructions are tangible like the white-capped waves Joshua Slocum found in the Milky Way or the pressures Ike and Bev had faced to pay their bills when they were young. Other obstructions exist in our minds, reinforced by habits, beliefs, emotional states and relational patterns. For Bev and Ike these included the hopelessness they occasionally experienced and the dramas into which they were so frequently pulled.

When life changes appear on the horizon they can bring a sense of moving from one chapter of life into another. At such times, many find themselves reflecting on larger questions. How have I lived my life?

How have I treated others? How will I handle these changes? Is this how I want my life to be? In the swirl of such questions, Bev and Ike had been allowing a williwaw of misunderstanding and hurt feelings to foster separation. The time had come to chart a new course.

They had spent years drifting apart and the currents that separated them were difficult. In such cases meaningful change, the kind that creates a lasting transformation in who we are and in our relationships rarely comes in an instant. It usually follows in the wake of slow and steady movement over time, often amidst heavy winds and numerous setbacks. Knowing this helped them keep their situation in perspective.

When Dean's condition worsened Ike decided to retire and began helping with his care. It was another step in getting reacquainted. As the days passed, small steps accumulated. They made headway. Tempers still flared, misunderstandings still occurred, but the havoc these created was less destructive and abated more quickly.

When Dean died, Bev's pain was intense. It was, she thought, "about the hardest thing I've ever had to go through." Ike tried to be supportive but questioned the value of his efforts. For years he'd fixed things down at the shop. He was good at it, but there was nothing he could do to fix Bev's sorrow. No belt he could replace or part he could install would counter the deep hollows of her grief. They would have to be patient.

Without Dean at the center of her life, the world seemed strange and unfamiliar to Bev. It helped, though, that she and Ike were no longer leading separate lives. She was beginning to see, as she had years earlier, his gentle spirit as he stood by her in her grief. In the disorientation of Dean's death, Bev had rediscovered the instinct that had told her long before that Ike was the perfect companion for her life's voyage. Storms would hit, but she now knew she was safe. Slowly, the lens of distrust through which she had long filtered the events of her world began to lose its distorting tint. "I still don't trust people, especially men," she said when I called a month or so later to check on them. "But I'm learning to trust Ike. I should have done it a long time ago."

As for Joshua Slocum, in June of 1898 he was safe as well. He sailed the *Spray* into the Acushnet River and on to Fairhaven where he tethered the plucky ship at the same dock he had left nearly three years earlier.

Section Two
Looking Deeply Into the Shadows
Facing the Past

The secret of life is in the shadows
not in the open sun; to see anything
at all, you must look deeply into
the shadow of a living thing.

Ute saying

When death arrives on the horizon it's not just our present and future that are shaken, it's also our past. Along with questions about how our lives have been disrupted and what tomorrow will bring, we may find that memories, feelings, thoughts and beliefs associated with our past are stirred and press into awareness. Some will recall happy experiences. Other memories may bring guilt, unresolved grief, or regret about strained connections or unrealized hopes.

Among the challenges of coming to terms with our mortality is the impulse to reflect on the nature and meaning of our life. When we feel ourselves running out of time we may see our journey as a whole including not just experiences about which we are satisfied but also, however we may try to avoid them, those with which we have struggled.

To be human is to be imperfect. Few can look back on their lives without finding things left undone, hopes unfulfilled for one reason or another, choices or behaviors about which it might be tempting to self-criticize. Whatever the challenges of such reflections, facing them may also bring the opportunity to grieve, find or give forgiveness, see more clearly, or develop what psychotherapist Tara Brach calls 'radical acceptance', a deep compassion for ourselves and others. Paradoxically, we may even find that it is our rough edges, those things we have tried to avoid, that best bear witness to our humanness, resilience and courage.

To face the present and the future it is often necessary to face the past. The stories in Section Two illustrate this theme.

Chapter Four
Innocents on Witch's Hill
Moral Courage

Luke's grandmother had helped raise him while his parents toiled as sharecroppers in the sandy clay of eastern Georgia. She'd been a strong presence in his life and he'd been thinking about her since being diagnosed with pancreatic cancer. Her example had helped him survive an operation and seemingly endless rounds of chemotherapy. Now that the disease was spreading, thinking about her fortified his resolve to die with dignity, but it also raised painful questions.

She had often predicted Luke would do great things. As if preparing him for his destiny, she'd passed down stories and ongoing instructions for life in the form of pithy anecdotes, Bible verses and earthy aphorisms like: "You can catch flies with honey but use a strong poison when it comes to rats" or "Bow your head to the Almighty but make everyone else look up." There were two injunctions in particular upon which Luke had tried to forge his life: Never sell your soul for silver or a pat on the head; stand for what's right even if no one else is standing with you.

For a young boy growing up with black skin in Georgia during the 1930s and 40s, her message was empowering and defiant. Nurturing a core sense of self-respect and inner-power, he simultaneously learned to wear a mask in the presence of white people, especially the ones who owned the stores, held title to the land or worked at the sheriff's department. He concealed his confidence and developed self-restraint especially when irritated. Despite, or perhaps on account of, his grandmother's prophecy of greatness, he lived with the constant threat that he might become a target if he were to stand out. "Something bad happens," he said, "I would have had a bull's eye on my back if I hadn't been careful." His wife Norma had grown up in the same community. She likened such flashpoints to witch hunts. "Whenever white folks back then went looking for someone to blame for something, you knew it was going to be a black man."

Despite many ups and downs, Luke had had an adventurous life journey. Looking back, he was troubled by what he saw. Or, to be more precise, he was troubled by the story he told himself about what he saw.

48

When he measured his life against the standards of his grandmother's expectations he concluded he had "messed things up and let people down." He hadn't done the grand things she'd predicted. Living by the core values she'd instilled had been difficult. More than once it had brought consequences that had been disastrous.

Opposition and false accusations had often been his reward when he'd challenged injustices. The good things, he'd come to believe, went to those who didn't ask questions. Life, it seemed, often came down to a frustrating choice. Either you preserved your integrity and risked attack and ostracism by speaking out, or you kept your mouth shut and shared what benefits came to those who conformed while sacrificing your integrity. The choice had never seemed fair. Now, he was questioning the sacrifices of the path he'd taken, wondering if he'd made a mistake.

Luke's memories were condensed into stories that, like his grandmother's, were rich in personal meaning and replete with personal truths. Often they underscored the hardships he and his family had faced in pursuing lives guided by conscience such as the one about his "other than honorable discharge" from the military. As a young man looking for a direction he'd surprised his family by joining the army. There had been few opportunities in his hometown and after watching his parents break their backs tilling someone else's land he had no intention of becoming a tenant farmer or sharecropper.

"I was ready to get as far away as I could," he recalled. "Truman had integrated the army and I thought maybe it was a place I could be judged for who I was without being expected to use a separate restroom."

"I thought he was crazy," Norma laughed. "I told him, you never took orders from anyone but your grandma and now you're going to join the army?" After pretending to be angry with him, she packed their bags and warmed to the idea of seeing some of the world beyond the loamy Georgia low country.

They wound up stationed in Japan on the island of Okinawa where Luke developed affection for the Japanese people who worked on the base. After a few years, he was able to carry on a basic conversation in their language. Norma also developed an affinity with her host country, regularly blending the disparate cuisines of mainland Japan with the Sea Islands of her childhood. A conspicuous minority of unruly soldiers, however, harassed the locals and occasionally committed crimes against them. When civilians complained, their concerns were dismissed often with negative consequences for those who dared make such reports. Most soldiers accepted this as the way things were. Not Luke.

He complained to his commanding officer, requesting an investigation into the reports and allegations. When his protests fell on deaf ears he went higher in the chain of command and wrote a letter to a lieutenant colonel. "When they finally got back to me," he said, "it was like getting pushed into a hornets nest."

Luke was upbraided for breaking the chain of command. "They really came down on me after that. Harassing me and trying to intimidate me and Norma." He was falsely accused of using government property without proper authorization and threatened with Court Marshal. In truth, he had used a jeep with proper authorization but the requisition had suspiciously wound up missing. His commander, claiming Luke had stolen the vehicle, hauled him before the metaphorical gallows reserved for those brave souls who stand against injustice. "They were after me," he said, "from the time I started protesting until the door hit me on the way out."

Luke was dismissed from the military and he, Norma, and their twin daughters, Ruby and Rita, returned to Georgia with no money and no jobs. "If I'd kept my mouth shut I'd be living on a military pension right now." Instead, he had fought the good fight and been railroaded.

Other events followed that further disillusioned him. He found work at a funeral home and did odd jobs as a welder (a trade he'd learned in the military). Norma cleaned houses. Somehow, they managed to make ends meet. In the early 1960s, Luke "got the call" and began preaching occasionally at their church. "I thought I was going to be a minister for sure," he remembered. He studied the Bible with a burning desire to unlock the secrets of every parable, verse and psalm. "He was good," Norma recalled, laughing as she pretended to stand at the pulpit, imitating his authoritative bearing and raising her arm as if pulling back a curtain separating this world from the Divine. "Whenever he raised that arm," she said with a smile, "I knew the heavenly spirit was rising and the Holy Ghost was coming down."

At last he'd found his niche. It was a role well suited to his passion for social justice, moral courage and qualities as a leader. With the civil rights movement building momentum and churches often serving as the nuclei of protest and strategy, he believed this was where his grandmother's prophecy would be fulfilled.

He found, however, that many of the parishioners at his church were less eager to push for reform as openly as he was. "I really got people riled when I planned to take a group of young folks with me to attend the white church across town," he said. "I figured all these folks were desegregating soda counters, buses and movie theaters, why not the house of the Lord?" Looking back, he had more compassion for the temperate stance of his pastor and church deacons, but at the time he was impatient with what he saw as their foot-dragging. Amid perplexing and impassioned church politics, he was pressured to fall in line or find another place to worship. With Norma's support, he chose the latter. Once again, his stand on principle had led to ostracism and misunderstanding. It did not, however, dilute his resolve when it came to raising his voice when something violated his conscience.

In 1968 Ruby and Rita were in ninth grade and, for all practical purposes, the schools were still segregated despite a Supreme Court ruling, over ten years prior, ordering them to integrate as quickly as possible. "Near as I could make out," Luke said, without a hint of humor, "that meant sometime around when hell froze over."

He went down to the local school board and asked to see the superintendent. When the secretary said he was unavailable, Luke sat in the office all day before the man snuck out the back door. When Luke showed up the next day with the same request the secretary called the police and he was taken to the sheriff's office for several hours and "questioned." Word travels fast in a small town and within a week three of the women whose houses Norma cleaned had informed her they no longer needed her services. One even suggested she put a muzzle on Luke before he got into trouble. "I told her," Norma recalled, "if I had a muzzle I knew just where I'd put it and it wouldn't be on my husband."

Luke wasn't easily discouraged. He wrote letters to President Johnson and Supreme Court Justice Thurgood Marshal complaining about his state's resistance to desegregation. Norma searched for other work but was unable to find anything. When the welding jobs dried up, they worried.

Things got so difficult they decided to move to Newark, New Jersey, where Norma had some cousins. "We were a little fearful," she said. "We'd seen Newark on television when they had a big riot up there and people got killed. But we wanted a fresh start and we could stay with my people till we got settled."

They stayed in Newark for five years but never felt at ease there. It was a big, noisy place. Something always seemed to be boiling just below the surface. Luke got a job collecting coins from washers and dryers in a chain of Laundromats. Norma decided not to work so she could keep a closer eye on the kids. Without her income, it was difficult paying the bills. During winter, their apartment was so cold Luke collected empty bleach bottles and brought them home so Norma could fill them with hot water, wrap towels around them and tuck them into bed with Rita, Ruby, and their son Lemeul.

Luke's job required him to carry large amounts of cash, so he was vigilant and kept meticulous records of the daily collections. He noticed the man who owned the Laundromats associating with people reputed to be criminals and became concerned that the numbers related to his collections just weren't adding up when he happened to check some of the company bank records. He suspected his boss was using the laundry business as a smoke screen to hide profits from petty theft and possibly the heroin trade. "I guess they took the phrase money laundering seriously," he observed acidly.

Once again he was faced with the choice between remaining silent and tacitly accepting something he believed was wrong, or speaking out. "I actually thought about keeping my mouth shut that time. I was tired of having the rug pulled out from under me, plus I was worried about my family. I mean, these guys were rough." After agonizing about the situation and talking it over with his wife, he decided to confront the man. "I pulled out the heavy artillery," he joked, "and asked grandma's spirit to walk beside me that day and keep me from getting shot."

His boss insisted Luke's concerns were ungrounded, that he was imagining things. Luke was mollified enough to admit he may have been over-reacting. "I thought maybe I'd been watching too many detective shows." Nonetheless, he began asking questions around the neighborhood. His suspicions increased and when he confronted his boss again he was fired on the spot. Fed up with city life, demoralized and missing home, he and Norma moved the family back to Georgia.

Their subsequent years were relatively uneventful compared to earlier chapters. There were no gut-wrenching choices to be made, no large moral battles to be fought, just ongoing labors to survive and provide for their family.

Luke never forgot his grandmother's emphasis on improving the lives of others and her expectation that he do things on a scale larger than his own backyard. When his children left home and finances eased up, he convinced Norma to set something aside each month to donate to charities serving the poor or fighting for social and economic justice.

For years they sent whatever they could to charities and advocacy groups.

When Luke was diagnosed with cancer, the bills (even with his health insurance) were so overwhelming they were forced to stop their giving in order to try to keep pace with the stratospheric cost of treatments and medications. When they reached the end of his medical options, he and Norma moved in with Ruby and her family, in North Carolina. "I came here to be around my family until I die," he explained. Lemeul worked nearby as an English professor. Rita lived in Georgia and visited regularly.

He was resigned to death but worried about Norma, money and being dependent on others. His biggest concern, however, could be traced back to the words of his beloved grandmother. More than anyone, she had strengthened his resolve to live in accordance with a higher law governed by moral principles and courage to speak against injustice regardless of the consequences. He'd done his best to uphold these standards and had paid a high price. His stridency had caused anxiety and distress for people he loved and had often left him floundering. It had ended his career in the military, closed the door on his aspirations to become a minister, alienated friends and created enemies.

Looking back, he wondered if it had been worth it. Wouldn't it have been better, not to mention easier, if he'd simply acquiesced and reaped the social and material rewards claimed by those willing to go along? As far as he could see, he hadn't made the world any better. He'd only caused his family bouts with poverty and uncertainty.

"What good did it do?" he scowled, as though daring me to try to convince him the sacrifices had made a difference.

For many of us, when we look back, there are things we would do differently or choices we would reconsider. For Luke, it was his entire life that was being questioned. Whether he affirmed or renounced it was more than an abstract exercise in homespun philosophizing, it would determine the way he lived his final weeks, even the way he died.

Norma and his children had reassured him that he had lived well. As far as they were concerned his life had been a model of unassuming virtue. Its meaning resided in the example he'd provided others and the many lives he had touched. They believed it, but he didn't.

When he imagined what his life might have been like he saw himself as a brigadier general, respected by straight-backed soldiers and a grateful nation. He imagined himself pacing near his pulpit before a thriving congregation, a leader in his community and among his peers. Such fantasies are a pass-time most of us have engaged in, but for Luke it crossed the line from harmless daydreaming into the realm of painful rumination.

"If only I'd been able to change things. Then I'd know I've done the right things." Time and again such thoughts returned like spectral visitors impervious to reason. When he was younger, he had believed that good works and humane intentions would, in the long run, be validated and appreciated by others. Now he doubted it, and in so doing he questioned the value and meaning of his life.

It's hard to look back on your life and wish you had lived in a different way. We had several conversations exploring these inner churnings. I asked what he'd say to his grandmother if he could speak with her again. After thinking about it, he returned to her two ironclad rules. Along with his spiritual beliefs and the welfare of his family, they had formed the sturdy pillars upon which all of his choices had been made.

The first rule – don't sell your soul for silver or approval – was an admonition against striving for material or egoistic rewards because, in the end, these were mere illusion. Viewed through this lens, his life was a resounding success. Several times he had sacrificed comfort and security in pursuit of higher principle, always trying to focus on deeper truths.

The second rule – always stand for what's right whether or not others stand with you – had been a hallmark of his life. He'd embodied this imperative with integrity and courage.

"If grandma was here now," he said, "I'd ask how I did, and how come all those great things I was supposed to do never happened?"

I asked what he thought she would say. He thought about it and smiled. With eyes slightly glassy from unborn tears, he said, "She'd tell me we're not promised great things just for doing right, and if we're expecting some kinda reward we better look inside ourselves, or to God, to find it."

I suggested that doing our best to uphold a law higher than our own self-interest is synonymous with doing great things.

"I'll have to think about that one," he said in a fatigued tone that suggested it was time to move on.

He was tired and told me to do some of the talking for a while. There was a dog-eared copy of the play, *The Crucible*, on a nearby table which one of Ruby's daughters was reading for a high school class. I picked it up and thumbed through it. I told him it was based on the Salem witch trials of 1692. Arthur Miller had written it as a cautionary tale after the hysterical excesses of Senator Joseph McCarthy's witch hunt against alleged communists in the 1950s during which only brave souls with moral courage had stood up.

I suggested that the events in Salem, Massachusetts more than three hundred years earlier had a striking relevance to his life and struggle. Many innocent people had been killed because they had chosen to stand up for their principles and act in accordance with conscience rather than give in to pressures to conform and accept injustice. Though they were pressured to back down, many chose to die rather than compromise their integrity or betray friends and neighbors.

I asked if he wanted me to tell him about what had happened.

"After a build up like that," he smiled, "you're not leaving till you do."

*

When the first ships loaded with English Puritans landed along the stony coast near present-day Boston in 1630, they set to work building what they believed would be a "city on a hill" standing for all to see. It would be a beacon in the wilderness for those who sought to live a Godly life. In a world full of conflict, temptation and vice, they intended to hold themselves to a higher standard and live in accordance with strict moral principles.

They inhabited a world where God's presence was personal and immediate, infusing everything from the first shoots of corn rising from spring ground to the pang of conscience following a selfish thought. The devil was also a real and palpable presence constantly probing the hearts of men and women, searching their faith for weakness and lack of resolve.

The existence of witches was unquestioned. Anyone with the temerity to doubt their reality might wind up hauled before a magistrate to explain such dangerous thinking. The veil separating this world from the supernatural one was thin and porous. It was the job of every good Puritan to be vigilant and root out those, such as witches, who conspired with evil.

By 1692, although some of the religious zeal of the first settlers had waned, this was still the world of Salem, a thriving seaport north of Boston and its adjacent community known as Salem Village. While the town was a busy commercial center, the village was oriented toward agricultural pursuits and had recently petitioned to become a separate municipality. Town officials had denied the request, but the village was allowed to establish its own church and, at the time, it was shepherded by Reverend Samuel Parris.

In the dark, frigid days of January 1692, Parris's nine-year-old daughter and one of her friends began exhibiting strange and frightening behaviors that the minister was at a loss to explain. The girls' bodies contorted into odd postures, they gesticulated in seemingly unnatural ways, and, according to a witness, uttered "foolish, ridiculous speeches, which neither they themselves nor any others could make sense of."

Parris called physician William Griggs who couldn't find any organic cause for the strange behavior. When other young women began experiencing similar fits and spasms, the doctor surmised they were being tormented by *maleficium*—evil magic, possibly conjured by witches.

When Parris learned that a slave named Tituba had been spending time with the girls engaging in what appeared to have been acts of divination he was irate. He called on fellow ministers and influential members of the village for advice. By then several other girls were experiencing the same mysterious convulsions. When pressure was put on them to identify their tormentors they accused Sarah Good, Sarah Osborne, and Tituba.

On February 29, the three bewildered women were charged with witchcraft and jailed in Salem Town. The next day they were hauled into a meetinghouse full of spectators and interrogated by magistrates John Hathorne and Jonathan Corwin. From the start, the officials considered them guilty and harangued them in accusatory tones with leading questions. Sarah Good was the first to be questioned. A snippet from her ordeal, recorded by an eyewitness in the form of questions and answers, conveys what lay in store for the accused.

Q. Sarah Good what evil Spirit have you familiarity with?

A. None.

Q. Have you made no contract with the devil?

A. No.

Q. Why do you hurt these children?

A. I do not hurt them. I scorn it.

Q. Who do you employ then to do it?

A. I employ nobody.

Q. What creature do you employ then?

A. No creature but I am falsely accused.

During questioning some of the accusing girls were again convulsed with fits and seizures. In the face of such drama, the crowd became so fearful that before the hearing was complete even Sarah Good's husband had joined the accusers, offering testimony against his besieged wife whose pleas of innocence were drowned out.

The interrogation was representative of what was to recur during the next several months as more people were accused and more hearings held. The presiding magistrates and judges assumed the accused person was guilty and tried to force him or her to confess. The core group of young girls leveling many of the accusations was present and magistrates often addressed questions directly to them as though their testimony was authoritative. Often, the girls appeared to become captive to dramatic displays of bewitchment that were attributed to the accused or to Satan acting on their behalf.

Spectators participated spontaneously, defendants were tortured and harassed, exculpatory evidence was dismissed. Fear was so pervasive that testimony that would never have been allowed in a legitimate legal proceeding of the time became the basis upon which suspects were condemned. Most significant was so-called, "spectral evidence," in which accusers claimed that a person's apparition had appeared before them trying to convince them to become a witch. Puritan courts usually barred such reports because these claims were impossible to prove and an accuser might have ulterior motives. With emotions high and fear running rampant, Salem became a deadly exception to this time-tested legal practice.

At the end of the first hearing, all three women were found guilty and shipped to jail in Boston to await criminal trials. The crisis might have ended there but Tituba, under intense pressure, confessed that she and her co-defendants were guilty of plotting with the devil. She said there were seven other witches in Salem and Boston, though she didn't know their identities.

She later tried to recant her testimony because, as witness Robert Calef put it: "her master did beat her, and otherwise abuse her, to make her confess and accuse." Despite accusations delivered under duress and her attempt to recant, Tituba's allegations were taken at face value and intensified people's terror, sparking further accusations.

Although the band of apparently possessed girls remained at the forefront of the accusers, others joined them. By the time the next hearing was held, Salem resident Deodat Lawson wrote people were so frightened that all who attended were "struck with consternation, and they were afraid, that those that sat next to them, were under the influence of witchcraft." In this ocean of panic, simply being accused of practicing the demonic arts was tantamount in many people's minds to guilt.

Some brave souls were more cautious. Most of these held their tongues or expressed their concerns in a manner calculated not to arouse suspicion. One of the few who spoke out defiantly against the hysteria was John Proctor, a sixty-one-year-old tavern keeper. He was critical of the judicial proceedings and openly stated his disbelief that so many of his neighbors could be witches. When his wife, Elizabeth, was accused, he vehemently defended her innocence.

Proctor's courage to speak out was rare. The social pressure against doing so was great and most people, including the magistrates, believed that the accused were guilty. In their minds, Proctor's willingness to publically question the court and attack the credibility of those who bore witness against Satan's conspirators, much less defend the accused, were acts worthy of condemnation. By speaking out against injustice he had placed himself at risk of being hauled before the magistrates as well, and ultimately, the gallows. Not surprisingly, he was soon among the accused.

By summer, more hearings had been held and the magistrates had judged everyone guilty, including John Proctor. But these were not the criminal trials necessary to dispense ultimate judgment. No such trials could be held until the new colonial governor, William Phips, arrived from England. The prior governor had been ousted in 1689 and thus, throughout the first months of the crisis the legal system of Massachusetts was in a state of confusing interregnum.

Week after week innocent people were accused, warrants issued, arrests made, hearings held and alleged witches thrown in jail, yet not a single criminal trial had been held. When Governor Phips finally sailed into Boston Harbor thirty-eight people were packed into the jails at Salem and Boston suspected of witchcraft. Five others had succumbed to the dogged pressures of the magistrates and simply confessed they were witches. Hundreds of aroused Salem residents had stepped forward and joined in the hailstorm of accusations against their neighbors.

Phips quickly established an official court composed of nine judges. Within days they had convicted Bridget Bishop of witchcraft. A few days later, in a scene that would be repeated in the months to come, she was placed in a wooden cart and rolled up the rocky bluff to "Witch's Hill" and hung.

She went to her death knowing she was innocent, refusing to confess to a crime she had not committed despite the concerted efforts of an intimidating array of learned judges bent on making her do so. She could have saved her life by confessing to the crime and giving the court a few more names. Instead, she chose to abide by a higher law, higher even than self-preservation. And she refused to turn on her neighbors the way others were doing.

In the wake of her execution, murmurs could be heard that the proceedings, and the accusers, were going too far. Several ministers, perhaps sobered by the legal killing, sent a letter to the court urging "a very critical and exquisite caution" in any future judgments. Although the clergymen applauded the judges' zeal to root out and prosecute Satan's minion, they advised against placing too much weight on dubious forms of evidence such as spectral visitation. This, they warned, might result in a "long train of miserable consequences."

In an act of conscience, Reverend William Milborne circulated two petitions defending several of the accused as "persons of good fame and unspotted reputation." In light of what the court had allowed to stand as evidence, one petition stated that the signatories had "great grounds to fear that the innocent will be condemned." When Governor Phips got wind of what Milborne was up to, he quashed the petitions before they could be submitted.

Another petition was circulated defending the innocence of Rebecca Nurse. Others began questioning the credibility and motives of the young accusers. Despite social pressure and the threat of dire personal consequences, people of moral courage began standing up. Such objections, however, were anemic compared to the power of fear that gripped most of those living in Salem. The vocal majority remained intent on making sure that all who were accused either confessed and recanted or dangled from the end of a rope.

When the court next convened all five defendants refused to admit guilt despite intense pressures to force confessions. Once again the court considered animated testimony accompanied by the dramatics of the seemingly tormented girls. The defendants were found guilty and sentenced to death. Even on the scaffold they refused to give in to last minute demands to confess. Sarah Good retorted to a minister that, "I am no more a witch than you are a wizard, and if you take away my life, God will give you blood to drink."

Six innocent people were dead for refusing to confess guilt. In contrast, none who had confessed were in danger of being wheeled out to Witch's Hill. By then it was evident that the surest way to save one's skin was simply to confess to the crime. Historians Davidson and Lytle describe the dilemma: "Those who were wrongly accused quickly realized that if they did not confess, they were likely to be hung. If they did confess, they could escape death, but would have to demonstrate their sincerity by providing details of their misdeeds and names of other participants. The temptation must have been great to confess and, in so doing, to implicate other innocent people."

In addition, a confession would spare one from the tortures legally employed under English law. John Proctor, for example, complained that when his son William was arrested for wizardry, "he would not confess that he was guilty, when he was innocent," and colonial officials "tied him neck and heels till the blood gushed out at his nose."

Before the witch hunt ended at least fifty people had confessed to crimes they had not committed. Robert Calef chided that, "though the confessing witches were many, yet none of them that confessed their own guilt, and abode by their confession, was put to death." Others had shown profound integrity and moral courage, choosing to die rather than violate their morals, implicate others or validate the workings of a court wracked by paranoia. More than any in Salem, those who were killed on Witch's Hill exemplified the values and hopes of their Puritan ancestors who had intended to live their lives in accordance with the highest spiritual principles.

It seemed nothing could stop the feverish momentum of anxious persecution. Next it was the Proctors and four others who were sentenced to hang. Elizabeth Proctor's execution was postponed in consideration of the fact that she was pregnant and it was ordered that she be hung after the child was born. Before their executions, the condemned were allowed to address the witnessing crowd. When George Burroughs flawlessly recited the Lord's Prayer (something a witch was supposedly not able to do), Calef reports that many were so affected that "it seemed to some that the spectators would hinder the execution." Had it not been for Reverend Cotton Mather's demands that the hangings proceed, and claims by the accusing girls that they had seen an apparition put the words of the prayer in Burroughs' mouth, the crowd might have stopped the executions on the spot. As it were, the hangings proceeded without further incident, leaving five more innocents dead.

Despite multiple executions, the prisons continued to fill and anxiety floated freely like leaves dispersed in an angry wind. To some, including a growing number of ministers, the number of accused defied believability. Moreover, the strange behavior of the afflicted girls began looking more like malicious mischief than Satan's work. Even Cotton Mather began to suspect that the devil's goal was not to convert witches, but to set the people of Salem against one another.

When the court next convened some two hundred persons stood accused, including many of the colony's most reputable and pious members. During this session, five persons were found guilty but pardoned when they chose to confess. Ten others refused to do so and were sentenced to death. One of these, Dorcas Hoar, confessed at the last minute and was reprieved, another escaped from jail and fled Salem altogether.

On September 22, the remaining eight were hung. One of them, Mary Easty, sent a letter to the court before her death. "I petition your honors," she wrote, "not for my life, for I know I must die, and my appointed time is set; but…that no more innocent blood be shed."

Perhaps it would have consoled her had she known that theirs would in fact be the last innocent blood spilled. In all, fourteen women and five men were executed, one man died while being tortured and several others perished awaiting judgment in the noxious air of prison. More than twice as many had confessed and added their voices against the innocent.

Though vilified at the time, we now know that those who were executed were among the most courageous and self-sacrificing members of the community. They chose to live in accordance with the highest moral and spiritual principles even though it meant suffering unjust consequences and opprobrium. Many left behind children and spouses rather than betray their consciences and friends. It is a bitter irony that, looking back, we can see that those who were executed were most likely the most devout people in Puritan society. It was they who had most faithfully lived up to the ideals of their ancestors who decades before had built their city on a hill.

They had endured brutal treatment, as well as the psychological violence of false accusations and condemnation rather than betraying their core values and religious faith. Falsely confessing, though it would have saved them, was, in the understanding of the time a form of blasphemy. They had refused to succumb to earthly pressures, lie under oath, betray their friends or renounce their trust in God. In the end, their steadfast willingness to stand on principle and sacrifice their lives to a higher cause was an important reason Salem's collective hysteria finally subsided.

*

All of us have an inner place of strength, wisdom and fortitude. Though it may be outside our awareness as we go to work, raise children and pay the bills, when we are challenged we may find ourselves reconnecting with this place. Luke had done his best to make this the center of his life. Doing so had given many rewards but had also created crises and suffering he might have avoided had his integrity and sense of justice not demanded action regardless of the personal risks.

He was captivated by the plight of those in Salem who had refused to yield to a phalanx of false accusers. They were examples of the values that his grandmother had instilled in him.

"They knew they were going to die," he said, shaking his head in admiration, "and they stuck to their guns."

We talked about the sacrifices they'd made, knowing that standing firm would not only endanger them but might harm their loved ones – children might grow up without mothers, husbands might be left without wives, reputations could be ruined and property seized.

I asked Luke if he thought they had done the right thing.

"Yeah, they did."

"Wouldn't it have been better to just go along?"

"And sell your soul? No way. Then you're nothing but a slave."

"But their lives were turned upside down. Their families suffered."

He thought about this, smiled, then threw his hands up in mock surrender, "You set me up for that one didn't you?"

Laughter was followed by silence as he organized his thoughts. Finally, he said, "I've tried to do what's right. I've paid for it, but I stood firm."

"Was the price worth it?"

"It was hard. You shouldn't have to suffer for doing the right thing."

"Was it worth it?"

"I can't imagine having to face myself in the mirror or talk to my kids about right and wrong knowing I didn't stand up. I can look back with a clean conscience knowing I tried. You know, I had folks here and there that backed me up. There are always at least a few others who catch up with you and watch your back."

By the time the last eight "witches" were hung in September 1692, the people of Salem were beginning to catch up as well. It was obvious to many that things had gone too far. From the beginning there had been isolated protests. People had signed petitions, defended a neighbor's innocence or questioned the reliability of the accusers. Eyes were opening.

Reverend Increase Mather (father of Cotton Mather) wrote an essay called, *Cases of Conscience Concerning Evil Spirits* in which he warned the court of grave consequences if it persisted in legitimizing the persecution of innocents. When Mather's essay was signed by fourteen other ministers and printed as a book, its impact was significant.

Governor Phips forbade any more arrests on charges of witchcraft and dissolved the court. By then, it was clear that a horrible injustice had occurred. Echoing Mather's objections, Phips acknowledged that "several persons who were doubtless innocent" had been executed.

It was a few weeks before I saw Luke again. During that time his decline had been rapid. He hadn't eaten anything in several days and was taking only miniscule amounts of fluid. He was dying and Norma knew it.

Most of the visit was spent talking with her at Luke's bedside, reflecting on his life, legacy, and their impending separation. Although he appeared to be sleeping Luke could hear our voices as evidenced in facial expressions, alterations in the rhythm of his breathing and a few barely audible sounds as we spoke. Often when people are near death, though they do not have the energy to interact and appear to be sleeping, they hear what is being said and can feel the touch of a loved one's hand.

Norma teased out the themes of his life – commitment to family, faith in God and fair play. At times she spoke to him directly to underscore a point or make sure he knew how much she appreciated and loved his gentle spirit. And like him, she refused to gloss over their hardships.

"He could be as stubborn as a snapping turtle and bite twice as hard," she said. "And when he thought he was right, you better watch out."

She smiled when I asked her, as I had Luke, about the cost of acting with moral courage.

"The cost would have been worse not doing it."

I asked her to hold Luke's hand and tell him what she meant. Slowly, she recalled times during which she'd been especially proud of him, assuring him that, "every time we had the rug pulled out from under us, I found something more to love about you. Your grandma would be proud of you."

A few days later, Luke died surrounded by his family. When I talked to Norma afterward, she said he had seen his grandmother during the last two days of his life. "At first we thought he was just confused but he kept talking to her, asking us if we saw her and telling us what she was saying. After a while, we just figured she had come back to take her grandson home."

Experiences like these are common at the end of life. Though the prevalence and origins of such paranormal visitations is subject to debate, research as well as reports from family members like Norma and medical professionals suggests that a majority of those who experience such deathbed visions respond with a sense of peace or joy. Related experiences (sometimes spoken of broadly as deathbed phenomenon or transpersonal end-of-life experiences) such as near death and out of body experiences, synchronicities and after death communication appear to be a common part of the continuum of events which may occur at the end of life.

I asked Norma if Luke's grandmother had conveyed any messages to him.

She nodded, "She told him he did a good job."

Chapter Five
Adrift in the Pacific
Old Wounds

Nell was terrified of death. Even at ninety-three, the mere mention of the word was enough to start her on the road to a panic attack. Twice, after the subject arose, she'd wound up in the emergency department in the grip of anxiety so acute her breathing had become shallow and erratic. Since then, her niece Cleo had avoided mentioning anything related to death including Nell's cardiac disease.

Beneath her fear Nell harbored a quiet, though less visible, nervousness about loss in general which had accompanied her throughout her life. She had always been afraid of losing people and things she cared about. She'd avoided romantic relationships because she didn't want to get hurt; friendships because something always went wrong sooner or later. Despite her love for cats she'd refused to have pets because "they only die and leave you heartbroken." It was a soft refrain in the long song of her life: When you get close to someone, sooner or later things fall apart. Now that she was dying – in a sense, losing her self – this refrain and its accompanying sense of fear and foreboding had intensified.

In other regards Nell appeared self-reliant and more-or-less free from anxiety. She had worked for decades as a pediatric intensive care nurse, respected by colleagues who marveled at her ability to handle the pressures of a difficult job with flexibility and ease. She'd lived alone until she was ninety, managing her own affairs. Her mind was absorbent and creative. Despite describing herself as a loner, she enjoyed being around others and was lithe and engaging in conversation.

She had remained in her home for as long as she could but when her needs began multiplying Cleo and her husband Sam had invited her to live with them. After much protest, negotiation and delay, Nell had agreed on the condition that she pull her weight financially by turning over her social security check to the household expenses.

Cleo had offered her the guest room but Nell preferred living in the basement where her little room had become a tiny sanctuary in which she felt safe and in control. In her weakened condition, it was *terra firma*, the only place where she seemed to stand on solid ground and which she was very reluctant to leave.

Part of her reluctance was due to the tremendous effort it took to climb the stairs. The main reason, however, was her underlying anxiety. As her illness progressed, nervousness about leaving her safe place became more pronounced. In fact, the principal reason she'd agreed to hospice care was that she would no longer have to go to the doctor's office.

The afternoon I met her Nell was cheerful and told stories about her childhood. She was careful to stick closely to the central theme of her reminiscences, which was that her life had been happy. She had fond memories of growing up in a New England fishing town. The vivid detail of her recollections was astounding: the tiny school house with the iron furnace; the old sea captain who taught her to tie nautical knots; the little boy who liked to jump out from the bushes yelling "Thar she blows" while brandishing a stick as though it were a harpoon. Though it sounded like an idyllic time, she never mentioned her family and glossed over the first years of her life without comment.

Neither of us mentioned her heart disease or the fact that I was there because she was dying. Having talked with Cleo I suspected she may have experienced some kind of psychological trauma at some point in her life and I didn't want to push too hard on our first visit. Besides, she was eager to focus on other things and seemed skittish that I might try to steer her away from her picturesque narrative, so I did not. There would be opportunities later to explore what might be locked beneath the stories of her happy childhood.

Over the next several weeks as her body was steadily ground down by illness Nell went through taxing mental contortions to appear happy. She even convinced herself that she just had a bad case of the flu. All she needed was to increase some of her many nutritional supplements, maybe the iron or vitamin B. Despite losing her ability to move independently and needing a nursing assistant to help her bathe and dress, she continued talking about getting better.

She was sleeping more, eating less and using what strength remained to mask her growing fear. She told herself that if she just kept a positive attitude she'd get better. Although she managed to push her anxiety away, it emerged in nightmares and the sudden onset of a fear of the dark. Whenever members of her hospice team tried talking with her about her changing condition her respiration increased and sweat appeared on her forehead – signs her nervous system was ramping up into a fight, flight or freeze response. She refused to talk about anything other than what she called "happy thoughts." Death was a taboo subject and she instructed me and the rest of her hospice team to "talk with Cleo if you want but leave me out of that kind of talk."

Despite her determination to hold back the emotional leviathan swimming beneath the surface, it proved impossible. I received a telephone call from Sam one morning telling me Nell had suffered a panic attack during the night. Since then, she'd been crying and withdrawn, repeating the phrase, "I don't want to die." Cleo had talked with the nurse about increasing her anti-anxiety medication. Now, they wanted me to talk with her to see if it would do any good.

When I arrived, Cleo told me that Nell had been "staring into space" for more than an hour without saying a word. As I entered her corner room, she remained silent. I asked if I could sit beside her and she nodded her head. Her face appeared listless and distant, like an ebbing tide. I wondered if she was dissociating, something that can happen when someone is overwhelmed. Asking questions might have further overwhelmed her so I sat silently and waited. After several minutes, tears welled up in her eyes. As they trickled down her cheeks, she said, "I'm dying, aren't I?"

"What is your answer to that question?" I asked gently.

She hesitated then, drying her eyes with the bed sheet, whispered, "I think I'm going to die."

"Have you known this for a while Nell? Or is it just hitting you?"

Tears gave way to the voluble crying that would recur throughout our conversation like waves rolling in and out.

"Just hitting me," she whispered.

Our visit that day was full of silent pauses as she struggled to find words or waited for tears to subside. At times I had to help her stay grounded using de-escalation techniques intended to settle her nervous system, interrupt cascading catastrophic thoughts or connect her to an inward place of strength.

She knew she was dying and she was terrified. She didn't know why she was so afraid much less how to find peace. She'd had fear throughout her life but it had never been this paralyzing. No longer able to avoid it or distract herself from her weakening condition, she was shaking in terror and wanted it to stop.

For someone who had gone to such great lengths to avoid talking about or even acknowledging her terror, Nell's willingness to do so now seemed sudden. Cautiously, I asked her if I could ask some "hard questions." When she agreed I made sure she knew that she was in control of how far we went and whether or not she wanted to continue.

"When you think about death, what's the first picture that pops into your mind?"

She said she saw in her mind's eye a bird of prey descending on a tiny rabbit, gripping it in its talons and snapping its bones into little pieces. "I can hear the bones snapping."

"Would you be willing to tell me your first experience with death Nell?"

The question opened the floodgates and again she began sobbing. I was heartened that she was able to do so without moving toward a state of panic. The sobbing this time seemed penetrated by sadness more than fear. When the tears subsided she diverted her gaze downward to avoid making eye contact and said in a deflated voice. "Daddy was killed when I was little."

It turned out that Nell's life had not begun in New England nor had her childhood been idyllic. She'd been born in the mountains of western Pennsylvania where her father had worked in the coalmines. Like other mining families, she and her parents had lived in an uninsulated shack owned by the coal company. Mining was grueling, dangerous work and the company had little concern for the safety of their workers. Injuries and deaths were common. There were cave-ins, she said, and people died in explosions. Others died from inhaling poisonous gas or were killed by run-away coal cars.

For years miners had pushed for safer conditions, shorter hours and better pay. They had tried to change the exploitive arrangement where families were forced to pay whatever prices the company charged for housing and basic supplies, racking up debts and further tightening the company's control over their lives. Although such things were not discussed with children, Nell learned later in life that her father had been involved in organizing for the United Mine Workers. As with many labor organizers, he attracted the attention of the company's goon squad.

When Nell was five they murdered him. As is often the case with traumatic memory, when Nell spoke of that night the images were fragmented and, at the same time, layered with multi-dimensional detail of what she saw, heard, felt, thought, even smelled.

She recalled her pregnant mother walking back and forth on the floorboards of their shack, repeatedly saying, "Oh no." A man came to the door and talked in a whisper. Her mother began screaming. Two women came in and rushed her mother out the door. The man lifted Nell into his arms and carried her to a nearby home. As they walked, she heard men's voices and the metallic sound of lanterns swinging back and forth over railroad tracks. She remembered the smell of kerosene and a harsh-sounding voice say, "Lift him up." Then she heard the sound, very clear and distinct, of what she said were bones snapping. Later in life she came to believe this had been the sound of her father's bones cracking as men lifted his lifeless body from the railroad tracks where company thugs had placed his corpse and crushed it with a locomotive to make his death look like an accident.

I was stunned, not only by Nell's story but by the fact that she was able to recount it without spiraling into panic. By the end, her voice was a trancelike monotone as though viewing herself from far away.

"Who have you told about that night?" I asked.

"No one."

"Never?"

"Never."

"Why not?"

She searched for the words, "I guess I thought if I didn't talk about it, it would go away."

She motioned that she didn't want to continue. She sobbed quietly for a minute or two then blew her nose and forced an unconvincing smile, "I'm over ninety years old. When I think about that night I feel like a helpless five-year-old."

When repressed traumatic memories break into consciousness they can release a storm of thoughts and emotions as intense as those during and in the aftermath of the original trauma. Sometimes near the end of one's life there are sensations or experiences – physical pain, for example, or a sense of immobility, vulnerability, helplessness or being close to death – that trigger painful memories and associated feelings and thoughts. I was concerned that the sudden reemergence of this trauma might be an emotional volcano.

I offered her some strategies for managing any intense thoughts, emotions or physiological states associated with these memories. With her permission, I promised to consult with Cleo before I left to make sure she knew about our talk.

Nell was tired. She closed her eyes, "Am I crazy or something? I thought if I buried it, it would go away. I never thought it could've outlasted me."

"There's no expiration date on something like this," I said. "Maybe talking will lower the pressure you've been carrying inside."

Weeks before, she'd told me about a whale-watching trip she had taken on a vacation. It was another of her "happy memories" and she'd spoken rhapsodically about the thrill of being so close to these magnificent creatures. I asked if she'd like to hear a story about a young man who had struggled with a similar challenge. He'd suffered a horrible ordeal on a whaling voyage to the Pacific and, for much of his life tried to bury away the pain and pretend it hadn't happened only to have it reemerge as he faced his twilight years.

Closing her eyes she whispered, "Thar she blows."

*

If Owen Chase could have seen the future in the rippling waters of Nantucket harbor in the summer of 1819 he would have given up whaling and headed off in search of a new vocation. Chase, however, was busy overseeing preparations for an upcoming whaling expedition and had no time for such aquatic divinations.

Nantucket, a small island off the coast of Massachusetts, was homeport for over sixty whaleships equipped for journeys that usually lasted two years or more. As whaleships went, the eighty-seven-foot *Essex*, commanded by Captain Pollard was relatively small but had served well on prior voyages. First Mate Chase knew the ship in its smallest detail. Having recently returned on the vessel with a hold filled with barrels of whale oil, he was eager to set out for more.

Like all whaleships, the *Essex* was an industrial mill on water. Aboard a rolling foundation of wood propelled by canvas sail were large brick kilns, huge iron pots and a mind-boggling array of specialized hooks, knives and spades. Men were organized into crews so work could go on around-the-clock. Their entire focus was finding, killing, and extracting oil (used in lamps, paraffin candles and to lubricate machinery) from as many whales as they could catch.

Once underway, crewmembers took turns standing in the mainmast night and day watching for signs of their quarry. When whales were spotted, three twenty-five foot whaleboats were lowered into the water and six-man crews rowed feverishly in pursuit. They hunted with lances and handheld harpoons affixed to a long rope called a whale-line. Once the harpoon landed, the whale-line connected boat and whale until the men were close enough to use their lances. After a whale was killed, the massive carcass was towed back to the ship and prepared for "trying-out" in which the tough blubber was cut and removed in huge sheets, chopped into smaller pieces, thrown into metal try-pots and boiled to remove the oil.

By November 20, 1820 the *Essex* had rounded Cape Horn and entered the Pacific where the barrels in its hold were filling steadily. That day they spotted a pod of Sperm Whales and the whaleboats were quickly deployed. The men in Chase's boat narrowly escaped being swamped by a flailing whale and had to return to the ship. As his men worked to repair the boat a large Sperm Whale, weighing perhaps eighty tons, charged the ship, accelerating as it approached. As Chase remembered it, the whale, "came down upon us with full speed and struck the ship with his head, just forward of the fore-chains. He gave us such an appalling and tremendous jar as nearly threw us all on our faces."

Those aboard ship were dumbfounded. Such behavior from these giant mammals was unheard of. They were there to hunt their prey and now the tables had been turned. They quickly surveyed the damage and found a gaping hole in the ship's side below the waterline. Chase ordered the men to prepare the emergency pumps but before they could comply the whale charged again. Bearing down on them with what Chase described as "tenfold fury and vengeance in his aspect," it rammed its powerful brow again into the ship. This time the *Essex* was done for. In mere minutes the lives of every man aboard had been forever changed.

Chase and his small crew lowered their hastily repaired whaleboat back into the water and jumped in. By the time Pollard and the rest of the men reached the site of the disaster the *Essex* was a wooden corpse bobbing in the aftermath of the whale's inexplicable assault.

Dazed and in shock, the whalers had the presence of mind to salvage what they could – fresh water, navigational instruments, tools, guns and several hundred pounds of dry biscuits. As darkness fell, the disconsolate men circled the floating debris. The next morning, with the crippled *Essex* still bobbing in the water, Chase recalled that they "wandered around in every part of the ship in a sort of vacant idleness."

Although barely afloat, the whalers were reluctant to leave the *Essex* behind. It had been their home in the empty vastness of the Pacific. They had trusted its strong oak walls as they would have a fortress of rock. Thomas Nickerson remembered how they clung to the wreck as though "it were possible that she could relieve us from the fate that seemed to await us."

Reluctantly though, they realized that remaining with the wreck would only lessen their chances of survival. If they were to reach land, they would have to move. Using cedar planks, they raised the sides of each whaleboat by about six inches, fashioned masts from spare timber, and sails from a patchwork of canvas. There were six men in Chase's boat and seven each in Pollard's and second mate, Matthew Joy's. They planned to sail south for about 1,500 miles where they might catch the friendly winds that would take them east to the distant coast of Chile. Given the vagaries of weather, limited provisions, and their reliance on dead reckoning to estimate their position, it was an optimistic plan at best.

The frightened men spent the next several days buffeted by waves and pelted with rain. Water splashed over the sides of their boats, tossing them about like splinters of driftwood. It must have seemed like a nightmare incarnate, helplessly adrift in tiny lightweight craft amid the darkness and thunder of a powerful storm. In danger of capsizing or being separated from their companions, the men bailed until their arms burned, then bailed some more.

By the end of November, thirst and hunger were constant. With daily water rations down to a half pint per man they learned, as Chase put it, that the "violence of raving thirst has no parallel in the catalogue of human calamities." The sun bore down, reflecting off the water as though they were in a giant solar oven. Nickerson, traveling with Chase, later wrote that with no way to screen the sun, "our suffering became most intolerable as our short allowance of water was barely enough to support life."

After surviving more horrific storms the leaky whaleboats became stalled by a calm that lasted almost a week during which not a wind stirred. Baked by the sun, too weak to row, depleting what little supplies remained and not moving any closer toward the distant sanctuary of Chile, the men were pushed to the limits of their endurance. "Our suffering during these calm days," Chase later wrote, "almost exceeded human belief."

When the wind finally resumed, the men were nearly dead. Their water was almost gone. Physically and emotionally they were crushed beneath the pitiless accretions of trauma and privation. Nathaniel Philbrick captured the scene:

> Their physical torments had reached a terrible crescendo. It was almost as if they were being poisoned

by the combined effects of thirst and hunger. A glutinous and bitter saliva collected in their mouths that was "intolerable beyond expression." Their hair was falling out in clumps. Their skin was so burned and covered with sores that a splash of seawater felt like acid burning on their flesh. Strangest of all, as their eyes sunk into their skulls and their cheekbones projected, they all began to look alike, their identities obliterated by dehydration and starvation.

On December 20, while the dying castaways floated listlessly, they sighted land. It turned out to be Henderson Island, a tiny non-descript outcropping of coral, but to the desperate whalers it looked like salvation. Looking back years later, Nickerson wrote, "Never have my eyes rested on anything so pleasingly beautiful."

After beaching their battered boats they surveyed the island on weak, wobbly knees and found some birds, eggs and crabs but no water. They decided to conduct a more thorough search, an arduous task since, as Chase reported, "Our bodies had wasted away to almost skin and bone and possessed so little strength as often to require each other's assistance in performing some of its weakest functions."

Their efforts paid off when they found a modest spring with enough water to fill their empty casks and temporarily satisfy their thirst. Unfortunately, there wasn't enough food on the island to sustain them. They would have to resume their agonizing journey. Three men couldn't bear the thought of returning to the rigors of the sea and decided to stay behind, preferring the thin chance that they could survive on the island's meager fare long enough to hail a passing ship to the unsympathetic and ill-named Pacific.

On December 27, the determined survivors launched their boats into the oncoming waves. Despite their filled water barrels, the situation was as dire as when they had first sighted Henderson Island. Matthew Joy was the first to die. Starvation killed him on January 8, 1821. A few days later the sky once again bristled with lightning and the boats were dashed about in a punishing storm. The whalers had little strength to fight the gale. When the storm finally broke the men in Chase's boat had been separated from their companions, unsure whether their friends were dead or alive.

They were still over a thousand nautical miles from Chile with little food to sustain their flickering lives. They desperately needed to extend their food supply but there was no way to do it other than cut their already inadequate allowance. It was a dilemma Chase summed up as a choice to "either feed our bodies – and our hopes – a little longer or, in the agonies of hunger, to seize upon and devour our provisions and then coolly to await the approach of death." With stoic discipline, they decided to reduce the ration to less than three ounces of hardtack a day.

On January 20, Richard Peterson died. The rest, "were so feeble," Nickerson recalled, "that we could scarcely crawl about the boat upon our hands and knees." Several days later, Chase, sullen and losing hope, increased the rations. "Our sufferings were now drawing to a close. A terrible death appeared shortly to await us. Hunger became violent and outrageous, and we prepared for a speedy release from our troubles."

When Isaac Cole died Chase broached the subject of eating his emaciated remains. When the others agreed, the hungry men somberly ate the whaler's sun-scorched corpse. Whether this is what sustained them is hard to know, but on February 18 Benjamin Lawrence spotted an English merchant vessel, the *Indian*. As if awakening from a long nightmare, the three dazed survivors were soon on their way to Valparaiso, Chile, traumatized and starving, but alive.

When Chase arrived back in Nantucket, despite what he'd gone through, he was intent on putting the *Essex* behind him and moving on. As soon as his physical condition allowed, he signed on as first mate for a New Bedford whaleship. To outward appearances, his life continued along on the same path it might have taken if the wreck had never occurred. He eventually earned command of a whaleship and plied the waters of the Pacific searching for Sperm Whales until he retired in 1840. Appearances, however, are a poor measure of the inward effects of trauma.

When Chase was in his sixties, perhaps once again feeling the tenuous thread of his mortality, his long submerged anxiety exploded into view. He developed an overwhelming and obsessive fear of starving. He began hording food in his attic, convinced that without ample supplies his life was in jeopardy. Nothing could reassure him or diminish the force of his compulsive behavior. As he neared the end of his life the once fiery captain was plagued by intense fear and panic as the haunting specter of starvation intensified.

Sadly, he was so inconsolable, his anxiety so crippling, he was eventually judged to be insane. His suffering continued until he died in 1867. Like a dormant memory awakened and revived, the horrible experiences of his youth had reentered his awareness as he reached the end of his life. He'd tried to press it out of his mind, like oil pressed from whale blubber and hidden away in the hold of a ship, but as his life neared its end the hold had broken open.

*

Although we may try to forget painful or frightening experiences often the more we struggle to deny them, the more creative they become in how they influence our lives, affecting us in subtle and not-so-subtle ways until we find a way to make peace. After Nell's father died, she and her mother had moved in with distant relatives in New England. It had been a confusing time and the details in Nell's mind were blurry. She hadn't been allowed to speak about her father and was isolated in her grief, left to sort out the terrible events on her own. In her confusion, she had attempted to bury the memory in a place deeper than any mineshaft.

In some ways her efforts had been successful. She had lived a meaningful, productive life. As a nurse she had positively impacted patients and families, shared in their joy and comforted them in their despair. But currents of her early trauma had run through her life like an underground river. The fear of loss which had separated her from others; nervousness that some catastrophe was always lurking around the corner; her insistence on banishing all but "happy" thoughts and feelings from her life, were just some of the costs of her self-imposed amnesia.

During the next few sessions, she found other things buried along with the memory of the horrible night her father had been murdered. As a child, for example, she had believed it was her fault that her father had been killed. She should have been the one to die instead. Though irrational, such thoughts are common among survivors of events in which others are killed or injured. As an adult she was still shadowed by survivor guilt and a gnawing sense of shame that she was a "bad person."

Like Nell, Owen Chase had done his best to put the terrible experiences out of mind. Seasoned by the ocean's constant reminders that life can be hard and unpredictable, the idea of dwelling on these things was akin to rubbing salt into an open wound. But if we look more closely, we can see that his life too had been marked by the traumatic events. Shortly after returning from the ill-fated expedition of the *Essex*, he began having merciless headaches which plagued him the rest of his life. At times, they were so incapacitating that they reduced the tough-shelled mariner to sobs. He recognized that these headaches had begun during his struggle for survival. Such physical complaints can grow out of lingering anxieties and emotional pain related to post-traumatic stress and can become chronic and persistent, especially when one attempts to repress inner pain (something referred to as somaticizing).

Despite the matter-of-fact style of his written account and tendency to minimize what he'd endured, the immediate aftermath of Chase's return suggests indications of post-traumatic stress disorder – nightmares, flashbacks, intrusive memories and vivid ruminations seized his mind and interrupted his sleep. It's impossible to know how long these symptoms persisted. Whalers in the 1800s were not inclined to tease out the nuances of their long-term psychological response to crisis. We can only wonder about his inner life and speculate without certainty about the nature of his personal struggle.

In terms of healing, Chase had advantages Nell had lacked. He had returned to a close community of friends where he didn't have to keep his tragedy a secret (his experience was well known and others were interested in hearing his account). He was an adult at the time of the events and thus had the mental and emotional maturity and verbal sophistication to make sense of what had happened. Despite these advantages, the subtle pull of his hellish struggle for survival remained ever beneath the surface, pulling him into another storm before he died, characterized by crippling headaches and unrelenting fears about starvation.

For Nell and Chase, their traumas had been cumulative. Things that were equally challenging had followed in the wake of the initial critical events. For Chase, the wreck was prelude to the savagery of starvation and exposure. For Nell, her father's death had led to a chain of events that had separated her from friends and community, leaving her confused, frightened and alone in her grief.

In the last weeks of her life, Nell's fear of death persisted but lost some of its charge. To her surprise, talking lightened the burden of her longstanding psychic pain. Freed from pressure to appear happy all the time she was able to ask questions about the dying process which she'd secretly assumed would be physically painful and leave her gasping for air as though being drawn underwater. Once she began communicating openly about these fears, she realized they were unwarranted. Her pain could be controlled and her breathing eased with medication. Death, which had once seemed like a rapacious bird of prey, though still frightening, lost its bloodthirsty power. Tentatively, she was able to view it as the natural culmination of a long and meaningful life rather than as a predatory assailant.

She never had another panic attack. The nightmares disappeared as her anxiety lessened. Ironically, when she stopped trying to elude her past, it lost much of its influence over her. Talking openly also allowed Cleo to better understand Nell and drew them closer.

As Nell looked back on these early experiences she was better able to contextualize them into her larger life journey. They were a heartbreaking and tumultuous part, of course, and one that affected her in many mysterious ways, but a part which had also deepened her resilience and courage and given her a passion to serve those who, like her many patients, were vulnerable and suffering.

Chapter Six
Behind the Walls of Tohopeka
When Defenses Become Traps

There were two things Paul made sure you knew. The first was that he was brilliant. The second was that he was an alcoholic. He was aware of the apparent contradiction but another thing you quickly learned about Paul was that he loved contradictions, gleefully referring to himself as a walking paradox.

Unusually sensitive and able to feel empathy for others, he often behaved aggressively and intimidated those around him. He was full of bravado and assertions of his own importance but harbored a lingering fear that whatever he might have accomplished was of no real value. Eager to inform others that he was unconcerned about their opinions, he was hungry for acceptance and lived with secret anxiety that he was unlikable. Gifted with tremendous mental focus and discipline, he was capable of impulsive and destructive acts. He could be brash, loud and competitive one minute, kind and gentle the next; humorous and charming in the morning, sullen and combative in the afternoon. In reality, Paul only pretended to like contradictions – they had often made his life torturous and bewildering. The problem was he had no idea how to resolve them.

He'd been a writer and journalist specializing in social and political criticism, particularly outspoken on abuses of power and the ways vulnerable groups and individuals are vilified, marginalized and made scapegoats by those in privileged positions. He'd spent decades advocating for women, poor people and African Americans with an eye to equity and social justice.

Paul attributed his concern for social justice to his grandfather who had been a Tuscarora Indian, telling me about how the Tuscarora had nearly been wiped out by whites and Cherokees in the early eighteenth century. He was proud of the Tuscarora blood flowing in his veins and he identified with those tenacious survivors who had fled north to the land of the Iroquois.

He lived near his ex-wife Janice. His home was filled with books stacked from floor to ceiling, many containing scribbled comments in the margins expressing Paul's disdain for an author's viewpoint or the shoddiness of his or her research. Although Janice had gotten the house as part of the divorce settlement she rented it to him so, as she put it, she wouldn't have to "deal with all the books, bad art and raggedy furniture."

Despite countless battles and disappointments they had remained friends, something Janice said had been possible only after she "stopped relying on him for anything other than a laugh now and then." When Paul was diagnosed with advanced cirrhosis of the liver she began helping out. When his doctor recommended hospice services she started coming by daily.

Paul, on the other hand, scoffed at the idea that he needed hospice. According to him, he was simply feeling the negative effects of the journalistic grind. He just needed some extended rest. He knew his liver was damaged but was convinced a regimen of distilled water and milk-thistle would allow it to regenerate. Within a few months he'd be back at his computer lambasting state and national politicians, exposing their lies and hypocrisy.

It was a sunny day in early summer when we met. He was a large man with thinning gray hair, pale complexion and bright blue eyes. He conveyed an air of amused detachment, as though our interaction had an element of gamesmanship, the rules of which he understood and I did not. He liked to laugh and talked excitedly about his work and ideas, deftly avoiding questions about his inner experience and illness.

He passed his alcoholism off as "the family disease," something which warranted no further discussion. It was an incidental fact of his life, passed down like the long spidery fingers that also ran in his family. He was an alcoholic because his father had been one and that was all there was to it. When I said this seemed like a strangely simplistic explanation coming from someone who'd spent his life studying the psychological complexity of human experience and looking beneath the surface of things, he laughed, looked up as if in thought, and told me a story.

His father had been in a unit responsible for collecting military intelligence during World War Two. In June 1944, he and a small group secretly made a night landing on Omaha Beach in northern France where they dug into the sand near the foot of massive German defensive works and waited for the D-Day invasion – a massive assault by American, British and Canadian forces on the Normandy Coast. During the initial wave, thousands of Americans fell dead or wounded. According to Paul, his father's job had been to photograph the entire landing, capturing every savage detail. When his father returned from the war he began drinking heavily and was prone to paroxysms of rage and periods of moody withdrawal. Reflecting on what he may have seen that day, Paul acknowledged with dry humor the theoretical possibility that other factors may have been behind his father's drinking. As to his own, he was noncommittal.

He frequently spoke about his deceased parents, describing his father as an honest, hardworking man. He'd been demanding, critical and emotionally aloof and had always seemed uneasy in the world, even before the war. His mother had been strong, reliable and loyal to family but beneath the surface Paul had sensed an undercurrent of disappointment with her life and those around her. Both had been difficult to please. Rare words of approval were quickly qualified by warnings about pride and countervailing criticism intended to keep Paul from getting an "inflated opinion" of himself.

He was not judgmental when talking about their lives. His own personal challenges had taught him that life is a messy business, full of imperfections and unintended conflicts. From his parents he had drawn several lessons: success depends on hard work and persistence; you must improve yourself every day; never rest or become satisfied; emotions are to be controlled not expressed. He'd also learned that life was hard, unfair, and there were two basic groups of people: those who fail and those who succeed, or, as his father had been fond of saying, the nails and the hammers.

It had been a rough blueprint for a sensitive young man to follow, but it had helped him earn status and excellence in his profession. Combined with his mother's admonitions to live in service to others, it had helped him positively affect many lives. It had also led him to develop a fierce exterior which covered an inward sense of vulnerability and aloneness.

Paul used our visits to reflect on his life. Despite a tendency to minimize his illness it seemed to have evoked an impulse toward introspection. In the course of these reflections he began looking at his twin defenses of using his intellectual power aggressively on the one hand, and muting painful thoughts and emotions with alcohol on the other. He acknowledged that his intellectual competitiveness had often masked anxiety, fear of failure, not being good enough or of being rejected by people he cared about.

It was difficult for him to talk about such things. For him, fear had connotations of weakness. It was something to be overcome or, at very least, denied. He'd learned to outmaneuver his fear by intimidating others and showing them how brilliant he was. This, of course, hadn't eliminated the feelings or silent beliefs underlying them, it had only moved them to a slightly more comfortable psychological distance. The only time fear and self-doubt seemed to entirely vanish was when he was numbed with alcohol. In a moment of lucid insight he realized that he drank to feel less scared.

Alcohol may have temporarily anesthetized these internal churnings, but it had grabbed hold of his life and left a trail strewn with hurt feelings and broken relationships. Beneath a veneer of brilliance and success, his private life had been a wreck.

Not surprisingly, Paul drank most heavily when his fear was threatening to break through the surface of his other defenses. This, it turned out, happened not only when he felt threatened but during times most would associate with joy like the day he and Janice were married or when he sold his first big story. He'd missed the first three days of his daughter's life lost in a drunken fog. On another occasion he'd been slated to accept a major journalistic award which Janice had to receive on his behalf because he'd disappeared on a bender. The list was long and sad.

As our conversations unfolded it became apparent that Paul's decision to explore rather than avoid painful thoughts, memories and feelings had potential risks. He was plainspoken about the fact that he was still drinking. Digging up painful inner material as we were doing could easily backfire if his craving got the better of him. We agreed that if his urges for alcohol increased he would tell me. Throughout our sessions I checked in with him about whether our discussions were causing any increase in his typical consumption.

Moving toward his hidden doubts, shame and feelings of inadequacy proved much harder than running away to a whiskey bottle. When such emotional pain is unearthed it can intensify as it dashes from psychological cages devised to keep it away from our awareness. This was true for Paul. He became uncertain about whether or not he wanted to continue our explorations. The more sadness and fear we uncovered the more he became tempted to "call one of my old drinking buddies and disappear." With his permission, we enlisted the support of Janice and his hospice team and shifted the gears on our sessions to focus more on connecting with strengths and resources, leaving aside more loaded topics.

Eventually, we discussed whether he wanted to dig deeper or simply, as he put it, let "sleeping dogs lie." By then he had realized he wasn't getting better. Time was running out. He was struck by the paradox of his circumstances. He'd spent his life trying to understand others and develop strategies to create meaningful social change, yet he'd been stuck in patterns of self-destructive thoughts and behaviors driven by secret fears and emotional pain. The more he thought about this, the more certain he became that this was one paradox he needed to resolve before he died. Healing his disease was not an option but maybe he could find some measure of psychological and emotional healing before he died.

With surprising energy, he renewed reflecting on his life from his earliest memories to more recent experience. We focused on his interior world, his secret life, rather than the formidable facade he'd tried to present to others. His innermost self, it seemed, had long ago retreated beneath the pressures and clamor of a dangerous world. It was this deeper self, beneath the surface defenses and longstanding automatic thoughts and beliefs, to which he began to listen.

This was the part of him that had tried to connect with others. It was the part that had been concerned about social justice and which wanted to make the world around him more humane. It was the part that was sensitive and empathetic. Maybe it had been the part that had gotten overwhelmed amidst the violence and injustice of a rough world in which the hammers seemed to always be slamming away at the nails. This deeper voice had hidden quietly behind the wall of Paul's pugnacious intellectual prowess and assaults against those in power.

Like Paul, all of us have multiple voices inside us. Psychologist Richard Schwartz calls these our "internal family." Depending on circumstances, one voice or another may be in the driver's seat. Paul had spent much of his life listening to voices urging him to project confidence and dominance or those which were easily angered, wounded or prone to escapism. Inside, often unheard, there was a deeper voice, a deep self, which held the promise of wisdom and equanimity. In the last weeks of his life, despite weakness and difficulty concentrating, he focused on connecting with this deeper self.

For Paul, there was no eureka moment of sudden transformational clarity, just the cumulative momentum of his heartfelt attempt to piece together the fragmented shards of a complex life into a mosaic through which the light of his true self might shine. He realized that his aggressiveness, inflated ego and drinking were merely smokescreens.

Since early childhood the world had seemed scary and uncaring. He'd secretly expected to be crushed beneath its weight unless he appeared fearless. Ultimately, his intellect and success had not cured his anxiety. The greater his outward success, the more he worried. When brilliance and charm had failed to protect him, alcohol had succeeded, or so he'd thought. In the belief that he was protecting himself he had actually been destroying himself or, as he put it, "The walls I built to protect myself have become a trap that's killing me."

I commented that he was in a very human predicament. Many have found themselves up against these kinds of walls.

"Give me an example," he said earnestly, seeming to genuinely want to know he wasn't alone.

"Have you ever heard of the Battle of Horseshoe Bend?" I asked, remembering his affinity for Native America.

*

By the early 1800s, the Creek nation was in trouble. There were tensions among the tribes and intruders from the United States were hungry for their land. Uncertainty and fear floated freely through the pine trees of their homeland in Georgia and Alabama like snow falling on weary shoulders. Decisions had to be made about how to defend themselves from the threats of a changing world. Even strong and boisterous warriors ready to fight could feel anxiety churning down in their bellies.

Though Americans called them Creeks, they were a loosely knit confederation of tribes such as the Tallassee, Alabama, and Coweta. They included remnants of what had once been large chiefdoms like the Apalachee, nations driven from their homes like the Yamasee and blacks escaped from slavery, drawn together by the force of shared experience and their close proximity to an expanding United States.

A split had emerged between the tribes known as the Upper Creek and Lower Creek. The former lived mainly in present-day Alabama, the latter in Georgia. The United States, though a new power, wanted control over the southeastern fur trade and were intent on stealing Creek land in order to get it. Many Americans were already squatting on Creek territory and demanding more. The Creeks argued about how to respond. On one side were those who believed the best strategy was to accommodate the Americans. Others argued for resistance and, if necessary, war.

The groups were further polarized in the winter of 1811 when the Shawnee leader, Tecumseh, arrived with a vision of drawing all Indians, regardless of tribal affiliations, into a grand alliance to resist white expansion stretching from the Great Lakes to the lower Mississippi. His presence was like a lightning rod that galvanized the war faction. British operatives stoked the flames further, encouraging the Creeks to take up arms, promising guns, powder and lead.

This resistance faction, composed largely of the Upper Creek, intensified its calls for battle and became known as Red Sticks – a term that may have come from the red sticks handed out by Tecumseh or which was perhaps a reference to "vermilion war clubs, and the red sticks, supposedly magic ones, used by their shamans." Whatever its origins, everyone knew that in traditional Creek symbolism red was the color of war.

On July 27, 1813 Red Stick warriors fought a battle with soldiers at Burnt Corn Creek. In August they attacked the palisade of Fort Mims on the Tensaw River in Alabama. By the time the fight was over the fort was burned to the ground and two-hundred-fifty of the people inside, including Creeks who had sided with the Americans, were dead.

When word of the attacks spread, militia from surrounding states moved into the Upper Creek heartland. About fifteen-hundred Georgians and their Lower Creek allies pushed west and were repulsed. From Mississippi and Louisiana joint militias, supported by Chickasaws and Choctaws, advanced east and they too quickly withdrew. From Tennessee, Andrew Jackson moved south from Nashville with twenty-five hundred volunteers joined by groups of Cherokee and Creeks. Heading into Red Stick country, he described himself as "Determined to exterminate them."

By early November Jackson and his men had assaulted the Creek town of Tallushatchee where they'd killed women and children as indiscriminately as they had Red Stick warriors. The Tennesseans, however, were in a precarious condition by then. Winter was closing in, food was scarce and they were deep inside Red Stick country. Jackson dug in his heels to tough out the winter.

By spring, about five thousand new militia itching for a fight had augmented his force. In late March, scouts found a large Red Stick village built on a small peninsula formed by a loop in the Tallapoosa River called Horseshoe Bend. About thirteen hundred men, women and children were gathered in a hastily constructed village they called Tohopeka, or "the fort." Among them were several hundred warriors eager for battle. Others, frightened and bereft, had come seeking safety from the terrors of war.

The fort was protected on three sides by the river and was accessible by land only along the eastern neck where the bend formed. The Creeks had constructed a sturdy breastwork across this narrow gap consisting of a zigzagging wall. It was a formidable defense, unmistakably designed to withstand a frontal assault. Even Jackson acknowledged, "It is difficult to conceive a situation more eligible for defense than the one they had chosen, or one rendered more secure by the skill with which they had erected their breastwork."

The Creeks were confident in their defenses as they watched Jackson's men prepare for attack on the morning of March 27, 1814. Their shaman had assured them the Master of Breath was smiling on them. They were sure the wall they had built – and the wall of water that surrounded them – would keep them safe. Amidst the dislocations and heartrending grief of war, they had retreated to this place. Believing their wall was impregnable, they readied for Jackson's assault.

The ensuing battle was horrific. Jackson's main force attacked the wall with a bloodthirsty fury but found that the breastwork, as intended, was very effective. Creeks fired through portholes, placing the attacking troops in a menacing crossfire, cutting them down as they tried to advance.

Unfortunately for the Red Stick warriors, the river proved to be less protection than they had assumed. While the fight raged at the wall, Jackson's Cherokee allies (as well as Creeks not allied with the Red Stick faction) swam the river, stole some canoes and began crisscrossing the river bringing others to attack from behind. The Red Sticks realized too late that the wall they had built and the river they had chosen for protection had become the jaws of a trap. Their defenses had become their undoing. All directions for the Creek were blocked. Blocked by the river that had so recently reassured them, and a wall of their own making.

Even Jackson was aware of the irony. On the day after the battle he gloated that, "their walls became a snare for their own destruction." In the end, their defenses proved to be their undoing.

*

It's natural to seek ways to feel safe amid the uncertainties of life but constructing defenses is a tricky business. The best ones are porous and flexible enough to allow for growth and change, capable of nourishing rather than impeding relationships. They expand and change as we become wiser or simply fall away lest they impede our passage. When we cling blindly to our defenses or when they keep us from greater awareness, they become traps. As such, we are wise to be careful about the walls we build. Whether intended to protect us from external enemies or uncomfortable internal thoughts or feeling states, there is always the possibility they may leave us paralyzed or constricted.

As with Paul, many defenses are learned so early in life, often unconsciously, that we don't even recognize them for what they are. As we talked about the Battle of Horseshoe Bend, Paul wondered what it might have been like behind that zigzagging wall with the world about to cave in under a powerful and implacable foe. For him, being crushed had always seemed like a real possibility and he understood the impulse to build strong walls. The plight of the Red Sticks placed the paradox of his own behavior into a larger human context. "I guess we've all built walls or found ways to feel strong which have blown up in our faces," he mused.

His self-examination in the preceding weeks had allowed him to see that he had built a wall out of his arrogance and ability to intimidate. And like the waters of the Tallapoosa, he'd allowed a river of alcohol to further separate him from others, leaving him huddled on a spare, lonely spit of earth afraid to venture out (despite his often grandiose pretensions). He'd worked so hard trying to escape his fear that he had become disconnected from his deepest and sanest inner voice.

Paul saw that the Creeks had realized the danger too late. "Maybe it's too late for me too."

"Too late for what?" I asked.

"Too late to live in a different way, I guess."

"Is it really too late to live in a different way?"

"I don't know."

I asked if he thought his recent efforts at understanding himself and his situation had been a waste of time.

"No," he said empathically.

"Why not?"

He thought about it for a moment. "I guess it's not really too late. I mean, yeah I'm going to die, but I can live the rest of my life in a different way. Even if I've just got a day left."

A day was more than most behind the walls at Tohopeka had. By nightfall so many Creeks had been killed that soldiers cut the noses from corpses in order to count them. When Jackson asked how many noses they had gathered, he was told, "Five-hundred-fifty-seven here at

86

the fort, and three-hundred-fifty in the water, but we can't find all that are in the water."

After the battle, the Creeks were forced to cede twenty-three million acres of their homeland. This was true for all Creeks including those who had sided with the Americans. These White Sticks, as they were called, had believed the best way to defend their families was to befriend the Americans. Ironically, like their Red Stick comrades, they had contributed to their own demise by assisting Jackson at Horseshoe Bend and paving the way for the crushing demands that followed.

Not all were killed or captured during the battle though. Some escaped. Maybe Paul could escape his self-imposed trap and live his remaining days in a way that better expressed the wisdom of his deeper self. The fear, regret, sadness and shame he had hidden for so long were not an enemy from which he needed to flee or defend. They were simply a part of his life. Not the definitive part. That part he discovered in the voice that had been barricaded behind his invisible walls. In the shadow of his dying, this voice grew stronger and gained his trust.

We created a vision of what Paul's final days might be like if he allowed himself to be anxious without labeling it as weakness or reaching for a shot of whiskey. How might it change things if he could communicate his love to Janice and his children without allowing fear of rejection to close his heart? What if he could feel sadness without chiding himself for being weak, experience joy and connection without a voice in back of his head warning about pride? What if he allowed himself to be seen as he was rather than trying to project an image of who he thought he should be?

This kind of envisioning, as long as it does not become just another high bar against which to judge one's imperfection, can be an avenue toward expanding beyond the limits of one's defenses. It can even help change internal stories we tell ourselves about what is possible. I encouraged him to move in the direction of this vision as best he could without becoming attached to outcomes or judging. It was a final paradox that in the process of losing his life he might step out from behind the walls and express who he really was.

Though he liked the vision, he wasn't convinced. Would people take him seriously without his facade of loud and quick-witted extravagance? Was it really safe to feel his feelings without numbing them with alcohol? He worried about losing his independence and trusting others with his care and protection.

As it turned out, he didn't have much time to sort these things out. His condition deteriorated rapidly. Without a live-in caregiver, he was transferred to an inpatient hospice facility. For Paul, who had always kept his own counsel and desperately wanted to be seen as independent, leaving his home for a building filled with strangers was hard.

His need for physical assistance removed any possibility of projecting indestructibility. Though this initially increased his anxiety he eventually found it to be a source of relief. "I don't have to worry about people finding out I'm a wreck and expending energy trying to outsmart them. Now they know I'm a wreck and it's alright." With a smile he added that he was starting to suspect we are all wrecks in one way or another.

With his vulnerabilities transparent, he was amazed to find people liked him anyway. It didn't matter that he was afraid, needed help or had little stamina for conversation. In fact, these needs made his humanity all the more compelling. For Janice, Paul's transformation allowed them to reconnect in a way neither had thought possible.

"He's like the Paul I fell in love with," she said as we sat at his bedside. "The Paul that has been buried for so long has come back. It's the best part of who he is."

"What part?" I asked.

She grabbed a tissue from a cardboard box and searched for the words.

"His compassion and gentleness and humility. And all his crazy insecurities. I knew he was still in there under all the bravado. I was afraid I'd never see that part again."

She likened him to a caterpillar that had spent much of his life plodding clumsily through a forest trying to convince the birds and spiders hunting him that he was a rattlesnake. In the end, he'd emerged shortly before his death as a beautiful butterfly.

"He may only get to fly a little while, but what a wonderful sight," she said.

Paul died quietly in early autumn, before the first frost. Janice was sitting on the front porch of the hospice building when the nurse came out and told her his heart had stopped. According to Janice, just before the nurse arrived "an amazing blue and black butterfly landed on the back of my rocking chair then on my arm. When the nurse stepped out on the porch it just flew up into the sky."

Section Three
Hold onto My Hand
Staying Connected

*Hold onto my hand
even when I have gone
far away from you.*

From a Pueblo prayer

Faced with the separation of death, the importance of loved ones becomes as clear as polished glass. Ironically, we may better appreciate these connections at the very time they are about to be severed. This appreciation may lead us to give thanks, alter our priorities and even deepen our relationships during the time we have left.

For some, each day, however hard or stressful, is cherished in the shadow of life's gathering sunset. On the other hand, when feelings of regret or of time misspent are unearthed, or as one contemplates actions that cannot be undone, words that cannot be taken back, some may guard themselves or retreat behind old patterns of distance and alienation.

Either way, as energy ebbs and fatigue sets in at the end of life, relationships can still heal or strengthen. Such healing is not dependent on words and verbal processing; it is dependent on love and intention. Tending and mending important connections is another of the opportunities that attend times of upheaval and change.

Chapter Seven
Adams and Jefferson
Reconciliation and Forgiveness

As a child, Frances's family called her "the brain." Her perceptiveness was as apparent as her dissatisfaction with superficial answers to the questions she constantly fired at adults who wandered within range. It began as a playful nickname but had become the central metaphor of her life. By fifty, she'd earned two doctorates and published several scholarly books on intellectual history and political philosophy. As a university professor, she'd sharpened her questions into darts which she flung at students and faculty alike. Now, at seventy-two, living alone and feeling the effects of incurable cancer, she was flinging them at herself and piercing holes in a thin veneer of success that no longer insulated her from a deep sense of loneliness.

While climbing the academic ladder she'd had many successes and made many sacrifices. The eggshell colored walls of her apartment were full of books stacked tightly onto shelves. Awards and ornate diplomas hung in spare metallic frames. Tables were cluttered with stacks of journals. There were no mementos from vacations or postcards from friends traveling in distant lands. No photographs of family or crayon drawings from grandchildren. Fact was, she had never taken a vacation, had no friends, hadn't spoken with her daughter in years and had never even met her grandchildren.

Being a professor had demanded emotional control, determination and assertiveness. This had been especially true for women of her generation for whom academic positions had been rare. Competition and the clamoring, often sexist, criticism of colleagues could be harsh and disparaging. Succeeding in this environment had taken focus and long hours of work, leaving little time for family or friends. This all-consuming focus had destroyed her marriage and driven a wedge between Frances and her daughter. "It's like they just slipped away one night while I was preparing a lecture."

She had been married nineteen years. Although she glibly described the experience as a mistake, I learned that this was a facade to encourage people to move onto another subject. In truth, she remembered Ted as a kind, good-hearted person who was "much better at being a father than I was at being a mother." She described their years together as remote and disengaged. Even when she was home, she had usually been sequestered away in her study. "I spent more time with the essays of Thomas Jefferson and James Madison than I did with my family."

After the divorce, Ted moved to California with their son. Her daughter, Martha, lived on her own in Ohio near the university where Frances taught. "I thought I'd feel liberated," she recalled, "but I was sad when they left." Thinking she could outrun her sadness, she buried herself in her work. Without family, she became isolated. Surrounded by the sprawling crowd populating her university, she felt strangely alone.

Martha was the only person with whom she interacted without the common denominator of work. At her daughter's insistence they met at least once a month. Although Frances wanted to see her, she felt awkward during their visits. For all her mastery of the verbal arts, she was uncomfortable with simple conversation, unscripted as it were and without time for preparation. "There's a reason," she joked, "that my parents called me the brain and not the socialite."

She kept up to date about Ted and her son Kyle through Martha's reports. A few years after the divorce, she learned Kyle was planning to visit some colleges in the area and he was hoping to get her advice. Frances phoned him that night and they agreed on a plan for his impending trip.

Looking back, she recalled her excitement. It had been a long time since one of her children had asked for help and she'd been eager to assist. The silences between Frances and Martha dissolved as they discussed Kyle's "grand tour."

As the time neared, Kyle telephoned to let her know he would arrive the following week. It was the last time she ever heard his voice. He was killed in an automobile accident a few days later.

Few tortures can rival the death of a child. For Frances, it was like a descent into hell. Questions exploded like searing embers landing on exposed flesh. Why had it happened? How could she continue living when her son had died at such an early age? Why hadn't she been a better mother? Why hadn't she spent more time with him? Why couldn't it have been her instead? What was Kyle thinking when he died? Was he afraid? Did he suffer? These questions stood stark and unanswerable as if taunting her with the uselessness of her powers of analysis.

Despite the intensity of her sadness she kept her grief private. There were signs that something was wrong. Her mind was dulled. Her concentration flagged. She had none of her former gusto for arcane academic debate. In the department of her university with its tight schedules, emphasis on matters of the intellect and respect for personal privacy, her struggle, if noticed at all, went unacknowledged.

Martha had no idea of the depth of her mother's pain and didn't understand her attempt to use work as a distraction from sadness. For Martha, grief was a public event to be shared with anyone who would listen. Tears flowed easily; talking about Kyle loosened the shackles of her despair. Frances, on the other hand, wound everything into a tightly compressed ball and swallowed it whole. Talking about Kyle only heightened her fear that this ball would explode like a coiled spring and tear her to pieces. The languages of their grief were as different as Sanskrit and Gaelic and neither knew how to translate the other's unfamiliar tongue.

Misunderstandings ensued, compounded by raw emotions and the haunting thoughts that often come to those who have lost a child or sibling. The more Martha searched her mother for signs of sadness, the more Frances camouflaged them in apparent detachment. Martha yearned to know that her pain was shared and to connect with her mother in the midst of their loss. Frances was afraid that if she loosened the vice-like mental contortions through which she confined her grief, she would become lost forever in the sorrow. Eventually, they stopped meeting. Telephone calls became infrequent.

Frances recognized that she was in danger of losing contact with her daughter but had no idea how to bridge the widening chasm. Instead of talking openly with her, she fell back into the habit of making work the pillar around which she organized her life and stopped returning Martha's calls. Looking back, she recognized her tendency to retreat into the disciplined chambers of her mind during times of crisis. At the time, however, she blamed Martha, concluding that she was emotionally unstable and that it was impossible to reason with her.

Years passed. There were sparse words now and then. When Martha got married, for example, she sent Frances a wedding invitation. Though she toyed with going she convinced herself she couldn't miss an important research symposium. In retrospect, she admitted feeling ashamed of her role in their relational cold war and being apprehensive about running into Ted. Occasionally a card was sent on a birthday or holiday, but the unpredictability of this only served to accentuate the long silences. Over the years their separation became a habit both came to view as inevitable and unchangeable. Like mortar holding brick, silence hardened into a baffling wall of separation. Over time, sadness, anger and grief transformed into fear; fear of reaching out and facing the possibility of rejection.

When Frances retired to North Carolina, she sent Martha a card. After a brief exchange of cordial, though formal notes, contact again fizzled. It had been over four years since the last letter had been sent and no one in Frances's family knew she was dying.

When a terminal diagnosis signals the beginning of the last stretch of one's journey, it has a way of raising questions about what is most meaningful. Her legacy as an educator offered some solace but family was another matter. It had been nearly twenty years since she'd spoken with Ted and her break with Martha seemed irreparable.

During failed chemotherapy, Frances had begun experiencing the terrifying chill of what she referred to as "absolute aloneness," the kind of aloneness that comes when the sands beneath one's feet are shifting and loved ones are far away. It was as if all the various alloys that harbor loneliness and sorrow were drawn into a single blade left dangling precariously above her head. This time she had no university or scholarly pursuits to distract her.

By the time we met she'd been thinking about writing a letter to Martha. "I suppose I have no right to hope for one of those deathbed reconciliations. But I'd sure like something better than this," she said as she motioned around her arid townhouse.

She was hardnosed enough to know that the possibility of she and Martha coming together bathed in forgiveness and love after lives spent struggling to get along was probably an unattainable fantasy. Even so, it was a fantasy pointing toward her deepest hope.

"It's a crazy idea," she said.

"Those are the best kind. Besides, how do you know?"

"I've made my bed. I need to lay in it."

"Not even try? What's the worst that can happen?"

"My daughter tells me to go to hell or ignores me."

"If you don't take the risk you'll never know."

She seemed to regret having broached the subject and launched into a storm of rationalizations and dismissive sarcasm. It was too late. The rift was too entrenched. Hope was unrealistic and there was no use belaboring things. It would be more consistent, she concluded, to die without so much as lifting a finger toward bridging the separation.

"It'd be consistent," I agreed. "But is it what you want?"

94

We both knew it wasn't. I'd already asked her to tell me what the script would be if she could write one for the rest of her life. She'd admitted it would include mending fences with Martha and some type of "closure" with Ted.

"You can handle being rebuffed Frances. What really stops you from reaching out?" I asked.

"I don't know. I really don't."

She was still angry at her daughter for not pursuing her more persistently. Part of her relished the thought of Martha receiving the news of her death out of the blue. Would she feel guilty? Frances was also afraid. What if she reached out and was rejected? Why risk the disappointment? And if it went well, could she withstand the possibility that the years of separation might intensify her regret over the time she'd lost? Reaching out brought too many unpredictable variables and Frances hated unpredictability. She vacillated, lost in a maze of excuses, girded by fear and fear's shadow – longstanding habit.

"Have you ever read any of Thomas Jefferson's letters?" she asked. With Frances, any conversation could quickly turn toward history or philosophy. She was thinking of a particular letter Jefferson had written in the form of a dialogue between his head and his heart. She quoted parts from memory and concluded by expressing deep empathy with Mr. Jefferson whose head and heart, it seemed, were at war. She was likewise torn between her heart's longing to reconnect with Martha and her head's caution. Her head told her to forget about Martha and pack away her emotions. Her heart told her to reach out and, even if her effort came to nothing, find comfort in having tried.

We spent some time discussing this tension, searching for ways to enlist her head's assistance in pursuing the goals of her heart. She wanted to be convinced but her mind was full of doubt. After sputtering through fruitless attempts at finding an avenue for her to pick up the phone and call her daughter, I suggested we think about Jefferson's complex relationship with John Adams.

She knew the story better than I did but she encouraged me to tell it anyway.

*

In the winter of 1811, John Adams prepared to write Thomas Jefferson a letter. The two hadn't communicated in over a decade. Among the nation's aging patriarchs, Adams wondered whether the bitter conflicts that had severed their friendship might yet be put aside. They were growing old. Time for reconciliation was slipping away. For Adams, however, swallowing his considerable pride and picking up his pen was not something he would do without pangs of ambivalence and resentment. As he looked back on the events of his life he may have recalled the summer of 1776 when he and Jefferson had stood shoulder to shoulder. He may have regretted the way their friendship had been wrecked by political battles and a river of hurt feelings.

In June of 1776, the American Revolutionary War had completed its first bloody year. With the British army in route to New York, Adams and Jefferson were among the delegates of a Continental Congress meeting in Philadelphia. Both had been appointed to a small committee entrusted with writing what would become the Declaration of Independence.

They had developed a close friendship, though at first glance they were an unlikely pair. Adams was a pugnacious New Englander. Plainspoken and often argumentative, he was at ease speaking in front of large crowds and reveled in stormy debate. Jefferson was the consummate Virginia gentleman, reserved in public, controlling his emotions and impulses with the precision of a Roman stoic. He was uncomfortable speaking before groups and his words were often artfully ambiguous.

It was Jefferson's draft of the Declaration that the committee submitted to Congress for approval. During the ensuing debate, Jefferson's work was held up to great scrutiny as delegates argued and admonished each other over every detail. Jefferson sat in sullen silence, offended as they sliced up his sentences and removed others from the document altogether. Later, he wrote appreciatively that John Adams had stood firm, "fighting fearlessly for every word" and had been "its ablest advocate and defender against the multifarious assaults encountered."

Adams's faithful defense had solidified their bond, signing their names on the document drew them even closer. Placing one's signature on the Declaration was a gravely serious act. At the time, England was the most powerful nation on earth with an army and navy known for its remorseless lethality. Benjamin Franklin was speaking literally when he commented that all who signed must, "hang together, or assuredly we shall hang separately." Jefferson and Adams knew theirs would have been among the first necks placed in British nooses if things went wrong.

In 1784, after weathering the Revolution and helping found a new nation, Jefferson was chosen to join Adams as a minister to the French

Court. Adams was delighted when he heard the news. In a letter to James Warren, he wrote that Jefferson's appointment "gives me great pleasure. He is an old friend with whom I have often had occasion to labor at many a knotty problem, and in whose abilities and steadiness I have always found great cause to confide."

In France the two collaborated closely, relying on each other as they plied the shifting shoals of global politics. Representing the new American states to Old World powers was a delicate job. Negotiating treaties, trade agreements and the specifics of America's massive financial debt required great tact and seamless teamwork.

Adams had his wife, Abigail, son, John Quincy, and daughter with him in Paris. To Jefferson, who had suffered the deaths of his wife and four of his six children, the Adams household became a surrogate family. Years later, the elder Adams commented to his friend that during this time, John Quincy "appeared to me as much your boy as mine."

In April 1785, Adams was appointed Minister to England. As he and his family prepared to leave for London, he wrote Richard Cranch, "I shall part with Mr. Jefferson with great regret." In a letter to Adams shortly after his departure, Jefferson acknowledged his sadness, writing that, "The departure of your family has left me in the dumps. My afternoons hang heavily on me."

The steady flow of letters between London and Paris attests the continued importance of the friendship. Though these letters contain much discussion of critical political events, they are also filled with reports and inquiries about family and expressions of loyalty and friendship. In the hustle and bustle of foreign courts and exciting news from their fledgling nation, Adams proclaimed to Jefferson that their correspondence was "one of the most agreeable events in my life."

In 1788, Adams was summoned back to the United States. Sailing across the Atlantic, he professed to have no political ambitions and anticipated a quiet return to his farm in Quincy, Massachusetts. By the end of the year, however, the constitution had been ratified, George Washington was President and Adams had been elected Vice President. When Washington appointed Jefferson his Secretary of State soon Adams's old friend was on his way across the Atlantic. When the two reunited in New York (the temporary capital), they may well have anticipated a continuation of their fruitful collaboration and a deepening of their friendship.

Such was not to be. Without the King of England to rally against in a common cause, sharp differences quickly arose among the nation's leaders regarding the scope of the constitution and proper direction of the new nation. Though Adams and Jefferson had agreed on independence they had different visions for the nation's future. Throughout the 1790s, as this debate intensified, two views emerged: Jefferson's, which envisioned an agrarian nation with strong independent states and a strict construction of the constitution; and Alexander Hamilton's which saw an America with a robust centralized federal government, thriving urban centers and a more flexible, dynamic understanding of the constitution.

Debate descended into attacks of a mean-spirited and personal nature with Adams and Jefferson on opposing sides. Historian Joseph Ellis is not exaggerating when he writes that, "in terms of shrill accusatory rhetoric, flamboyant displays of ideological intransigence, intense personal rivalries, and hyperbolic claims of imminent catastrophe, [the 1790s] has no equal in American history. The political dialogue within the highest echelon of the revolutionary generation was a decade-long shouting match."

Although Adams attempted to remain above the fray, Jefferson came to see him as a satellite orbiting dutifully around a Hamiltonian center of gravity. In 1793, a frustrated Jefferson resigned as Secretary of State and retreated to his estate at Monticello. Despite his claims that he was through with politics, he quickly took aim at his old friend and surreptitiously encouraged scathing attacks on Adams's politics and character.

By the time Adams was elected President in 1796, conflict and misunderstanding had nearly battered their friendship into an empty shell. Harsh words had been spoken and actions committed that made the gulf between them seem unbridgeable. As the smoke rose from a burning landscape of distrust and recrimination, their old bond had become a casualty of repeated political and personal collisions.

In a strange twist of fate, due to the electoral process of the time, Jefferson was elected Adams's Vice President and the two were thrown into a moment of decision. Could they repair their friendship and rise above the rancor of political factions or would this be the final note in the dirge of their dying affections? Instead of rapprochement, antagonism grew hotter. By the end of Adams's term, Jefferson had privately funded some of the basest personal attacks on him by one of the most unscrupulous mudslingers of the day. For his part, Adams had signed a law allowing the government to throw his political enemies in jail if they dared publish criticism of his administration. The Adams-Jefferson friendship was done.

When Jefferson was elected President in 1800, Adams didn't bother staying for the inauguration. He left the capital before dawn and headed home, disgusted with the rapid erosion of the high-minded idealism of the Revolution into backbiting political gamesmanship. When he crossed the threshold of his home in Quincy he had every reason to believe that he would never communicate with Jefferson again.

In 1804, on hearing of the death of Jefferson's daughter, Polly, Abigail Adams sent a note of consolation to him without her husband's knowledge. If any hope of reconciliation had been behind her gesture, it was quickly dispelled by the short, belligerent exchange of letters that followed between her and the Virginian. Their short correspondence ended as abruptly as it had begun, their mutually caustic pens only reinforcing the divide.

Both men were wounded, proud and stubborn enough to believe the responsibility for the rupture rested squarely on the other's shoulders. There would be no more direct contact between either of the Adamses and Jefferson for several years.

As time passed, silence calcified into habit. Adams busied himself on his farm, Jefferson retired to Monticello. Their worlds remained as distant as if they were living on separate planets. They had stood together during troubled times, protected and consoled each other in times of grief and uncertainty. They'd helped forge a new country. In 1809, their mutual friend, Benjamin Rush, was hoping their bond was not completely dead.

Rush had signed the Declaration of Independence and weathered the same political storms as his feuding friends but had somehow remained on good terms with both. From his home in Philadelphia, he carried on a flourishing correspondence with each, hoping to spark one to reach out to the other.

In October 1809, with feigned innocence, he told Adams about a particularly interesting dream he'd had during which Adams sent a letter to Jefferson. "This letter," Rush reported, "did great honor to Mr. Adams. It discovered a magnanimity known only to great minds. Mr. Jefferson replied to this letter and reciprocated expressions of regard and esteem. The letters were followed by a correspondence of several years." Whether this was a real dream or a sly ploy is unclear.

Rush was open about his hope that the men would put their animosity aside, carefully crafting his good-natured prodding to their different temperaments.

Adams made it clear that Jefferson, not he, would have to take the first step, telling Rush that if he were to receive a letter from Jefferson he would, "not fail to acknowledge and answer it." Mildly encouraged by this, Rush began working on Jefferson. "I have ardently wished," he told him, that "a friendly and epistolary intercourse might be revived between you...I am sure an advance on your side will be a cordial to the heart of Mr. Adams."

Jefferson's response was a long letter blaming Adams for everything. He would not take the first step but he encouraged Rush to continue his affable cajoling, assuring him that, other than being the first to reach out, he would do whatever he could to "second [Rush's] efforts."

With Rush as intermediary, both men were gingerly probing the edge of the chasm separating them, each convinced it was the other's job to be the first onto the tenuous rope bridge Rush was attempting to construct. For over two years Rush softened them to the idea of communicating. Whenever he drew kind words or lingering affections from one, he reported them to the other. He was like a human telegraph through which Adams and Jefferson sent and received guarded expressions of respect, regret and hope.

By December 1811, they had been leavened with steady doses of Doctor Rush's unflappable optimism and refusal to believe their friendship was dead. They were aging, their careers were over and many of their contemporaries were already gone. Each had seen children die and friends whisked away by illness and old age. Perhaps, as they neared the end of their lives, they saw the window through which they could break their silence closing.

On January 1, 1812, John Adams set aside his wounds and sent a letter to his old friend at Monticello. Whether Rush's dream was prophecy or fantasy remained to be seen. However, one thing was certain, Adams would make the effort. The rest was out of his hands.

*

Bridging the gulf between ourselves and a loved one with whom we have grown apart is no easy matter. Too often our minds learn to accommodate separation and transform it into something that seems normal and routine, transmuting sadness, regret or a general sense that something is amiss, into detachment, avoidance or blame. When death

100

approaches, however, the sadness of separation is often unmoored from its deep anchorage and floats to the surface in search of resolution.

Such was the case with Frances. She was weary of pulling a heavy chain of loneliness and regret. She didn't need me to tell her how things turned out for Adams and Jefferson. She knew that Adams's note was the opening chapter of a fourteen-year correspondence now regarded as one of the most extraordinary in American history. Jefferson's first response, though carefully proper, closed assuring Adams that all the bitter pain and recrimination of the preceding years had not "suspended for one moment my sincere esteem for you; and now I salute you with unchanged affections and respect." If Adams hadn't swallowed his pride and reached out there would have been no reconciliation, no ambling reflections of kindred spirits connecting in their twilight years; just grave-dead silence.

About a week after my visit with Frances, I got a call from Martha. She wanted to know what the heck was going on. Her mother had called "out of the blue." They'd had a strained conversation which had left her confused and ambivalent. Questions poured out: How sick was she? Why was she getting a call now? How long did her mother have? Did Frances expect her to drop what she was doing and race down to North Carolina? Why shouldn't she let her mother die alone? What did Frances say about her? Could she tell me her side of things? Did I understand how hard it was to get a call like that? Did I know Frances didn't even come to her wedding?

She talked fast, as if trying to digest decades of hurt feelings. She was angry, scared, concerned, hopeful, cynical, relieved, ashamed and elated. Despite internal conflict, one thing became clear as we talked; she missed her mother and wanted to see her.

Frances called me the next day and informed me she and Martha had arranged a visit the following week. "We decided we need to talk about practical things," she said, "like power of attorney, my will, and the insurance policies. I don't want anybody having to clean up after me." Given the circumstances, it was about as safe an agenda as could be hoped for. As the visit neared, Frances prepared herself for disappointment.

Although Martha arrived with low expectations as well, she wound up extending her stay. The practical things they had planned to discuss offered a convenient sanctuary from which to venture into the more difficult subject of the preceding years. Martha had many unanswered questions and, in the absence of an opportunity to understand Frances's experience and intentions, she'd decided on some answers that had been troubling. Frances was surprised to learn that Martha had interpreted her silence over Kyle's death as indifference. She was equally puzzled when Martha explained that when her mother had withdrawn, she'd concluded Frances didn't really care about her.

These were difficult conversations. Frances occasionally became overwhelmed and retreated into heady abstractions; Martha's temper occasionally got hot. It was a mutual surprise when they realized they had both wanted to remain connected but layers of misunderstanding, false assumptions, different personalities and communication styles had confused them.

When Martha returned home she began calling several times a week. By then Frances had learned Ted had suffered a stroke and was confined to a wheel chair. She mulled the idea of contacting him but settled on relaying information and messages through Martha. Like Benjamin Rush, her daughter became a human telegram through which Frances and Ted culled out what had been good about their relationship and let the rest drift away.

Frances was shocked when Martha offered to let her move in with her family and she turned the offer down flat. But as her condition worsened, her desire to be with family and finally meet her grandchildren, grew. The next time Martha offered, Frances accepted.

When Frances transferred her care to a hospice in Ohio, neither expected the move to be easy. After years of chilly silence, Martha and her family would have their lives turned upside down. Martha would become caregiver for a mother she, in some ways, barely knew. Frances would have to relinquish her precious privacy, independence and the familiar architecture of her careful routine.

I'm not sure where they ended up. But I know that the direction in which they were headed was profoundly different than the one toward which they had been moving when Frances and I met.

As for Jefferson and Adams, as they grew older, writing letters became more challenging. Adams's hand trembled, his eyesight dimmed. For the last eight years of his life he had to dictate his letters. Jefferson suffered physical pain and moving even short distances left him exhausted. In 1817, when Adams's beloved wife died, he wrote Jefferson that he found consolation in the thought that their "separation cannot be so long as twenty separations heretofore." Jefferson also thought of death, writing that with their bodies wearing out they, "must expect that, worn as they are, here a pivot, there a wheel, now a pinion, next a spring, will be giving way, and however we may tinker with them for a while, all will at length surcease motion."

In 1826, as July Fourth dawned, both were dying. As he drifted into his final sleep, John Adams's last words were, "Thomas Jefferson survives." He was unaware that his friend had died earlier that day, the fiftieth anniversary of the Declaration of Independence.

Chapter Eight
Mountain Man Rendezvous
Invisible Community

Buddy's life revolved around his wife, Flora. For years he'd watched her deteriorate mentally and physically from the effects of Alzheimer's disease. For Flora, the worst part had been when she had known what was happening but couldn't stop it. Few things are more agonizing than descending into a fog of confusion, knowing that eventually you will become unable to find your way out. "She tried to make me promise," Buddy recalled, "that when she got like she is now I'd give her an overdose but I told her no. I promised to keep loving and protecting her no matter what."

For Buddy, the worst part had been when she began forgetting his name. It had been as though the history they shared was being stolen one memory at a time by the winnowing blade of dementia. The doctor suggested putting her in a nursing home but he recoiled at the idea. She had nursed him back to health after three heart operations and he intended to take care of her at home until she died. "I'll do it," he said, "even if it kills me." Which was exactly what the doctor was worried about.

Given the state of his cardiac health, every morning Buddy prayed for one thing: that he lived one day longer than Flora. The thought of relinquishing her care into the hands of strangers was enough to bring him to tears. Though he preferred to focus on other things, the prospect was ever in the back of his mind.

Aside from Buddy's brother, he and Flora had no family. Other siblings were dead and they had no children. Years earlier, they'd had a few friends but when Flora's mind had begun slipping she had become self-conscious and they had withdrawn from everyone but each other.

Buddy had equipped the doors of their home with alarms when she started wandering outside and getting lost. When she got her days and nights mixed up he spent afternoons cooking and cleaning while she slept then stayed up all night keeping her company. Despite the fact that she was now bed-bound, he kept motion and sound monitors throughout the house and made sure the alarms all worked. "I know it's crazy, but it makes me feel better. I told her I'd protect her and I meant it."

His love for her was unbending. He loved her even more as she disappeared into a wilderness of dementia. As he explained it, you come to realize just how much you love someone when you see them slipping away.

Despite many moments of tenderness, Alzheimer's disease had trampled across their lives like a herd of buffalo sweeping across a mountain meadow. As it did, Buddy's world shrank along with Flora's. His brother offered to help out but Buddy would have none of it. Until hospice care began there had been no one with whom he would talk about his challenges and complex sadness.

Being a caregiver had not come naturally and he'd mastered the multiple, often simultaneous tasks through trial and error. As his and Flora's isolation increased, Buddy had had few opportunities to gain perspective on the intense, sometimes contradictory inward thoughts and emotions that arose daily. With no one with whom to compare notes, he often doubted the value of his efforts and frequently second-guessed himself.

When something went awry, as often happened, he invariably blamed himself. If she was in pain, he blamed himself for not giving her additional medication in time. If he was unable to assuage her tears, which came spontaneously and often, he blamed himself for not knowing the right words or gestures. If she wanted something and he couldn't understand what it was, he berated himself for not comprehending. It was like a trap with springing jaws: He wanted to do everything perfectly, but her many needs, confusion and impaired ability to communicate, not to mention his limitations as her sole caregiver, made perfection unattainable. When he fell short of his impossible expectations, he felt guilty and ashamed.

When I met him, isolation and self-doubt were as much a part of his life as his boundless love for Flora. He jumped at the chance to talk about their lives. Sharing memories brought her back, if only momentarily, strengthening the unbreakable links that still connected them. No matter the degree of her mental erosion, nothing could break their bond as long as he remembered who she was beneath the web of her disease.

They'd met late in life when each had been resigned to living alone. Buddy was driving a bakery truck that afternoon when he'd stopped at a country store along his route. Flora was standing at the counter. He was instantly drawn to her smile and soft-spoken manner. Before the bread was on the shelves, he'd invited her to a fish fry that Friday night. "I was running early that day because I was training a new driver and there were two of us to do the unloading," he remembered. "If the new guy hadn't been there I'd have missed her. Funny the way little things can change your whole life."

He remembered how the store's florescent ceiling lights reflected off her glasses and made her eyes sparkle. In his mind, she was still the person he had met that day. On particularly bad days, he liked to think about that moment and remind himself that beneath the burdens of their current circumstances, she was still with him, sparkling.

Though modest and unassuming, Flora had been adventurous and self-possessed. Buddy had stock stories he liked to tell illustrating her independence. One of these had to do with fur trapping. Before they married, Buddy had trapped small fur-bearing animals near a creek meandering through woods owned by his brother. He sold the pelts to a friend in the mountains who made them into hats and sold them to tourists. When he met Flora he assumed his trapping days were over, but to his surprise and delight she insisted that he show her how to bait the traps and cure the skins.

It was one of the many stories in which he and Flora were the only characters. Occasionally there were others, but they were always tangential. In her company, he needed nobody else. "When you saw one of us," he said, "you saw the other."

As with many who have a loved one with Alzheimer's disease, his grief was complex. In some ways, Flora had already left him. Memories they'd once shared were now his alone. And yet, he had not lost her. She was still with him. Whether she remembered him or not, he was certain she knew that he loved her. Some messages have ways of getting through, even when nothing else does.

Dementia was like a trackless wild into which Buddy and Flora had stumbled without a compass. As her condition deteriorated, he'd kept his thoughts and emotions on a tight rein, rarely giving them vent. Occasionally they gathered into perplexing storms where sadness and love, helplessness and determination, guilt and courage, blended into an internal cascade of anxiety which could leave his heart pounding, sweat pouring down his forehead. Buddy simply rode these times out. For Flora such storms were over; her bouts with anger and fear anesthetized by pervasive disorientation. Her days were spent sleeping, her face a blank page rendering her inner world all but unknowable.

In the absence of direct feedback, Buddy continued doubting himself. He dissected every thought, feeling and behavior for signs of failure. If, in his frustration, he momentarily raised his voice, his response was not to see this as a normal, human, response, but as confirmation of his ineptitude. If he had a passing hope that Flora's life would finally come to an end, he saw this as proof of his imperfect loyalty rather than as a reflection of fatigue or of love for someone grown tired in her suffering. He seemed impervious to assurances that he was doing a good job. His refrain to all who tried to chip away at his doubt was that they didn't understand because they hadn't been through what he was going through. If his efforts to reassure Flora were unsuccessful, it seemed, he would not be consoled by the efforts of others to reassure him.

Underlying his belief that others could not understand was a sense of aloneness and separation. Given the emotional roller coaster of his daily concerns and anxieties, his life seemed far removed from the mundane rhythms of 'normal' life. "Sometimes," he said, "I feel like I'm living on out in the woods far from everyone else in the world."

He kept his own council and drew his own conclusions. Unintentionally, this tendency placed him into another trap: He took no comfort in the assurances of people whose lives were untouched by Alzheimer's but he had no opportunities to talk with those who knew what it was like. As such, his tendency to expect the impossible from himself and attribute normal thoughts and frustrations to pettiness and weakness could not be tested against the experience and perspective of others.

Occasionally, he talked about people he'd met in the waiting room at the clinic where Flora had gone in the early years of her illness. There were a few people in particular whose spouses or parents had Alzheimer's disease with whom he'd had significant conversations. Now and then he recalled something that reassured him or helped him make sense of things. "One day I was feeling real angry at God about all that was happening and I was mad at myself for not having more faith. I was talking to a fellow in the waiting room whose wife had Alzheimer's and he said he got mad at God all the time."

"What impact did that have on you?" I asked.

"I felt like I wasn't all alone."

"Do you remember the first thought you had?"

"Yeah, I thought, I'm not going crazy after all. Maybe I'm normal."

I offered to get him a hospice volunteer so that he could attend a local support group for caregivers of people with dementia. He declined and the matter was put aside. Several weeks later, however, he asked about the group again. He wondered what it would be like to talk with people who might understand. He had spent a long time huddled with Flora in their home, rarely venturing out. The thought of talking to strangers about such a delicate subject was both intimidating and compelling. He wavered, as though walking a tightrope between his fear and his desire to feel less alone.

As we bounced the idea around, he warmed up to the prospect of attending the group. "Even if I just went once," he thought, "it could help knowing there are others out there and I'm not as alone as I feel."

Just when it looked like Buddy was set on going, fear returned bringing its panoply of excuses about why he couldn't leave the house. As we disentangled these, he grew exasperated. Seeing his frustration, I reminded him about how he and Flora used to go fur trapping.

"Ever hear of the Mountain Man Rendezvous?" I asked

*

Most Americans in the 1820s never came anywhere near the Rocky Mountains. The chain loomed like a jutting wall of massive rock and earth as if warning any would-be travelers to reconsider their itinerary. Aside from a handful of Indian nations only a few fur trappers, known as mountain men, entered the mountains in search of beaver pelts. Trappers lived lives so remote and unfamiliar to people in the eastern states that it would have been all but incomprehensible to them. Only other mountain men understood the challenges.

In earlier years most trappers had worked for large operations like the Hudson's Bay or American Fur Companies but the number of freelancer working independently had increased since 1825. That was the year William Ashley and Andrew Henry had held the first Rendezvous during which they brought goods and supplies from Saint Louis and rendezvoused with trappers for trade and comradery. Since then, the Rendezvous had become a much-anticipated annual event.

Men were drawn to the mountains for different reasons. Some, like Pennsylvania farm boy, Zenas Leonard, simply wanted to "make my living without picking up stones." Jim Beckworth, whose mother was a slave, was escaping a future that had promised to be bleak. Others were looking for a fresh start. Whatever their differences, they all shared an ambition for profit, a strong sense of independence and an aptitude for living in isolation.

They also possessed an array of survival skills without which they would have perished. An accident or momentary lack of vigilance, however small, could prove fatal. In addition to paralyzing snowstorms in the winter and ferocious grizzly bears the rest of the year, the mountain man's life was filled with constant physical toil and ongoing struggles to stay warm and dry and to find food.

Sudden, often violent deaths were common. Men died from accidents, infected cuts and diseases; they were killed by Indians, grizzly bears, rattlesnakes, and occasionally other trappers. Some drowned; others died from exposure to the elements or simply vanished. On occasion, men even starved to death and many could relate personal stories of near starvation. Joe Meeks, for example, was once so hungry he plunged his hands into "an anthill until they were covered with ants, then greedily licked them off."

Historian Bernard DeVoto points out that there were things one needed to know as if by instinct. "Why do you follow the ridges into or out of unfamiliar country? What do you do for a companion who has collapsed from want of water while crossing a desert? How do you get meat when you find yourself without gunpowder in a country barren of game? What tribe of Indians made this trail, how many were in the band, what errand were they on?"

Beaver traps were set in streams and lakes during the coldest months when pelts were at their most lush. Frostbite and hypothermia were common. Aside from his traps a mountain man's most important possession was his gun, nearly always loaded and ready for use. To service his rifle he carried a bullet mold, lead, flints, percussion caps and gunpowder. Along with his traps he carried anchor poles and castoreum (a scent used as bait taken from glands near a beaver's tail).

Although trappers often traveled in small groups, wintered together and occasionally married Indian wives, it was a solitary existence. Ever restless to find new streams and be the first to trap virgin ground, they roamed across vast stretches between the Rockies and the Pacific, rarely staying in one place more than a season before moving on. Threading their way along steep spines of earth, dwarfed by mountain spires with cloud-covered peaks, it was easy to feel disconnected and lost within the endless spaces.

The rigors of survival and demands to bring in pelts made opportunities for gathering into a larger community rare. When the men emerged from the shadows of the wild Rockies once a year to attend the Rendezvous they were lured not only by cash and supplies, but the opportunity to be with their fellows. For a few weeks they were woven into a visible community, connected with those who understood what it was like to live as a wilderness trapper. It affirmed who they were and what they were doing. It allowed them to ventilate emotions usually tightly reined in by the mountain's demand for self-control, and fortify themselves for another year in the rocky streams and passes.

The Rendezvous was held in the summer when the beaver's coat was thin and of little interest to merchants. All that was required was an open meadow, a good stand of trees for firewood and a nearby river. Between 1825 and 1840 its location rambled through the present-day states of Wyoming, Utah, and Idaho. Trappers were informed of each year's location at the preceding Rendezvous or by the "mountain telegraph" which transmitted news by word of mouth throughout the region's camps and among Indian nations.

Trappers came from far-ranging corners, wandering in on foot, atop mules or horses, or in axe-hewn canoes. Along with mountain men, Indian men and women arrived eager to participate. It was common for over a thousand people to converge on an otherwise quiet meadow to create a temporary town. It was the only time during the year so many mountain men would stand in the presence of one another in a single, albeit rowdy, community.

Usually a sizable number arrived before the wagons and mules that carried trade goods, supplies, and cash. This offered time for what Alfred Miller, an artist who attended the 1837 rendezvous, referred to as "high jinks," which he described as "a species of Saturnalia in which feasting, drinking, and gambling form prominent parts." The peripatetic trappers found old friends and shared news. They told stories about the year's close calls and enjoyed practical jokes played at one another's expense. There was a competitive side and drunkenness and fights were common, as were wrestling matches and shooting contests.

Whatever tensions there may have been, however, were usually dissolved within the otherwise festive atmosphere as men enjoyed the rare opportunity to rest from their burdens and be with others who shared their difficult way of life. DeVoto speculates that the trappers' "solitude had given them a surpassing gift [for] friendship" with those who understood their hardships and triumphs.

After a year in the wilderness, necessities like gunpowder and lead were typically running low. Little things like tobacco, sugar, and whiskey were scarce luxuries. Jim Beckworth remembered, "the arrival of such a vast amount of luxuries from the East did not pass off without a general celebration. Mirth, songs, dancing, shouting, trading, running, jumping, signing, racing, target-shooting, yarns, frolic, with all sorts of extravagances that white men or Indians could invent, were freely indulged in."

Fur company operatives pitched tents and opened for business. They paid cash for pelts then quickly took it back in exchange for watered-down whiskey, overpriced supplies or the beads, fabric and jewelry prized by Indian women. Amid the rough carnival-like air, serious matters were discussed. Men formed groups for the coming year and strengthened bonds that would bring help in times of need. They planned explorations into new territories. Some sought medical help for injuries or afflictions they had been unable to cure themselves. At the 1835 Rendezvous, for example, Marcus Whitman, a missionary whose wagon company had traveled west with the trade caravan, removed an arrowhead that had been in Jim Bridger's back for almost three years.

By the time everyone dispersed, the trade goods were distributed and the fur companies were in possession of all the pelts and most of the money. The summer gathering was a time of solidarity and affirmation otherwise unknown in the lean life of a mountain trapper. Their contests of strength and skill mirrored the abilities they needed to survive on the mountain frontier. The songs they sang and stories they told related directly to who they were, how they saw themselves, and the lives they were living.

The two or three weeks sprawled together in the meadow reinforced their connectedness, the choices they had made, and their commitment to a unique and difficult way of life. As the fall cold returned, friendships forged at the Rendezvous might ease the occasional pangs of loneliness. In times of doubt and isolation, this awareness might temper one's uncertainty in the knowledge that there were others out there walking the same path.

*

No matter how difficult our journey or how isolated we feel, we are never alone. There are others who understand, an invisible community of kindred souls threading their way along similar paths. We may never converge on a picturesque mountain meadow to tell the stories and sing the songs of our shared journeys, but they are with us.

Buddy identified with the mountain men. The dementia caregiver support group, he thought, was "probably like a Rendezvous for people taking care of someone with Alzheimer's." The opportunity to talk with others in similar straits held a strong appeal but logistical concerns made going to the group impractical. The conversation, however, left him with the consoling awareness that he was not alone. His tribe was out there.

Buddy asked me to tell him what it was like for others, especially men I'd known, who had spouses with Alzheimer's. In a sense, he was asking me to introduce him to some of his fellow caregivers through stories. When I offered a few (carefully protecting privacy) he realized that his occasional anger, second-guessing and frustration were normal. The complex grief, the taxing physical and psychological demands, while incomprehensible to most, were known intimately to the people of his far-flung, invisible community. Whether their loved one was home or, as was often the case, in a nursing facility, there were others who understood his emotional and psychological pain, as well as his enduring love and commitment.

Shortly after our conversation Flora contracted a respiratory infection that caused her lungs to fill with fluid. We discussed whether or not he would treat the infection with an antibiotic or simply focus on keeping her comfortable as she died.

"Part of me wants to keep her here no matter what," tears welled in his eyes.

"Is there another part?"

He nodded then lowered his head as though disinclined to continue.

"What does that other part want?" I asked gently.

He shook his head, wiped his eyes and said, "I don't know."

He asked me what others did in situation like this. I told him there was no right or wrong decision. People assessed each situation on its own merits and did what they felt in their hearts was best for their loved one, or which best reflected wishes that loved one may have expressed.

"Buddy, can I ask you to try something?"

He nodded.

"Let yourself feel the love you have for Flora. Take your time, feel your breathing, relax. Let me know when you're in touch with it."

He took a moment then nodded his head.

"What would Flora say to you if she could give you a message?"

He whispered "Let me go."

Later that day Buddy called a friend on the telephone, a retired minister who lived in Delaware, to ask if he'd be willing to lead Flora's funeral. In a strange conjunction of events, he learned that his friend's wife had been diagnosed with Alzheimer's dementia and been moved to a nursing home. Without going into details, Buddy reported that, "We probably talked for an hour." It was clear they had quickly reconnected and found mutual comfort in their renewed friendship.

Buddy decided not to treat the infection. When Flora died his grief was disorienting. Taking care of her had been the center of his world. Along with losing his wife, he had lost a way of life that, despite its hardships, had provided him with meaning. For a time, his days became empty and unfocused.

Finding his bearings took time. Eventually though, he wandered out of the mountains of his solitude and began doing volunteer work. A nearby hospital was piloting a program pairing people who had experienced caring for a spouse with dementia with someone facing the same challenges. Schooled in the demands caregivers often face, Buddy overcame his reserve and signed up. In the months ahead, as his grief waxed and waned, his presence would be a source of encouragement and strength to those struggling through the same crags and ravines he had survived. Even though his responsibilities caring for Flora were complete, he remained loyal to others whose struggles he had shared.

By the late 1830s, the life of the mountain man was coming to an end. The beaver that had once seemed inexhaustible were nearly trapped out. Even the most remote streams had been depleted. In addition, the beaver hat, long a staple of aristocratic fashion, had been replaced by silk. In 1840, so few trappers attended the Rendezvous that it passed into the dust of history.

Chapter Nine
Rescue Line
Staying Connected

No one who met Sal was surprised to learn that he'd commanded a ship. Even confined to a hospital bed, unable to speak, he had the air of someone used to giving orders. If he could have given orders now he would have had a pistol delivered so he could blow his brains out. He'd made no attempt to conceal his desire to commit suicide rather than succumb to the lethal wasting of Lou Gehrig's disease (ALS). He'd demanded that his daughter and the nursing home staff assist him but the crew had mutinied and the captain was not pleased.

He'd joined the Coast Guard at seventeen over his mother's objections. His father had been in the Navy and, even though they rarely saw each other, Sal had grown up daydreaming about the sea and the strong sailors who faced its dangers and kept its secrets. His maternal grandfather had died in an Atlantic hurricane while stoking the boiler of a merchant steamer. For his mother this had been one of the most painful experiences of her life but to a young boy it was a romantic story of a heroic death worthy of a hardened seaman.

Sal had worked hard to master tasks quickly, eager for new responsibilities. Driven by an ambition to command, he had made sacrifices to move up the ranks. It was a family joke – in a family that rarely joked – that his idea of shore leave was to *leave shore* while most of his shipmates were still out in the taverns, in order to return to the ship to polish his shoes and study navigation.

The hard work paid off when he was given command of a Coast Guard cutter but by then his single-minded intensity had extracted a heavy cost. By the time he retired, four marriages had ended in divorce and of his seven children, only Diane was still visiting. Throughout his life he'd had a violent temper and been intolerant of anyone deemed incompetent, weak or disrespectful. After the Vietnam War, he started drinking heavily and his behavior had become erratic. Mood swings, long a source of anxiety for those around him, had become more intense and unpredictable, his rages more violent.

He was almost entirely alone. On one visit I asked if gaining command of a ship had been worth the price. Unable to speak because of a tracheotomy, he spelled the words "Hell no" by using a pen and pointing to letters on his communication board.

After he left the Coast Guard, Diane had talked him into moving to the coast of North Carolina. "I wanted him close enough that I could get to him," she explained, "but not so close that I'd have to see him much." When he began experiencing physical weakness and loss of coordination he ignored the symptoms thinking he could push them aside if he focused hard enough and stepped up his increasingly difficult walks on the beach. When he finally went to a physician and was diagnosed he told no one. It was his fight. He would go it alone. Besides, there were few people to tell and it was easy enough to keep Diane in the dark since she'd learned not to ask questions.

Sal assumed he could beat ALS the way he'd beaten other challenges, with discipline and hard fighting. He dug his heels in, pushing his doctors for experimental treatments. When told he was out of options he accused them of giving up and traveled to a hospital near Diane's home expecting they would offer more hope.

When Diane received his voicemail letting her know he was in town, she knew something was wrong. The next day she met him at the hospital and took notes as they consulted with a specialist. By dinner, they both knew he probably had less than a year to live. The next morning Sal returned to the coast, refusing Diane's offers to drive him home, traveling the same way he had arrived – by cab.

A week or so later Sal wound up in the hospital after falling and hitting his head. His physician was adamant that he was no longer safe living alone. After several arguments with her father, Diane got his permission for her to visit nursing homes near her home which, as she put it, "could handle Dad's temperament."

Despite initially agreeing to move, Sal refused. After a horrendous week during which he'd tried unsuccessfully to manage things alone Diane finally gave him an ultimatum. "I told him," she laughed, "that he needed to move to the nursing home or I was going to get all his ex-wives together and we'd pay him a visit." After more angry protest he agreed to try the nursing home, conditionally. Diane had braced herself for his arrival, and his wrath.

Shortly after the move, hospice care began and I was on my way down the hallway to meet him. His suicidal ideation had come up during the admission visit and he was disdainfully anticipating a visit from the social worker. As I approached his room a woman who appeared to be in her mid-fifties exited in a hurry. She looked upset. I followed at a distance, unsure what had chased her from the room. I found Diane sitting in a rocking chair on the outside porch. She motioned for me to sit as she searched her purse for a lighter to spark an unlit cigarette already dangling from the corner of her mouth.

"Why do I do this to myself?" she asked, lighting the cigarette. "He's impossible to get along with."

She had hoped they might be able to put the past behind them and spend less time arguing but had found that the past can be a tenacious companion. Frustrated and angry, she was tormented by the belief that they were wasting what time remained arguing and criticizing each other. She'd thought about throwing her hands up and walking away but he was her father. She wouldn't abandon ship. Maybe, she thought, having the help of a hospice social worker would make it easier for them to talk.

When we returned to Sal's room he stared at us without a gesture of recognition or greeting. His face was defiant. When I asked if I could sit down he slowly reached for his communication board and, his hand trembling from poor motor control, spelled the words "who cares?"

His room was filled with photographs and mementos of his days in the Coast Guard. Diane had created this space to convey a sense of who he was. There was a photograph of the ship he had commanded, another of him shaking hands with a high-ranking Coast Guard official. Medals and officer stripes were framed in a glass-covered box hanging beside photos of three of his grandchildren. On his dresser was a wooden model of a colonial frigate. On a table there was something that looked like a radio which played a recording of ocean waves and sea birds.

It was difficult for him to use his communication board and he was self-conscious about his lack of motor control. We sat and, without pressuring him to respond, I encouraged Diane to talk about his life. When he realized we weren't there for a confrontation and that I was interested in hearing about his life he picked up his board and filled in details now and then to supplement his daughter's reflections.

As he became more engaged I looked him in the eye and shifted our conversation. "You've been thinking about killing yourself."

"Yes." He tapped his communication board firmly as though warning me not to give him a lecture.

After asking him about the frequency, duration and intensity of such thoughts, I asked if he had a concrete plan to kill himself. He did not.

"Is it that you *want* to die or is it that you just want to stop living like this?"

He remained silent.

"Do you understand the question Dad?" Diane asked. He glared at her.

Finally, he spelled, "Don't…want…live…like…this."

"Do you want to die?" I asked.

"No."

"Is death the only way you can think of to stop living like this?"

Though his ability to move his head was severely impaired he nodded ever so slightly.

Suicidal thoughts are common among people with terminal illnesses. For some, they occur only briefly, for others they are persistent and can even lead to action. It's important to take such things seriously and allow people to speak openly so loved ones and professional helpers can better understand and offer effective support. As we explored his inner life it became clear that Sal did not want to commit suicide, he wanted to stop living in a way that he saw as "useless." It begged an obvious question: How might his life have meaning and purpose despite his physical limitations and complete dependence on others?

As he pondered this his eyes softened. He looked at Diane then spelled the words "More visits."

"More visits?" Diane raised her voice in exasperation. "You get mad every time I come by. You practically threw me out less than two hours ago. Now you want more visits?"

He spelled the words again – more visits – this time motioning as if to underline them for emphasis.

When he'd moved nearby Diane had hoped they might bury the hatchet, find a way to connect, but so far it hadn't worked out. His words suggested he shared her hope. Looking at him with sad, earnest eyes, she promised to visit more often.

"Why is it important to you that Diane visit more?" I asked.

His eyes glistened with tears then he spelled the word "sorry."

When we left the room Diane was skeptical. Memories of their relationship told a story of distance and rejection. As a child trying to gain his approval, life had been difficult and confusing. She and I agreed to meet separately now and then to help her sort things out and process how things were going as she visited her father.

During our visits she looked back on their lives, gaining a deeper understanding for a man who, although infinitely fallible and difficult to satisfy, had done his best to be a good father. She realized that, despite his discomfort with expressing emotions (other than anger), he had tried to show her he loved her. When she was a kid, for example, he would bring her aboard ship and show her how to use the signal lamps and radio. They had even invented their own secret code so they could communicate by hand signs when she was down on the dock. When she turned ten he sent her a special birthday telegram from sea. Before she went off to college he gave her lessons on how to physically incapacitate an attacker, concerned about her safety. These memories had been overshadowed by those freighted with emotional pain and resentment. Now they came floating to the surface like messages in barnacle-covered bottles sealed for decades and finally recovered.

The central message was that, whatever their struggles and hurt feelings, she and Sal had found ways to stay connected. When his drinking had become a problem she'd continued calling him despite his ill-temper. When he retired, she had encouraged him to move to North Carolina, enduring his complaints and using much of her vacation time to help him find an apartment. Over the years she had developed a knack for showing up just as he was about to get into trouble and helping avoid a catastrophe.

For his part, Sal had stood by her when she'd gotten divorced as well as during her son's hospitalization after an automobile accident. When she'd needed emergency surgery he'd hopped a plane the next day and made sure the doctors and nurses treated her like she was their only patient. Whenever trouble had arrived for one of them, the other had arrived on the scene.

Trusting in the power of metaphor, I suggested that the surfmen of the United States Life-Saving Service, forerunner of Sal's beloved Coast Guard, might be an image capturing their stormy bond. It was the Service's job to watch over ships moving up and down the coast and help them stay out of trouble. If a ship went down in a storm or grounded on a sand bar, patrolmen jumped into their boats, often amid enormous waves, to bring the passengers to safety. Throughout their lives, she and Sal had kept watch for each other, sometimes from shore, sometimes from the surf, when necessary rowing out into the storm.

They had never spoken about this; it was expressed in action. Indeed, there was much they had never talked about. Not surprisingly,

Diane had many questions. She decided to use their remaining visits as an opportunity to ask some of them. Did he miss her when she left home? Why did he yell at her so much when she was a child? Why did he and her mother get divorced? What happened in Vietnam? At first Sal dismissed her questions, bewildered that she wanted to dredge up such things. When she persisted, he tried to give her answers as best he could even as his ability to communicate eroded. Often, he didn't have good answers or wasn't able to find the words. Diane accepted this; it was enough that he was trying.

When Sal lost his ability to use the communication board Diane started bringing things to read to him. Overcoming her self-consciousness, she even bought a songbook of traditional shanties and sang to him as he slept. When he drifted into a light coma she knew the end was near. With the moment of separation fast approaching, she searched for ways to stay connected. Her father's illness had opened him up and made him "more human." The last weeks of his life had been the most loving and satisfying in their lives together. She didn't want to let him go. She likened it to watching him being drawn away from shore at the very moment she began to appreciate him.

There were things she wanted to say, things she wanted him to know. Although I told her she could say them even though he was not able to respond, she didn't trust that these messages would really get through. I asked if she recalled the lifesaver metaphor and told her about how surfmen would use a rescue line – a strong rope – to connect them with those who were otherwise unreachable. I suggested that during their recent visits she had fixed such a line between herself and her father. It would hold even as he was dying. She could say what she needed to say and trust that it would get through.

"Did people really go out into hurricanes like that?" She asked.

I told her that on a few occasions, when the line couldn't be landed using cannon, rescuers had actually brought it out by hand. In fact, such a rescue had occurred in the same North Carolina waters along which her father had walked each morning.

*

In October 1896, as Richard Etheridge and his crew of lifesavers watched the horizon through the storm, they could barely make out the *Newman* being ripped apart by the hurricane's punishing waves. There was no way they could reach the ship with the surfboat; the breakers were too high. They had dragged the beach cart down the shoreline hoping to fire a rescue line but the beach was flooded and there was no place to set up the Lyle gun. If they were going to get a line out to the terrified passengers on the *Newman* there was only one way to do it – they would have to swim.

For over two decades lifesavers with the U. S. Life-Saving Service had patrolled the Atlantic Coast, guarding its shores. Congress had created the Service in 1871 to operate stations up and down the coast. The original plan had been to build stations along the most dangerous parts of the shoreline at intervals about twelve miles apart and have crews available from December through March. As the value of the Service became apparent, the distance between stations was reduced and the season extended. By the time the *Newman* found itself in trouble there were around two hundred life-saving stations along the Atlantic from Maine to Florida as well as on the Great Lakes and the Pacific.

In North Carolina there were eighteen stations, eleven of which, like Etheridge's, were on the Outer Banks. Station houses varied little from one place to the next. The buildings were designed with an eye toward function and practicality, two stories high with a steep wood-shingled roof on which was perched an observation platform. The six-man crew slept upstairs. The station commander, or keeper, had a separate room. The first floor was used as the boathouse where the men kept a surfboat, beach cart, and tools of the trade such as cork life belts and rain gear. Although some stations maintained a stable for a horse or mule to help pull the heavy equipment, others relied on the backs of their patrolmen.

It was a dangerous job requiring men who knew the language of the surf and sky, strong swimmers skilled in the use of small boats able to withstand harsh weather while working long hours as part of a disciplined team. Etheridge's crew at Pea Island was not typical. They were the only African American station in the entire sixth district (which included all of North Carolina and part of Virginia). Many of them, including Etheridge, had been born on the Outer Banks as slaves.

To stay sharp, they trained constantly – hauling the beach cart, unloading and assembling the beach apparatus, firing rescue lines at targets placed offshore. They launched surfboats, honed their skills at emergency communication and learned how to treat everything from hypothermia to lacerations.

In addition to regular drills, surfmen kept a twenty-four-hour-a-day watch over the stretch of coast entrusted to their keeping. Every day, from sunrise to sunset, somebody was in the observation tower looking for signs of trouble, ready to relay important information to passing ships. At night, and on days when visibility from the tower was poor, men walked patrols along the shore.

The primary goal of watches and patrols was to steer ships away from danger and keep wrecks from happening in the first place. If a lifesaver in the tower could warn a passing ship about shoals, dangerous currents or a developing storm, he might prevent a catastrophe. Simply relaying longitude and latitude to a ship could help a navigator accurately fix a vessel's position and stay clear of treacherous waters.

At night, surfman warned ships away from danger using flares. In the spring of 1884, for example, Etheridge recorded in his weekly log that "Robert Toler discovered a vessel on the morning of March 30 about 1/2 passed 4 o'clock almost on the beach. He immediately burned his Coston Light and she immediately kept off from the beach. It is almost likely she would have struck on New Inlet Shoals had she not been warned."

Looking back on the history of the U.S. Life-Saving Service, the focus is often on the drama of crews braving storm-tossed waves to rescue those aboard sinking ships. But day in and day out, quietly and without fanfare, lifesavers watched over ships traveling near shore, connecting momentarily in order to relay information or warn of a potential hazard, then watching them pass safely out of sight.

When ships needed more help conditions were usually at their worst. Winds could knock down masts, tear up ship planks and floor boards, rip doors off hinges and lift cargo into the air, raining down a terrifying hail of splintered debris. Given the vast stretches of beach and limited ability of a small crew to cover it all, it could be hours before a sinking ship was spotted. By the time lifesavers pulled the thirty-six-foot surfboat and thousand-pound beach cart through wet sand, additional hours had often passed.

There were three ways to rescue passengers. The least desirable was to jump in and fish them out of the water after they had washed overboard or jumped from a fragmenting vessel. It was far better to use the surfboat, which had the advantage of allowing most or all of a ship's occupants to be removed in a single trip. Sometimes conditions were too rough to launch or maneuver a surfboat. In these cases, provided the ship was in range, the men turned to the rescue line.

The line was weighted to a grappling shot which, if landed on deck could be attached to a beam or mast. Firing it required the beach apparatus – a contraption containing ropes, wooden crossbeam, cannon (called a Lyle gun), twenty-pound grappling shot and a sand anchor.

Although pulling the beach cart containing the apparatus through sand was exhausting work, its contents could be unloaded and assembled in a matter of minutes. The keeper chose the place to set up, factoring in beach conditions, wind velocity and distance. Two men dug a hole and buried the sand anchor. Two others unloaded the "faking box," which contained the rescue line wrapped around wooden pegs in such a way that it could be played out without getting tangled. Others unloaded the two-hundred-fifty pound Lyle gun and prepared for the shot. Once the line was secured to a ship, a traveling block could be moved back and forth along the line holding the breeches buoy, a circular seating platform suspended above the water used to pull people to shore one at a time.

The *Newman* was a large schooner, blown off course after leaving Virginia with a cargo of coal. The weather that day was so bad patrols had been canceled. Theodore Meekins had only spotted the vessel from the stations watchtower when the *Newman's* crew had fired off a signal flare.

Sylvester Gardiner, captain of the *Newman*, was unsure of his location but he knew his crew, as well as his wife and three-year-old son, Tommy, were in trouble. The storm had grounded them on a sandbar. The menacing spray had matted the air into a thick gray haze making it difficult to gauge their distance to shore. Now, the tempest was dismantling the vessel, washing away sails, rails, anything not battened down. Water filled with black coal spilled from the wounded hull. All they could do was hang on and hope someone had seen their flare.

The Pea Islanders harnessed themselves to the beach cart and headed into one of the worst storms in anyone's memory. Etheridge didn't even try to bring the surfboat. Launching it under such conditions would be impossible. The rescue line was their only hope, although, as the lifesavers knew, in a storm like this one, it was a slim hope indeed. Wright and Zoby, historians of the Pea Island station capture the situation as the men splashed their way through the surging tide of the barrier island on their way to the *Newman*:

From the moment the keeper had begun shouting his orders, with water up to their knees and wet sand swallowing each step, not one of the men had uttered what they all knew was true: rendering any assistance under such unfavorable conditions would probably be impossible. Maybe they could help those who, still capable of bracing the surf, tried to swim to shore— those few who successfully completed the dangerous voyage. Or maybe they'd be forced to sit and watch as the shipwrecked sailors were washed out to sea, one by one, from the deck of their doomed vessel. Maybe by the time they arrived, it would already be done.

When they finally got the beach cart in range of the ship the beach was inundated. Sand melted away wherever the men attempted to dig. There was simply no place to set up the beach apparatus. Just off shore travelers were on the edge of death and they were powerless to fire a rescue line. There was only one option. They would have to enter the water and carry the line themselves.

It was a risky idea. The reason for using a line in the first place was to keep men out of the water under such deadly conditions. But there are times when rendering help and forging a connection, or strengthening one that already exists, requires us to enter the waves ourselves and stand by those in trouble. Keeper Etheridge asked for volunteers.

His plan was to tie two men together with an eight-foot rope connected to a longer rope capable of stretching all the way to the ship. This line would be held by the men on shore as the volunteers tried to reach the *Newman*. It was a bold plan. Such a thing had been tried only rarely and never in seas as bad as these. In 1878 the keeper at the Jones Hill station, a powerful swimmer, had attempted to carry a line out to the steamer *Metropolis* and nearly drowned. No one harbored any illusions about the work at hand. Even an expert swimmer could be quickly drained of all his strength in such surf.

Theodore Meekins and Stanley Wise volunteered. With the rope tied around their waists, they fought their way past gigantic breakers, over sand bars and water churned up by mighty gales. They disappeared under the water frequently but always somehow resurfaced, sometimes closer; sometimes farther away from the disintegrating schooner. As they got closer, they dodged splintered planks and fragments of debris flying through the air and floating in the water. Each object brought the possibility of a death-dealing blow to their unprotected heads. When they finally reached the schooner they managed to secure the line. Etheridge tied the other end to the beach cart linking those on board with those on the beach.

With no breeches buoy to pull the passengers and crew to safety, Meekins and Wise held the captain's son in their arms and slowly made their way back to shore, gripping the line for stability and protection. When they made it back, battered but safe, they had only begun the job. If they worked quickly, and if the creaking ship held together long enough, maybe they could save a few more of the *Newman*'s ill-fated passengers, but they'd have to do it one person at a time. Etheridge shouted above the winds, asking for two more volunteers.

*

Compared to the intensity of a hurricane, a rescue line seems a very fragile thing. Yet it can secure a connection that the most punishing waves cannot break. A connection that reminds us we are not alone; others care about us and are keeping us safe. In the murky waters of human relationships some lines are strong and flexible, able to stretch across the highest waves, others have become weak, unable to bear much weight and easily unbraided by any gale or billow. But once a line has been set, unless we choose to sever it, it can be made to hold fast in the hour of our deepest need.

For Diane and Sal, though this tether had been strained and frayed, it had always held. During Sal's illness it had allowed them to speak from their hearts and clear up old misunderstandings, forging a deeper appreciation for each other. As she tried to find a way to say goodbye they were still connected even as he was being pulled away by the gravity of his failing body.

In Sal's case there was no daring rescue to accomplish. It was his time to go. In the immediacy of his last days, however, the image of a connection in the storm was helpful to Diane. She could have walked away, avoided the nursing home altogether or hidden behind her anger. Instead, she'd found a way to enter the rough seas to stand alongside her father despite the undertow of painful memories and emotions. The connection held under pressure, as Sal, like his grandfather, went down in his final storm.

Sitting at his bedside, Diane spoke of their lives together, trusting that her words would get through. When she sensed that he was fighting to cling to life, she encouraged him to let go. For a man who had once wanted to kill himself, he seemed to be battling to hold on. Maybe he fought out of habit, a final affirmation of who he was, but Diane sensed something else was holding him back and she decided to make a few calls.

Nothing could hold Theodore Meekins back. When Etheridge called for the next pair of volunteers he insisted on returning to the ship. It would take eight more trips out to the vessel and back before all aboard the *Newman* were rescued. Meekins made every one of them. In his log, Keeper Etheridge ended his report by noting matter-of-factly that, "Although it seemed impossible to render assistance in such conditions, the ship wreck crew was all safely landed."

It surprised Diane when her stepbrother, Rick, called to tell her he was in town. "I told him," Diane said, "that Dad was dying but didn't think he'd come from Alabama." Rick hadn't seen Sal since he had moved to North Carolina. He was shaken when he saw Sal's skeletal body and sallow face. In a surge of anguish, he demanded his father be taken to the hospital where he could "get worked on." He refused to be calmed by the nurses and staff and only relented after Diane pleaded with him to let Sal die in peace.

The next day another daughter, Jackie, showed up. Diane had spoken to her but hadn't pressured her to come. Like her siblings, Jackie was plainspoken. As they sat around Sal's bed sharing stories they didn't gloss over the abrasive truths of his life or the way he had often pushed them away. They'd all felt his anger and coldness but they had also learned to decode the messages of love he had, often clumsily, attempted to deliver. Diane learned that Sal had been there at pivotal times for Jackie and Rick just as he had for her. There were lines connecting them to their father that had sustained them during difficult times and drawn them to his bedside. When Sal exhaled his final breath they were beside him, standing watch.

Richard Etheridge died in 1900. Having trained his crew well, his long-time friend Benjamin Boswer stepped in as station keeper during Etheridge's final illness. Bowser's daily record, like his mentor's, was matter-of-fact and left no question that the Pea Island Station would continue fulfilling its duties. "Keeper Richard Etheridge died at this station at 20 minutes to 7 o.c. a.m. today. The condition of the telephone at the station is good."

In 1915, the Life-Saving Service was merged with the Revenue Cutter Service to form the United States Coast Guard. By then, the powerful steamers that plied the waters of the Atlantic were making the need for rescues less frequent than in the days of wooden ships moved by sail. By the time the Life-Saving Stations were decommissioned in the 1940s and 1950s, the Lyle gun and rescue line had been replaced by motorboats and ship-to-shore radio.

Section Four
Ready to Depart
Letting Go

I warm'd both hands before the fire of Life;
It sinks; and I am ready to depart.

Walter Savage Landor

Few things are harder than saying goodbye. When the separation is caused by an impending death, many resist with all their might. Finding ways to say goodbye may become overshadowed by efforts to regain one's strength, find a cure or search for any hope, however slim, of reprieve. Though death may be pressed to the periphery, over time our bodies have ways of telling us when the time approaches.

Although the impulse to fight or avoid may continue until our final breath, others welcome death as a natural culmination of a life lived as best as one could, a moment of transition or simply as a time of rest from the burdens that have accumulated over the course of an illness. Though the challenge of acceptance, letting go and saying goodbye are common themes at the end of life, resistance or ambivalence may be fierce. The tension between a desire to live and saying goodbye is the theme of this section.

Chapter Ten
Death of a Warrior
Acceptance

Hap was no stranger to war. At eighteen he joined the army and wound up fighting in Vietnam. After two years of combat he returned to North Carolina with a heroin addiction and a head filled with violent images and painful memories which fueled the nightmares that still woke him up in a cold sweat. After the war, he oscillated between a desire to get clean and the persistent demands of his addiction, swinging between hope and despair. Making things worse, alcoholism became another enemy with which he battled. For fifteen years he barely made ends meet by doing odd jobs, talking his mother into "loans" they both knew he wouldn't repay and petty theft.

By the time he met his wife, Kim, he was broke, craving drugs, and about to be thrown out of the hotel where she worked as a cook. Though his fast-talking swagger didn't fool her, and in spite of his attempt to con her out of some money, she'd seen the "good person" beneath his abrasive appearance.

On the surface they were an unlikely pair. Hap was extroverted and talked rapidly like a machine gun. He could be rigid, impulsive and had a long memory for every slight or harsh word ever received. Fiercely loyal to family, he had few friends and was generally cynical about his fellow humans. He loved to tell stories about his life casting himself in the role of outsider and warrior. As he saw it, he went against the grain, spat at convention, and was usually under attack.

Kim was socially reserved, preferring to think before acting and measuring words cautiously before speaking. She had a relaxed manner and was slow to take offense. Where Hap's stories emphasized overcoming obstacles, hers underscored attempts to live a moral life. She was sensitive and adept at discerning subtleties. She saw more complexity in the world than Hap and didn't divide everything into antagonistic categories like friends versus enemies. She worked hard, paid her bills, didn't drink and had a small community of friends on whom she relied for support.

She calmed his tumultuous intensity and helped him open to the spiritual dimension of life, trusting in something beyond his ever-vigilant senses. With her, he felt safe and was less combative. From

Hap, Kim drew confidence and learned to trust in her strength and resilience. His sharp and playful humor often tempered her tendency to be overly serious.

By the time they were married Hap had joined her church, kicked heroin and was holding down a job at an asphalt plant. He continued to struggle with alcohol for which he attended a support group and saw a counselor at the Veteran's Administration but for the first time in his life he'd begun believing in the possibility of a better future. Maybe the smoke of battle would finally clear. Maybe he and Kim could raise a family and live happily ever after.

When their daughter, Allie, was born, it was the final motivation Hap needed. Within days he had given up the alcohol and emerged, as he put it, "Drier than a Baptist preacher who knows the congregation is looking." He knew he had to be on guard for a relapse, but he was sure the enemy was finally vanquished. Even Hap, whose life had been filled with disappointment, had to admit things were looking up.

Shortly thereafter he caught a pulmonary infection. At first he ignored it thinking it would go away but after a couple weeks he wound up in the hospital. He'd been working extra hours at the plant and figured he simply needed some rest. When blood tests revealed that he had Human Immunodeficiency Virus (HIV), the infection that causes Acquired Immune Deficiency Syndrome (AIDS), he and Kim were decimated (this was in the days before a new class of medication proved effective in managing HIV).

They insisted the tests were wrong and demanded they be redone. When the lab confirmed the initial diagnosis Kim was horrified. As she remembered it, the world took on a surreal quality that made the next couple weeks seem like a quagmire of intense emotions broken only by moments of numbness and confusion. Hap descended into wounded fury. "I blamed everyone but myself," he remembered. "I didn't want to admit that I got it from doing heroin. I even found ways to blame Kim."

When he realized he might have infected Kim and Allie he was immobilized by fear. "The day they tested my family for HIV," he said, "was the worst day of my life. If they'd been infected I couldn't have lived with myself." In the years ahead he would consider it a miracle that both were negative for the infection. At the time, however, his relief was short-lived.

His impulse to withdraw was strong. Soon after his family was tested, Hap disappeared. Kim's anger, already burning like a slow fuse, was incandescent. She was furious at him for abandoning her and Allie, vacillating between impulses to cut him entirely from her life and wanting him back. After long soul searching, she decided on the latter and gathered a few friends to help search Hap's old hangouts. They looked for him at bars, shelters, hotels, police stations, but he seemed to have vanished like a stealthy old warrior blending into an endless marsh.

About a week later, tearful and contrite, he called Kim begging to return home. "To this day," Hap said, "I don't know what I was thinking or why I got hijacked by a voice that told me to run." After getting a few things straight, as Kim put it, she picked him up at a local bus station and drove him home. "The first thing I did," she said with a mixture of seriousness and humor, "was let him know he'd run out of second chances. The second thing I did was make him take a shower." They prepared to fight the war together. There would be no more melting away into the brush, no more retreats.

One of the things they'd *gotten straight* was Hap's agreement to follow his physician's instructions to the letter. He went to the VA regularly, often bringing home pamphlets with information about his disease. Inured to war and familiar with its language, he began calling the clinic his base camp and described the combination of medications he was taking as his heavy artillery. Kim, it seemed, was his drill sergeant.

Although they attempted to keep his infection a secret, word leaked out. In their small community, news traveled fast and it was not long before everybody seemed to know. There was a great deal of ignorance about AIDS back in those days and the stigma was as virulent as the disease. They found themselves shunned by neighbors, friends, even members of their church. Despite Hap's good work record he was fired from his job. When he asked for an explanation he was given vague statements about health-related absences.

Paradoxically, the snubs strengthened Hap's resolve to beat the odds and survive long enough to see a cure. Survival became his focus and, not surprisingly, he likened it to his experiences in the Vietnam War. "When you're pinned down under enemy fire," he said, "you've got to hold on as long as it takes to bring in air support." He knew it didn't always arrive in time but the point was to keep fighting and hoping.

In the case of HIV, air support was not guaranteed. As his immune system weakened, he began experiencing a litany of opportunistic infections. Stays in the hospital became common. Amid the rounds of antibiotics and blood draws, the staff at the hospital stopped calling his condition HIV and starting calling it AIDS. Although they didn't talk about it, Kim and Hap noted the distinction. They were not entirely surprised when the doctor suggested they enlist the help of a local hospice. Initially they refused, mistakenly equating hospice with giving up, afraid it would hasten his death. As his condition worsened, however, the doctor broached the subject again. By then trips to the clinic had become so onerous that they agreed to give hospice a try.

When I met Hap he was standing in the dirt yard of their small cement block home. It was a warm spring day and he was leaning on a walking stick of twisted wood that had been sanded and coated with dark brown varnish. On top of the stick were some feathers and a small turtle shell attached with thin strips of rawhide. As it turned out, he carried the stick everywhere, even inside the house and on trips to the hospital. He told me a friend was a Native American shaman who had purified the stick with smoke and ritual prayer, infusing it with talismanic powers. He'd declared Hap to be a member of the turtle clan and said that when he carried the stick he would be protected.

Hap was thin and physically frail but exuded such tremendous determination that his wiry frame appeared to radiate vitality. He spoke at length about the many things he needed to do – plant the garden, fix the truck, on and on. The list was long. Kim joined us in the yard and offered her enthusiastic encouragement. The unspoken message was that he had too much to do and too many people counting on him to allow sickness to interfere.

Weeks passed. Hap planted the garden and fixed the truck then he had to cut firewood and fix the barbed wire out by the henhouse. Every time he took something off the list he added something else. In addition to projects he needed to do, there were events he needed to stick around for like Allie's sixth birthday or the Fourth of July. There was always something just ahead for which he needed to remain alive, something motivating him to fight harder.

In spite of his efforts to recover, by autumn he was so weak he couldn't go outside. Kim was terrified of new infections and cleaned the house every day trying to kill the germs she imagined were lurking everywhere. Searching for something to fortify him in his fight, Hap asked his Indian friend to visit again. When I asked how the visit had gone he was evasive. Pulling me aside, Kim whispered that his friend had suggested that Hap, "Ask God for help crossing the river." For a warrior like Hap, crossing the river was the last thing he intended to do.

Near the end of the year, he began having hallucinations and periods of confusion. To his medical team this was simply AIDS-related dementia, something common enough as to be more-or-less incidental to them, but to Hap and Kim it was like taking a trip into hell. Often his confusion contained elements suggestive of war. The illness, it seemed, had triggered long repressed post-traumatic stress. He saw snipers crawling on the ceiling and was convinced Viet Cong soldiers were digging beneath the floorboards of his home, intent on killing him.

As episodes of confusion intensified a disturbing theme emerged. He believed God and Satan were battling for possession of his soul and Satan was winning. He worried that God had given up on him because of all the "bad things" he'd done. Eventually, this war filled his entire field of vision, enveloping everything and everyone around him. He was convinced his hospice nurse was trying to poison him at Satan's behest and his doctors were spies and assassins. Everyone he met was on one side or the other; there were no neutrals.

He was terrified that if he died he would go to hell. When another respiratory infection invaded his weary body, Kim brought him to the hospital where he was diagnosed with pneumonia. Soon he was not responsive and appeared to be dying. Given his condition, she was hesitant to start another round of antibiotics and wondered if it might be better to let him go.

Such decisions can be agonizing, especially when a loved one has not discussed their wishes with family. It can be hard to know whether to keep fighting or to accept that death is near. Though Hap was a fighter, his life was clearly ebbing. The doctors painted a grim but realistic picture of what his life would be like even if antibiotics kept him alive for a few more weeks or months.

When faced with such decisions it's easy to feel guilty no matter what one chooses. Kim pulled her hair out trying to figure out what to do. After a sleepless night and much inner turmoil, she told the physician to treat the infection. Like Hap, she was unsure how to stop fighting even though she acknowledged that, "fighting doesn't make much sense anymore."

Despite her decision, while Hap was in the hospital he died – at least for a few moments. He went into cardiac arrest and, while a team worked to resuscitate him, he was dead. I visited the next day in the intensive care unit. Surprisingly, he was alight with energy and eager to talk about what had happened in those moments of death. He recalled that, just prior to his heart attack he had seen Satan at the foot of his bed. The spectral visitor was chiding him for fighting so hard, trying to convince him that God had forsaken him.

Hap searched for words to describe what happened next. Self-conscious about being misunderstood, he chose his words with unusual care. He said he had found himself back in the dense elephant grass of Vietnam in the middle of a firefight. All the soldiers in his platoon were dead and he was pinned down by an enemy he couldn't see. He fired his gun wherever he saw hints of movement in the grass. As the battle swirled, he searched frantically for the radio so he could call for backup but it was nowhere to be found.

In the corner of his eye he caught sight of a field of rolling grass and wildflowers removed from the battle. He tried to ignore it, but its peaceful allure was so incongruent with the violence of battle it drew his attention like a moth drawn toward the luminescence of a full moon. Looking more closely, he saw a small wooden building at the far end of the field which he took to be a church made of whitewashed planks. In front of the church stood a solitary figure in a simple brown robe smiling and waving for him to come over.

It seemed like an inviting place, but Hap was a warrior. Any distraction could be deadly, so he turned back to the fight. As he fired, however, his desire to go to the visitor on the hill became so powerful he did something that surprised him. He threw his weapon down, stood up, and began walking toward the field, unconcerned about the enemy's bullets.

The next thing he remembered, "Some guy from the hospital was shouting at me wanting to know if I could hear him."

Hap was convinced the figure by the church was a "holy man." Still, he was puzzled and unsure what it all meant. As we talked, Kim suggested, somewhat sheepishly, that "maybe the man was telling you that you've fought long enough and it's time to stop fighting."

As he thought about it, he got a far-away look, "I don't know how to stop."

He'd spent his life fighting. Anything else was tantamount to surrendering, something he resisted from his deepest psychic fiber. For him there was no distinction between surrender and failure. This left him in a dilemma. If, as he suspected, he'd received a direct message from some transpersonal realm then he certainly ought to pay attention, but doing so required him to do something he had spent his life trying to avoid. There were no clear answers. We agreed to think about things and meet later in the week.

Days later he was still mystified though he acknowledged for the first time that he was tired of fighting. His journey had been hard. He was exhausted. Yet, as soon as he allowed these thoughts to enter his mind they were countered by judgments that he was being cowardly and weak. He was stuck in a swamp of tension and contradiction. He'd been given permission to stop fighting but couldn't overcome his psychological mandate to resist.

Many times during the preceding months, Hap had spoken of his affinity for American Indian culture. He took pride in his membership in the turtle clan and seemed to draw strength from his mystical walking stick. Though guilty of stereotyping, he saw Native Americans as the embodiment of warrior culture and admired their fighting prowess. I asked if he'd ever heard of Osceola. He was familiar with the Seminole leader. When I asked if he knew how Osceola died, he wasn't sure.

*

In the winter of 1835, a long, bloody war was about to erupt between the Seminoles of Florida and the United States. For Osceola, a leader with growing stature among the Seminoles, war was nothing new. His entire life had been spent in a boiling cauldron of conflict. As he led a small band of warriors to the outskirts of Fort King, he was prepared for another battle.

He'd been born in Alabama in 1804, a member of the Tallassee tribe but the Americans had called him a Creek. As a boy, the Creek War had torn his tribe apart. In the horrible aftermath of the Battle of Horseshoe Bend he and his mother had fled into the wilds of northern Florida and joined the Seminoles.

Even here he couldn't escape the ravages of war. In 1817, Andrew Jackson invaded Spanish-held Florida and attacked the Seminoles, intent on capturing escaped slaves who had found shelter there and annihilating the Indians or driving them into the swamps. Osceola's adopted tribe had been fragmented during this First Seminole War and driven south.

In 1823, a few Seminole leaders signed the Treaty of Moultrie Creek, which stipulated that all Seminoles would move to a reservation in Central Florida. Despite much controversy over this treaty, many, including Osceola, agreed to move after being assured they could live in peace. Perhaps as he moved to the reservation he was hopeful that he might finally live without fear or the constant need to fight. Maybe he'd grown cynical about such hopes. Whatever his thoughts, any peace he may have found on the reservation had been short-lived.

The land turned out to be poor for growing crops, game was scarce, and the government's promised assistance never materialized. As whites gobbled up the surrounding land, the Seminoles had no choice but to leave the reservation in search of food. Time and again Indians and whites collided. In 1830, Andrew Jackson (who had become President by then) signed the Indian Removal Act which demanded that all Indians living in the eastern states be forced out of their homes and marched west of the Mississippi River.

The Seminoles had few choices. They could move or try to stall for time. They could melt into the swamps and pine-barrens or they could fight. During the debate, Osceola emerged as an uncompromising advocate of resistance. Speaking with a blend of charm, humanity, and incendiary aggression, his oratory frightened some and inspired others. He was a warrior and he would not move. He would fight, he would never surrender.

He drew together a band of ardent followers consisting of family, friends and those who shared his will to resist. These included many blacks that had escaped slavery and joined the Seminoles or formed separate communities. In fact, when the war commenced, General Thomas Jessup wrote, "This, you may be assured, is a Negro, not an Indian war; and if it be not speedily put down, the South will feel the effects of it on their slave population before the end of the next season."

Things reached a flashpoint in December of 1835 when Osceola led a small group to the walls of Fort King near present-day Ocala. Their goal was to kill the territorial Indian Agent, Wily Thompson, an act that was both symbolic and strategic. As Thompson strolled outside the walls of the fort, he and a companion were ambushed and killed. It was the first blow of the Second Seminole War.

Fifty miles south another fight was raging. One hundred troops led by Major Francis Dade had been crossing a seemingly innocuous stretch of pines just south of the Wahoo Swamp when they were ambushed by Seminole warriors. Recalling the first shots of the ambush, the sole survivor of Dade's men said, "I had not time to think of the meaning of these shots, before a volley, as if from a thousand rifles, was poured in upon us from the front, and all along our left flank."

The Americans quickly mobilized two-hundred-fifty soldiers and about five-hundred Florida volunteers near Fort Drane. When they reached the Withlacoochee River on December 31, Osceola attacked inflicting heavy casualties and sending them into retreat.

In a matter of days, Osceola and other headmen such as Alligator and Jumper, had killed the Indian Agent, destroyed Dade's column and sent an army scurrying. Whites panicked, fled their homes, and by summer 1836 had abandoned most of the interior of the state except for small concentrations at Micanopy, Newnansville and Garney's Ferry.

The Seminoles confounded the Americans with their lightning-like ability to appear, fight then vanish. Their knowledge of the wilderness and ability to travel quickly were formidable advantages. The Americans moved slowly and knew virtually nothing about the Florida terrain except for a thin toehold along the coast. General Jessup lamented that the land was "an unexplored wilderness, the interior of which we were as ignorant of as of the interior of China."

Although the initial battles of the war involved large groups of Seminoles working in concert, most subsequent fighting was in the form of small skirmishes and ambushes. Sometimes Indian leaders coordinated their actions but more often they acted independently. Though Osceola was regarded as an important leader he had no formal authority outside his group of followers. It was by virtue of his tenacity and abilities as a warrior that his influence grew.

Confronted with guerilla fighting on uncharted terrain the U.S. army floundered. General Winfield Scott was put in command and proved ineffective. Trained in European style drills and the tactics of massed engagement, he was stymied by an enemy able to appear and disappear quickly and which fought from behind trees, refusing to be drawn into the open.

Osceola seemed to be everywhere. He was there when General Gaines was pinned down for several days on the Withlacoochee River. He was there when warriors attacked Major Heilman's troops near present-day Gainesville. He was at the ambush of Captain Maitland's men in the Battle of Welika Pond. The army's strategy may have been muddled but Osceola's was simple. He wanted to inflict casualties while minimizing his own, displace settlers and disrupt the flow of troops and supplies. Above all he intended to survive. Maybe if the

Seminoles could hold out long enough the United States would grow weary of fighting and let them stay in their homes and live in peace. If only they could hold on.

Despite their toughness, after a couple years of fighting and staying on the run the Seminoles began to wear down. To stay ahead of marauding soldiers they had to retreat into hammocks, forests and swamps. Many of their towns had been destroyed. Growing food and raising livestock was nearly impossible. Hunger, disease, and despair became more devastating enemies than the Americans. Osceola was wracked by the symptoms of malaria and weakened by malnutrition. Though his fighting spirit was strong, his body was feeling the strain.

The Seminoles began to lose heart. Throughout 1837 small groups surrendered and were shipped west to "Indian territory." Late in the year, even Osceola was willing to parley and discuss peace. Under a flag of truce, he and about seventy warriors met General Joseph Hernandez at a mutually agreed upon place just south of Saint Augustine. Although the Seminoles had been assured a truce would be respected and treaty talks held in good faith this turned out to be a lie. Soldiers surrounded them and forced Osceola and his allies to surrender.

The stunned captives were marched back to Saint Augustine and imprisoned at Fort Marion. Seeing little alternative, Osceola sent word for the rest of his followers to come to the fort. Some fifty additional people, including two of his wives and a sister, arrived and were thrown into prison along with their friends. Two months later they were moved to Charleston, South Carolina and imprisoned at Fort Moultrie.

For Osceola, his body severely weakened by illness, captivity drained what was left of his waning strength. He'd been a wily and charismatic leader, respected by his people and intimidating to his enemies but his body had become frail, his power was ebbing. At Fort Moultrie he tired easily and needed assistance with things he would have preferred to do himself. In his weakened state, his immune system was unable to ward off infections. In January 1838, he caught quinsy, a virus characterized by acute inflammation in the throat. Once again he found himself fighting for his life.

It wouldn't have been a surprise if he had fought to his last breath. After all, he had been hardened by life's battles, learned to endure pain, survive at any cost and most importantly, never surrender. But by January 31, Osceola knew the time for clinging to life had passed. Accepting death was his final struggle, his final act of courage.

Declining the ministrations of a Seminole healer and a fort physician, the proud warrior called his wives and several friends to his side. Doctor Fredrick Weedon was present and recalled that Osceola "seemed to be sensible that he was dying." The Seminole leader was not able to speak but, using hand motions he asked for help getting dressed in his finest clothes. He painted his face in vermilion and then, according to Weedon, "shook hands with us all in dead silence, and with his wives and little children." Surrounded by those dear to him, the archetypal warrior prepared to accept death peacefully. Weedon recalled the scene in his journal:

> He made a signal for them to lower him down upon his bed, which was done, and he then slowly drew from his war-belt his…knife, which he firmly grasped in his right hand, laying it across the other on his breast, and in a moment smiled away his last breath without a struggle or a groan.

For Osceola the war was over. He had not willingly surrendered to American troops, but, in the end, he surrendered himself peacefully into the hands of the Master of Breath.

*

When death approaches some will fight until the very end while others grow tired of fighting and search for ways to accept and let go. Sensing when it's time to stop fighting and shift one's focus toward acceptance can be a formidable challenge for those who are warriors. It's easy to confuse acceptance with surrender or to equate surrender, which in many spiritual traditions is a sign of strength, with weakness or failure.

When I was done telling him Osceola's story Hap said, "I just figured he'd died fighting or disappeared into the Everglades." He was struck by the thought of this man – a fighter like himself – laying down his weapons and relinquishing the call to battle. Death was not the enemy.

As the physical effects of AIDS converged with the countless small indignities of illness, Hap also found himself 'ready for rest', as he euphemistically put it. At the same time, he still felt the impulse to fight, to survive. In hours of clarity, he would return to his near death experience and find solace in the thought that when he died he would be protected by the solitary figure of his vision. His life moved between fear of death, and trust that death harbored no real threat.

During one of our last talks he puzzled over Osceola's apparent acceptance of death while his loved ones were still "under fire." It was an important question since Hap agonized over not being able to protect Kim and Allie after he died. He wondered how Osceola could have relented, knowing the hardship that lay ahead for his people.

"What's your sense of that? What does your gut tell you?" I asked.

"I think it got to where it wasn't in his hands anymore. He just had to let it go."

"What about you?"

"I'm not there yet."

"Where are you?"

"I'm not sure."

To Kim it appeared that he would fight until his last breath. In the final days of his life he slept constantly but it was a light, fitful sleep. His body was restless and often moved as though startled. It seemed as though battles were being fought within and his sudden movements were shadows of the war being waged. Kim said and did all the right things – letting him know he was safe, that she and Allie would be okay, that it was alright if he needed to go. She provided physical care, sensitive to reinforcing safety, patience, gentle non-reactivity. Hap's restlessness continued.

The morning he died was icy, the sky a threatening gray. The roads were slippery. I reached the house before the hospice nurse which gave Kim and I time to talk. She told me that a few hours before Hap died, "He woke up briefly and was able to talk for just a little bit."

His mind had been clear. He told Kim it was time. He was ready to go. She asked if he was afraid and he asked her to forgive him for all that he'd put her through.

"I told him I forgave him," she recalled, "and asked him to forgive me too. Then I asked him again if he was afraid."

He responded by asking, "Do you know how much I love you?"

"I told him I did, and that I loved him too," Kim said. "Then I asked him one more time if he was afraid."

"No," he'd said, "Are you?"

She'd told him yes, but it was okay.

When he asked to see Allie, Kim brought her to Hap's bed where for several minutes they sat together quietly, holding hands as he stroked his daughter's hair. He told them he loved them then slipped into a deep, undisturbed sleep.

The Second Seminole War dragged on until 1842 during which time untold numbers of Native Americans died from battle, disease and starvation. Eventually, even the most strident warriors were forced to leave their homes and head west. By the end of 1843 thousands had been pushed onto reservations in Oklahoma.

The United States government was likewise exhausted. It had lost fifteen hundred men and wasted thirty million dollars on a senseless war. When several hundred Seminoles disappeared into the swamps rather than surrender, the Americans didn't have the stomach to hunt them down. For over a decade these Seminoles lived in the Everglades. By 1855 these holdouts were again under pressure as white surveyors, land speculators and would-be settlers cut paths into their territory. The ensuing conflict was called the Third Seminole War. By war's end only a handful of Seminoles, probably no more than three hundred, were left. These were never defeated, never surrendered.

Chapter Eleven
Building the Brooklyn Bridge
Legacy and Accepting Help

Mort was born in Brooklyn in 1911, the year fire swept through the Triangle Shirtwaist Factory in Manhattan, killing one-hundred-forty-six women. Many jumped to their deaths from sweatshop windows after finding factory doors locked and fire escapes inoperable. In his mind, the wrenching images of these poor women falling to their deaths blended with his birth to form a single inseparable event.

Maybe it was because his father worked in the apparel business and had known some of those who'd died. Maybe it had simply been an unforgettable reference point that gave immediate context whenever he told other New Yorkers, "I was born the year of the fire." There was, however, a psychological dimension. Throughout his life Mort had seen young people die quickly and unexpectedly: a schoolmate trampled by a horse-drawn trolley; a brother killed during the Korean War and a sister who died on an operating table during a botched mastectomy. As a marine in the Pacific during World War Two, he'd seen young soldiers die. The most painful loss, though, had been the death of his son, Mitch, who had suffered a cerebral aneurysm before his twenty-third birthday. "I was born under the death star," he liked to say. "It has been over my head my entire life."

He wasn't surprised when he was diagnosed with cancer or when surgery failed to cure it. At eighty-five, he figured he'd done well to outrun the death star for so long. It was time to 'face the music'. He expected to go downhill quickly but the doctors assured him his particular kind of cancer moved slowly and the surgery had bought him time. With luck, he might live four or five years.

Pondering the prognosis, he found himself wondering if it was better to die quickly without warning, like so many he'd known, or slowly, aware of what was coming. The former offered advantages – no anxiety about the future, no tedium from slow days of physical decline or dramas in doctors' offices. The problem was that dying quickly offered no time to prepare, savor the time or tie up loose ends. And there was no time to plan. For Mort, a methodical maker of master plans, this was the kicker.

By the time hospice care began, years later, he'd decided it was better to see death approaching. Those years had allowed him to use the time wisely and develop a game plan for what lay ahead. He and his wife, Alma, had traveled to New York to visit family, pay respects at a Brooklyn cemetery and return to the site of a theater (now high-rise apartments) where they'd met on a blind date. They'd visited Paris Island, South Carolina where Mort had been inducted into the marines and spent time with their daughter Ruth, and granddaughter, Rhea, in Washington, D.C.

In Eastern Europe they traced family roots. Everywhere they went they visited people and places that were significant to them. After returning, Mort often spoke of their "life-tour" with relish and enthusiasm, humorously referring to it as Phase One of his two-part, earthly departure plan. When we met, his disease was finally taking a serious toll and he'd already begun Phase Two.

In his mind, the plan was simple: spend as much time as he could with Alma, Ruth, Rhea, and his son Nate, write his memoir and prepare the family's complex estate for his death. He was certain it was a realistic blueprint and he intended to follow it to the letter. Ironically, for all his planning, he failed to factor in his illness. He just had no idea how strenuous and challenging activities would become or the toll they would take on his mental focus.

Spending time with family was his highest priority. Nate moved in with his parents to assist with practical concerns related to Mort's care. During the day Mort and Alma sat together talking, watching television and taking catnaps. There was no need for anything dramatic; it was enough to be together. Ruth and Rhea visited regularly and Mort's days passed with a rhythm that gave him some measure of comfort. Beneath the surface, however, he was finding it harder to concentrate, tiring easily and harboring worries that the rest of his plan might not be as realistic as he'd hoped.

His memoir fell by the wayside. He'd tried to get started but simply remembering the details of his life, much less organizing and writing it all down, was overwhelming. After gathering some old photographs and letters, the work languished. His consternation was heightened by the fact that the book he envisioned was as much a family history as a personal one. His parents were gone. His brothers and sisters were long dead. As he saw it, it was his sacred responsibility to tell their stories. He agonized that the memoir was stalled, his energy was diminishing and time was running out.

The estate planning was also stalled. He didn't have the stamina to analyze numbers and organize documents. As with his memoir, a larger agenda was in peril. For Mort, estate planning was synonymous with making sure Alma was protected and secure for the rest of her life. He worried about her constantly. It was causing him anguish that he was too worn out to meet with his lawyer in order to disentangle the many policies and accounts. In his mind, he was letting Alma down.

On the surface, Alma didn't appear to need his protection. However, behind the veil of competence and adaptability things were more ambiguous. After they'd left Brooklyn in the 1950s, she'd felt isolated in the rural environs of North Carolina and become prone to depression. When Mitch died, Alma had become reclusive, fearful of strangers and dependent on Mort for emotional support and reassurance. He'd long been the bedrock on which she had anchored herself and he worried that when he died she would be lost.

When I met Mort, Alma had recently broken her shoulder and been transferred to a local nursing home for a course of physical therapy. The doctor said she was there temporarily but no one believed him. "We all knew Mom was there to stay," Ruth later admitted, "but we pretended she'd be able to come home before Pop died." For Mort, nothing could have been more emotionally painful. He had expected to be with her for his remaining months and these hopes had been shattered. Making things worse, since arriving at the nursing home Alma had been sliding into deepening depression.

Mort's game plan had fallen apart at its very center. It's keystone, being with Alma, stolen away in an instant. The memoir was on hold and the estate plans were floundering. He worried constantly about his wife and felt helpless to comfort her. It was as though he was standing on a bridge that was crumbling beneath his feet before he'd made it to the other side.

On our first few visits Mort drifted in and out of deep sadness. Reflecting on things helped. When he realized his feelings were normal, not signs of weakness, his old optimism began to stir. It was time to reevaluate his game plan. It wasn't his fault Phase Two had fallen apart. There had simply been too many variables he couldn't control and hadn't anticipated. He needed a new plan that factored in his growing limitations.

Looking at the tasks to be accomplished it was clear that he needed help. Unfortunately, asking for help was a practice he'd long since abandoned. Even saying the words 'please help me' was like speaking a language so foreign it sounded nonsensical. Though he'd always been willing to give assistance to others, he refused whenever it was offered to him. Even on the threshold of death, the thought of asking for anything evoked strong anxieties. Rationalizations spumed forth: he didn't want to bother his kids; it was his job to take care of everything; he needed to work harder. Beneath these protests deeper injunctions emerged. Asking for help, he believed, was a sign of poor character and a lack of self-respect (at least when it came to him). The innocent act of asking for a hand, it seemed, had been sabotaged by automatic beliefs and judgments.

Ironically, his kids longed for tangible ways to show their affection and Mort had already rebuffed several offers of assistance. Nate was a mortgage broker with a logical mind and an eye for detail, well-suited to help sort out their labyrinthine finances. He was already his parents' power-of-attorney and executor of their estate and had asked Mort several times if he could help organize things, pleading with him to review the responsibilities that waited ahead. Mort always had excuses.

As for the memoir, Ruth was an editor and freelance writer. She excelled at organizing information and distilling it into engaging narratives. She'd done extensive genealogical research on Alma's side of the family but hadn't pursued Mort's in deference to his long-stated intention of doing it himself. In Ruth and Nate, Mort had a team that was ideal to help implement his plan and carry it through, even after he was gone. The problem was letting them do it.

Mort conceded as much but still refused to ask for help directly. Instead, he decided to seed his conversations with hints that he might now be receptive and wait for his children to offer. When they responded positively, he accepted. Over the next weeks he and Nate spent time going through accounts, insurance policies, reviewing documents. It was draining, frustrating work, but once the basics were covered Nate was able to begin sorting through the minutia on his own. Ruth came down for a week and took extensive notes as her father told stories about his life. She got the basics since Mort didn't have stamina for anything more. When added to the stacks of letters, photographs and yellowed postcards with which he sent her home, it was a rich trove of family history. Mort was relieved.

As the memoir and the estate plans slowly fell into place, Mort visited Alma when he could but each trip exacted a greater physical cost, requiring hours of rest afterward. For months he'd declined so slowly as to be almost imperceptible but as his cancer grew he seemed to cross a threshold beyond which things changed rapidly. Visits with Alma ended and he spent more time in bed. Knowing he was near the end of his life, he asked Nate to arrange for him to move to the nursing home. Being with Alma was more important than staying home and within a few days they were together again. By then he wasn't eating much and was sleeping most of the time.

Despite his somnolence, Mort's mind was clear. He vacillated between a weary acceptance of his situation and anxiety about how his family would cope when he "folded up my cards". He'd hoped to live until Nate had a solid grasp on all the particulars of the estate, Ruth had a rough draft of the family history, and Alma had outrun depression. He'd even hoped to outlive his wife and spare her the grief he knew would come, but such was not to be. His biggest fear was that his death would break his wife's spirit. His children reassured him that they would be there for their mother. He told himself not to worry. He worried anyway.

Our last visit was relatively brief. He was weak, talking was difficult. He expressed sadness about leaving so many things incomplete. Although he trusted his children to do their best, he worried that the work they'd started would collapse when he was gone. He found some solace in the fact that he had crafted a blueprint for them, but the work would need to be completed without him. He'd have to trust that it would be done well, but trust, like asking for help, did not come easily. He worried that everything would "go to hell when I'm gone."

On an earlier visit he had told me about how, as a child, his Uncle Saul had frequently taken him onto the promenade of the Brooklyn Bridge. I asked if I could tell him a story about the bridge. Still able to muster his dry humor, he said in a fading voice, "Make it good. It may be the last one I ever hear."

*

In 1869 John Roebling was at the peak of his career. Regarded as one of the great engineers of his day, he possessed tremendous physical and mental energy, creative vision and the practical skills to make his visions into reality. Now he was focused on building a bridge across the East River in New York between Brooklyn and Manhattan, and when Roebling focused on something it was all but impossible to distract him. His construction plan had been approved by the Brooklyn Bridge Company and work was about to begin. With blueprints in hand, it would have been inconceivable to Roebling that he would have to relinquish the project to others.

It was an undertaking beyond the scope of any bridge ever constructed. It would be a suspension bridge, a relatively new design never employed on this scale before. Roebling's plans were meticulous and comprehensive and he expected to be involved in all aspects of construction. The Brooklyn Bridge would be his masterwork. He rhapsodized that, "The completed work, when constructed in accordance with my designs, will not only be the greatest bridge in existence, but it will be the greatest engineering work of the continent, and of the age."

To create a foundation for two massive towers that would support the bridge, he intended to sink giant caissons to the bottom of the river, dig down to bedrock then fill the caissons with cement. The use of caissons was novel and controversial but Roebling had done the math and was convinced it would work.

He turned to his son, Washington Roebling, to assist him. They'd built bridges together in Ohio and New York and his son was a talented engineer in his own right. As a Colonel in the Union army during the Civil War, Washington had overseen the construction of bridges at Fredericksburg and Harper's Ferry. Together, they'd prove the skeptics wrong.

In the summer of 1869, as politicians squabbled over the financing, the Roebling's were completing surveys on the Brooklyn side of the river, mapping the location for one of the towers and a massive anchorage to be built on shore. Their work was interrupted when John Roebling crushed his right foot between a beam and some wooden pilings when a ferry docked against the pier upon which they were standing.

The wound was serious but Roebling figured he'd be back at work soon enough. Unfortunately, he developed a tetanus infection and found himself in a fight for his life. The infection spread. Fever and seizures ravaged his body. For three agonizing weeks he clung to life but finally reached the breaking point, dying before a single block of limestone had been laid, leaving nothing but plans for a bridge many thought could never be built. Some assumed the colossal project had died along with him.

But he'd drafted his designs in excruciating detail, covering everything from cost projections and time frame to the type of masonry and cable wire to use. The members of the bridge company turned to Washington Roebling to pick up the reins. Thomas Kinsella, editor of the *Brooklyn Eagle* and a member of the board, used the paper to give his seal of approval to the young engineer. "Not long since, before the accident which led to his death," Kinsella wrote:

> Mr. Roebling remarked to us that he had enough of money and reputation. And he scarce knew why, at his age, he was undertaking to build another and still greater bridge. His son, he added, ought to build this Brooklyn bridge – was as competent as himself in all respects to design and supervise it; had thought and worked with him, and in short was as good an engineer as his father.

Washington was already involved in the project and was one of the world's rare authorities on suspension bridges and caissons. No one was more motivated to bring his father's dream to fruition. Without delay, he was made chief engineer. John Roebling's vision and painstakingly crafted plans were in his son's hands.

The first order of business was to construct the caisson on which the Brooklyn tower would stand. Essentially, a caisson was an enormous box built of wood and iron with a heavy roof, reinforced sides and no bottom. Roebling intended to fill it with compressed air and sink it into the riverbed. Men would enter the caisson to dig out river rock and sediment until they reached bedrock. As they dug, huge blocks of limestone and granite would be piled on top of the structure, sinking it as the tower was simultaneously constructed. When they reached a firm foundation the caisson would be filled with cement. Given the novelty and magnitude of the job, the shipbuilders making the caisson demanded money up front and refused to guarantee their work.

By May 1870, the six million pound behemoth was floated to the site of the Brooklyn tower where a limestone block weighing about six thousand pounds was muscled on top of it. As more stone was piled on, the caisson began its descent, soon pressing into a layer of mud and river rock. After an initial survey Roebling concluded that the material "was of a very formidable nature, and could only be removed by slow, tedious, and persistent efforts." Digging all the way to bedrock, especially in an age of pick, sledge hammer and shovel, was going to be an arduous, time-consuming task.

Crews worked around-the-clock breaking boulders and hauling them away along with bucket after bucket of mud. They worked in dank air lighted by calcium lamps. Day after day they hammered and scraped while temperatures climbed into the eighties and nineties. As the caisson sank into the earth men began experiencing headaches, joint pain, dizziness and nausea. Something was making them sick but no one knew what it was.

Roebling was down in the compressed air more than anyone else, inspecting every detail and solving problems as they arose. By December, with the caisson sunk to forty feet and the tower climbing ever higher above the water's surface, conditions were beginning to affect him. One night he collapsed while surveying the work. By the time he was driven home in a carriage he was completely paralyzed. His doctor was called in. After a few anxious hours, the paralysis subsided but it was clear that his health was eroding.

Undeterred, Roebling returned to his grueling schedule. In March of 1871, the caisson reached bedrock at forty-five feet. By September, work was underway on the Manhattan tower; masonry going up as the caisson went down. The terrain on the Manhattan side was mostly sand and gravel and the structure sank more quickly. On the other hand, the caisson would have to descend much deeper before reaching bedrock.

Greater depth meant greater air pressure for those inside. Unbeknownst to them, every time the structure sank two feet the atmospheric pressure rose one pound. By the time it reached forty-four feet, the workers were again experiencing the symptoms that had afflicted them on the Brooklyn tower. As the tower sank, these symptoms became more frequent and acute. In addition to joint pain and vomiting, they experienced profuse sweating, paralysis, fatigue and lack of mental focus. In an attempt to protect his workers, Roebling shortened the workday and hired physician, Andrew Smith. Despite Doctor Smith's conscientious attempts to treat the men and understand the mysterious illness, his efforts were largely ineffective. By April 1872, two were dead from what people had begun calling "caisson's disease."

Caisson's disease is known today as the bends, a condition usually associated with diving caused by rapid changes in compression like those experienced by workers whenever they entered or left the caisson. Over time, repeated exposure can be debilitating, even fatal. There was no diagram or calculation in John Roebling's plans with which to anticipate this problem. He'd measured every beam of steel, every pound of mortar, but there was no logarithm factoring in the frailty of the human body or the limitations of the day's medicine.

149

Since his episode of paralysis, Roebling had continued going down into the caisson daily and his health had further deteriorated. As he struggled with mounting symptoms and the fact that two men were already dead, he made a startling decision. Even though they hadn't reached bedrock, he halted the digging at seventy-eight feet. He reasoned that, at that depth the sand was so compact as to be "good enough to found upon, or at any rate nearly as good as any concrete that could be put in place of it."

Shortly thereafter, he was seized by an incapacitating attack of the bends which left him in excruciating pain, paralyzed and near death. Eventually, however, he surprised everyone, rallying his strength and returning to work.

Attacks continued, arriving suddenly, sapping his strength and leaving him nervous and exhausted. He cut back on time spent at the bridge. By winter of 1872 his condition was so precarious he was spending most of his time in bed, unable to concentrate, exhausted after short conversations. Failing health gave him a keen awareness of his mortality; he worried that he would die before the bridge was finished and was haunted by fears that he would leave his work, and that of his father, incomplete.

In desperation, he took a leave of absence in April 1873 so he and his wife Emily could travel to Europe seeking treatment for his shattered body. They'd hoped the journey would restore him but he found travelling arduous and painful. By the time they returned to New York, Roebling was drained and demoralized.

His mind, however, was unaffected and his resolve to finish the bridge remained strong. He resumed his role as chief engineer even though he was too frail to visit the work site. He would have to rely on others and place in their hands responsibilities he would rather have shouldered himself. He would have to ask for help and trust that others could do the job.

Important among these helpers were assistant engineers such as C.C. Martin and Francis Collingwood who supervised crews and executed his orders. Later, Emily Roebling would comment that completing the bridge, "could never have been accomplished but for the unselfish devotion of his assistant engineers. Each man had a certain department in charge and they worked with all their energies to have the work properly done according to Colonel Roebling's plan and wishes."

Emily assumed a role equal to that of her husband's assistants. He relied on her to write his detailed instructions and reports, relay information and make regular inspections of the construction. As she became familiar with the science of engineering and the art of city politics, she spoke on his behalf and kept him apprised on all facets of the project. Though Roebling was still very much in charge, he would have been the first to admit he couldn't have overseen things without Emily.

By the time both towers were completed Roebling was in constant pain and moving around left him fatigued and frustrated. He was easily distressed and suffered from periods of acute anxiety. Emily provided the physical care and psychological support that sustained him through his most difficult times. Later in his life Roebling would write with fitting imagery, "At first I thought I would succumb, but I had a strong tower to lean upon, my wife, a woman of infinite tact and wisest counsel."

The next step in construction was to string steel wire between the towers and draw them into powerful cables. Reporting on the huge suspender cables, E.F. Farrington wrote Roebling that, "I have carried out your instructions to the letter." By then, Roebling had taken up residence on Brooklyn Heights from which, with the aid of a telescope, he could see the cables forming from the window of their home.

Emily visited the bridge almost every day. The project which had begun as the vision of John Roebling and which had become the center of her husband's life was now inextricable with her own. No communications reached or left Roebling without her awareness. When visitors from the site or the bridge company arrived, or when the occasional reporter stopped by, the visit was often spent entirely with Emily while her husband rested. She could answer their many questions and was skillful at asking her own on his behalf.

It's tempting to imagine Roebling in his room bolted to his telescope watching every trowel and rivet. According to his wife, however, this was not the case. His engineering skills were so good he could judge the progress with occasional observations. Physically, perhaps psychologically, he was a shell of his former self, but his mind was razor sharp. As steel cables slowly spider-webbed across the skyline, he must have wondered at times what his father would have thought.

By 1880 construction was progressing steadily though it had been six years since the chief engineer had visited the site. Work had been going on for over ten years and critics were becoming impatient. Some suspected corruption was behind the many delays. In truth, the bridge was a mammoth undertaking and early estimates for its completion turned out to be unrealistic. Simply getting enough rock, steel, and cable wire to the site required the energies and precision of a seasoned army. Perhaps inevitably, along with the delays, there was the politics.

The mayor of Brooklyn, Seth Low, went so far as to refer to the bridge as the "unsubstantial fabric of a dream" and attempted to have Roebling removed as chief engineer on the grounds that he "has been for many years, and still is, an invalid." Emily tried to insulate him from the more biting aspects of the fray and spoke eloquently as his representative but it was impossible to shield him from the controversy. Amidst the maelstrom of political posturing, scathing editorials and factionalism among members of the board, the bridge continued to emerge. By 1883 it was finally finished.

In April, Roebling was able to withstand a short carriage ride to the Brooklyn anchorage. Although he didn't leave the carriage, he finally got a close-up view of the great span crossing the East River. It was six thousand feet long with cables capable of supporting twenty-five-million pounds. It had taken much more time and money to build than anyone had imagined. At least twenty men had been killed in accidents during its construction. Its architect was dead and the health of its chief engineer was wrecked, but it was done. And as John Roebling had hoped, it was a masterwork.

*

No matter what the last days of a life hold, there are bound to be things left incomplete. Maybe it's a tribute to our ability to hold fast to meaning and relationships even as we move toward separation. For Mort there were bound to have been things undone no matter how long he lived.

Entrusting one's plans, hopes, and visions to others can be difficult. Letting go of such things can cause anxiety, even shame. At times, there may be no one to whom such things can be passed or maybe doing so is too difficult or time too short. In these instances, we must do our best to lay things aside and accept them as they are. Mort was fortunate that Ruth and Nate understood the importance of his projects.

He was nearly asleep when I finished telling him about the bridge. With his eyes closed, he said, "Uncle Saul must've taken me across that bridge fifty times when I was a kid." Before drifting off, he squeezed my hand and asked me to tell the story to his family after he died.

A few days later, I got a call from Nate concerned about his mother. Alma had asked why Mort wasn't in the hospital where he could get a feeding tube and be artificially hydrated. Although he'd been very clear about his desire not to have this done and Alma had agreed, now that he was near the end she wanted to keep him alive at any cost.

Conversations, such as the one Mort had conveying his wishes at the end of his life are important. They can relieve families of the pressure and responsibility of making difficult decisions under duress. Mort had thought long and hard about what he wanted and decided to forgo artificial feeding, hydration and resuscitation. While Alma had supported his wishes in principle, following through was hard.

I visited her that afternoon. When I arrived she was sitting by Mort's bed trying to wake him up so she could get him to eat some pudding.

"He has to eat or he'll never get stronger."

"Do you think he's going to get stronger?"

"He's bounced back before."

"Do you think he'll bounce back this time?"

She was silent then whispered, "He's got to eat something."

As a person dies, his or her body loses its need for food. Though Mort had reached this point, for Alma, food was laden with emotional and psychological symbolism. She equated food with strength and saw feeding Mort as one of the last acts of love left to her. She worried that he was hungry. He hadn't eaten in days and had "always loved food so much." It took time for her to understand that pushing Mort to eat might actually cause discomfort and put him at risk or choking and aspiration. Slowly she saw that *not* pushing was also an act of love.

Despite her questions about feeding tubes and intravenous hydration, she knew what Mort wanted. He had left a blueprint in the form of a living will. At the heart of her anxiety was the fact that he had always been the anchorage on which she had grounded during hard times. Now that he needed her help, she didn't want to let him down.

"What would he tell you he needs right now?" I asked.

She began sobbing, dried her eyes, "He's tired out. I need to let him go."

"What's the most important thing you can do right now?

"I can't do anything. I'm useless. I can't help."

"Do you love him?"

"Yes," she was emphatic.

"Do you think it's important for him to have someone here who loves him as much as you do? Does that matter?"

She nodded.

"Can you think of anything," I asked, "that's *more* important?"

She reached down and held his hand, "No."

Mort died a couple days after Alma and I talked. When I arrived at the nursing home she was alone in his room holding his hand and crying. After the death of her son she'd been filled with rage at God and had walked away from her synagogue. Now, in the midst of emotional pain and disbelief, what she wanted most was a Rabbi. After several telephone calls I found one who was able to visit. Hearing familiar prayers from childhood and the Rabbi's presence steadied her. It was as though the words, prayers, and rituals had traveled across some invisible bridge leading to an inward place of tradition and spiritual strength.

After the funeral, as Mort had requested, I told Alma the story of the bridge. It helped her, she said, accept not only the things Mort had left incomplete, but also to assuage her guilt about things she hadn't been able to say or do during his final days.

"I was afraid to talk about death," she said. "I wish I'd told him I was going to be okay."

"How does the story about the Brooklyn Bridge help you when you think about that?"

"It reminds me that we all leave things undone no matter how hard we try not to. The point is to do the best you can and let the rest be."

"Can you let it be? Let yourself be human?"

She paused in thought, "Yeah, I think so."

When the Brooklyn Bridge opened on May 24 1883, a newspaper reporter asked Emily if her husband was likely to undertake another such project. According to the reporter, "Mrs. Roebling elevated her brows and said decisively, 'Oh, no. This is his last as well as his greatest work. He will need a long rest after this is over. He needs it and he has certainly earned it'."

Alma asked how the characters in the drama had died. Surprisingly, Emily died some twenty-three years before her husband. "I bet he expected to go first, like I did" she said. "I didn't think I'd be the one left behind."

Her grief sunk deep. She had few opportunities to talk about her loss or her life with Mort. The routines and rhythms of the nursing home allowed only brief interactions with staff and other residents. Amidst the crowd, she felt isolated and alone. Moreover, the nursing staff confused her grief with depression (perhaps understandably, given her history of depression). After getting an order from her physician to increase the dose of a couple medications they considered the matter resolved.

But grieving is laborious and consuming under the best of circumstances. For those grieving in an institutionalized environment the challenges can be amplified. Although staff were kind and the nursing care competent, she had little privacy or control over her surroundings. The noise was distracting. She had no telephone with which to hear a familiar voice. Few people there had known Mort and those who had either did not want to talk about him or were too busy. She had little space for photographs and keepsakes and longed to return to her home just to sit in Mort's chair and breathe in the lingering scent of his cigars.

With her permission, I called Nate to discuss the possibility of her making a home visit. He was nervous that it might be too emotionally difficult for her but agreed to a visit on a weekend when Ruth would be able to join them.

It turned out to be a longer visit than they had expected. Rather than returning Alma in the afternoon, Nate called the nurse and arranged for his mother to spend the night. In the ensuing months, Nate brought her home every few weeks during which time they spoke about Mort and shared what they were experiencing in the wake of his death. Sitting in Mort's chair surrounded by things that reflected their lives together summoned her tears, but it also brought comfort and gratitude.

Initially, Nate had been overwhelmed by his responsibilities with the estate. With the help of an accountant, lawyer, and the right computer software, though, he sorted out the Byzantine intricacies Mort had left behind. The bills were paid. Alma was taken care of.

Ruth completed the family history within a year. Using the Internet, her father's memoir had led her on a fascinating journey into the lives of family she had not even known existed. She'd even talked with Uncle Saul's granddaughter, who lived in Atlanta. Saul had died shortly after her birth and she'd been delighted when Ruth shared some of Mort's stories. Mort had worried that the story of his family would vanish when he died but Ruth had not only captured it, she had reached across the waters of distance and time and connected it to the lives of others who would now carry the story with them.

Who knows to what extent Mort ever completely relinquished to others the work he had started? But he learned to ask for help and trust that his loved ones would do their best with the plans he handed them. If he'd lived long enough to see these plans completed, knowing Mort, he would have come up with a new set of plans, maybe a Phase Three.

He would have appreciated Washington Roebling who, despite daily discomfort and pain, lived until 1926. Years earlier, the same reporter who had interviewed Emily when the bridge opened had also asked Roebling if he thought he would ever build another bridge. He'd responded differently than his wife. "I don't know," he said "If I get well there is lots of big work in the world to do yet."

Chapter Twelve
The Nation's Hoop is Broken
Trusting One's Inner Voice

In the 1940s, when Miguel was a boy living in the mountains of Chile, his uncle showed him how to use the short wave radio in his family's attic. His uncle had run taped-up electrical wire onto the roof and fashioned a gizmo Miguel remembered as more fire hazard than antenna. The attic was off limits to Miguel's younger sisters who whispered about the radio as though it were a talismanic porthole through which adults passed in order to travel the skies.

The attic's light quivered from kerosene lamps, making it a surreal otherworld of vibrating shadow and illumination. For a boy with Miguel's poetic sensibilities, the radio invited him to look beyond the visible world into an unseen web of spirit connecting everything and everybody. Voices arrived from across the globe placing his life into the mosaic of a larger world. A world, he learned, that was in spasms of violent pain.

A great war was being fought and the entire world was bleeding. With no newsreels, magazines, or newspapers, he drew mental pictures of soldiers from Germany, Japan, and places like London, Moscow, and Guadalcanal. On nights when there was enough moonlight he'd slip out of the house and traverse the slippery footpath to a ridge overlooking his village where he could see the Pacific Ocean. There he would strain to see if Japanese ships were lurking on the horizon.

In the motionless morning hours he even heard part of one of Franklin Roosevelt's fireside chats. Though he couldn't understand English, the voice had soothed him. Beneath the jumble of static and strange sounding words, Miguel was able to hear a message, as though sent in secret code directly to him. "Don't worry Miguel. I will keep you and your family safe."

Decades later, unable to move without assistance, looking back on his life, Miguel longed to have that radio by his side. "If I could, I would listen closely in the night for the voice of my homeland." He imagined that beneath the wavy voices and popping transistor tubes he might hear another encoded message. "Miguel, it is not well to die so far from home."

He'd been having what he called life flashes – composite memories that flared with swirling images from his life in Chile. They arrived suddenly, plunging him into a world part real, part mystical. Like the attic of his youth, these flashes connected him to distant lands and people. They arrived in transient collages of sensation, emotion and imagery: the sound of water splashing off pebbles as it flowed down meandering mountain streams; the pungent smell of wet leaves hanging thick in morning fog; the clack of a wooden cowbell blending with the call of a seabird and the sound of his mother clearing her throat. These memories seemed to percolate from the spring of his innermost self, connecting him to a homeland from which he'd been forced to flee. They stirred a longing for home and feelings of sadness that the mystical connection he'd had as a child with unseen realms seemed to have been severed.

He and his wife Nica had been happy in Chile but when Augusto Pinochet seized control of the country in 1973 everything changed. Pinochet was an ironhanded dictator who used violence and force to intimidate, murder or exile those caught in the wide net of his supposed enemies. Miguel lived in Santiago where he worked as a doctor at a clinic in a poor neighborhood. He objected to Pinochet's seizure of power and spoke openly about his belief that if he were not stopped his reign would be a cataclysm of corruption, violence and paranoia.

"I should have known better than to speak so freely," he said.

Before he could elaborate, Nica interrupted him. "What you did was right, Miguel. I'm proud of what you did."

History is mixed when it comes to telling the stories of those who stand against the cruelty of false leaders. For Miguel and Nica, it meant exile. Soldiers with machine guns kicked open the door of their apartment one night and ransacked their home searching for evidence of disloyalty. When Miguel objected, he was informed that he was under suspicion of anti-government activities. It was a foregone conclusion that the men would find something flimsy upon which to hang their trumped up charge. In Miguel's case, they found it in a book that reproduced a map of Russia (which they claimed proved he was a communist). "I was surprised," Miguel said with a somber laugh, "that the soldiers knew what a book was much less how to read one. Perhaps that is why they were drawn to the pictures."

They were taken, along with their infant daughter, Mia, to a containment area; an antiseptic way of saying a prison. This part of the story was murky since neither Miguel nor Nica liked to talk about it. The memories seemed guarded by lingering sentinels wary of the suffering, humiliation and grief contained. When we approached this time of their lives they changed the subject, fast-forwarding the narrative to their departure for the United States several months later.

Although Miguel appreciated the U. S. as a refuge for his family, it had never been home. It was an inscrutable land and he'd remained mystified by its competitiveness and materialism. Despite living here for decades he still felt like a stranger. "It's different," Nica explained, "when you come to America because you want opportunity and you're motivated to be here. We came because we were ordered to leave a home we loved."

Nica's philosophy was to accept things that cannot be changed and go on with life. She claimed she rarely thought about Chile whereas Miguel thought about it constantly. As he reached the end of life he ruminated about having been driven from his home, separated from family and friends, insulted and abused, helpless to protect loved ones. As he put it, "I lost my past, present, and future, in a single day." From the time Pinochet's men arrived at his door, Miguel had harbored a sense that his life had gone irreparably wrong.

According to Nica, he was never the same after that. He was heavier, she said, as though carrying burdensome thoughts. He became anxious about the future and rarely laughed the way he had when they were younger. Even his deep spiritual life had dimmed.

As a child, Miguel had cultivated what he called "rapport with God." Maybe it was his mother's infectious piety or the fact that an uncle was the village priest. Maybe it was the preternatural attic and its evocation of mysterious connections. More likely, he thought, it was his immersion in the natural world. "Walking in the hills always reminded me that I was part of a larger realm of spirit"; a realm that had allowed him to see with the eyes of a mystic. As such, his spiritual life had remained inextricable with his homeland. "When they separated me from my land," he said "they separated me from God."

After leaving home with little more than a suitcase, Miguel hadn't been able to get a medical license. He worked odd jobs to support his family. For the rest of his life, he felt a deep loss of purpose, denied his role as a healer and community caregiver. "It was in those hills of my youth, communicating with God that I was told to become a man of healing. When the dictator arrived, I lost it all." Eventually he found a job assisting with medical research and they had a son, Carlos.

Reflecting on their lives, Nica was moved to tears. "I wish you could have met Miguel before he got sick." Despite his quiet sadness, she said, he had been loyal and affectionate with his family. "He was the wise one, always there for us to lean on."

As Miguel absorbed his approaching death thoughts of Chile swirled. Pinochet had died by then and, before his terminal diagnosis, Miguel had assumed that at some point he would return to his home. Now it was sinking in that he would never again look out across the hills of his childhood toward the Pacific.

One day, Miguel's gray eyes seemed to be looking beyond the walls of his room. He picked up a small red rock from his bedside table. It was flecked with silver and black. Turning it in the light, it seemed like a prism through which he might channel Divine power if he could only learn its secrets. Carlos had asked an aunt to send something from his father's village and the rock had arrived in the mail.

"There was a remote place, a sacred place, in the hills that only I knew about," he said. "This piece of stone reminds me of that sacred place." Lost in thought, he talked as if in a trance. "I would go there to talk with God. And God would talk to me. I think God is trying to tell me something with these life flashes I've been having. I wish I could go to that place to ask what he would have me do."

As we explored these thoughts it became clear that Miguel meant it literally when he said God had talked with him. He'd heard God's voice as clear as a bell the day he'd stumbled across his secret spot as a boy. It had frightened him and he'd run away. Later, he had a vision telling him that he was protected by God's love and should return to this secret place. Soon it became a retreat to which he would go to feel connected to the Spirit of all things.

At times he'd sit quietly, "waiting for the Spirit to send down poetry." Other times he prayed fervently for assistance with some knotty problem or asked forgiveness for perceived transgressions. Except for Nica and his kids, he'd never told anyone about this place. Now, in the confusion of a life unwinding to its end, he longed for that direct, immediate knowledge of God's presence. "If I could go there, I would ask God what happened to that little boy who has become such a tired old man. I would ask if that spirit still lives in me or if it died long ago."

He was tired to his very bones yet his spirit, his life-force, was strong. He was worn down from life's sadness and disappointments but the sadness was punctuated by moments of profound connection with his homeland and memories of a felt experience of God's presence. Two channels seemed etched into his heart, one leading into despair, the other peace. For Miguel it had long been so, but in his final weeks these competing trickles had become roaring cataracts pulling him in opposite directions.

"If I could only hear that voice again," he said with tears in his eyes. "If I could only know God is still with me."

I reminded him how he had once listened to Franklin Roosevelt's strange sounding words as they sparked from his radio, somehow decoding a hidden message. I suggested that perhaps the pulsations of memory he'd been having contained a message that was trying to come through. With his permission, I guided him through a visualization exercise using relaxation, imagination and sensate awareness to return, in his mind, to his secret place. Then I asked him to open his heart and wait to receive whatever message might arrive.

After a long pause he whispered, "God is telling me that he is with me even here, in this barren place. My spirit reaches my homeland. I need to listen for this voice more closely. I thought God had left me."

Nica had come in during the conversation and was sitting on his bed. She wondered if there was something more. She pointed out that not all of his recent multi-sensory flashes of memory had been of their lives in Chile (something he hadn't shared with me). Some had contained images from their lives in the United States, for example, times involving the birth of their son or moments of family closeness.

"I think God wants you to know that you have continued to walk your true path even in coming to this country," she said. "Even though you were denied your life as a doctor."

Miguel's face brightened. Maybe she was right. We spoke about how this perspective might transform the way he understood his life and, by doing so, transform the way he died. When I left that day he was beaming with relief and peace.

The next time I saw him this sense of peace had collapsed. As is often the case, the balm of healing insight rarely insulates us entirely from the icy fingers of doubt. In his youth, communication with God had been unambiguously clear. Recent messages seemed transient, even cryptic. He wondered if his spiritual connection had, after all, been severed. His belief that his life had gone off track was stronger than ever.

I knew Miguel was familiar with the history of Native North America. After his exile he'd made it a focus of informal study. Like him, Native Americans had been forced from their homes and sacred places, pushed into concentration camps and forced to watch helplessly as their families suffered and were abused.

I asked if he knew anything about a Lakota holy man named Black Elk.

*

Black Elk's people loved their homeland. It was as though the Great Spirit had tied them to the land using invisible cords. In the center stood the Black Hills – mountains rising from the plains like a beautiful poem, plentiful with animals of all sorts. Pine trees grew straight, providing everything from firewood to tepee poles. It was also a sacred place where the Lakota climbed its peaks seeking visions and guidance from the Creator. When Black Elk was born in the early 1860s, the Black Hills were the center of his universe.

He was an Oglala, one of seven tribes of the Teton Lakota (also known as the Sioux), and he was born into troubling times. By the mid-1860s, a flood of white prospectors was invading their land scrambling to get to the newly discovered goldfields in Montana. Black Elk remembered these early years as being "like some fearful thing in a fog, for it was a time when everything seemed troubled and afraid."

Making matters worse, relatives to the east, the Santee Lakota, had fought a disastrous war against soldiers in present-day Minnesota and many were arriving seeking protection. Black Elk recalled that when these refugees arrived, "everyone was saying that the Wasichus (Americans) were coming and that they were going to take our country and rub us all out." The Oglala drew strength from the land; it connected them to the Great Spirit. When the soldiers came, Black Elk's people would fight.

The epicenter of the ensuing war was the Bozeman Trail, a shortcut to the Montana gold mines running through the heart of Lakota territory. Fighting for their homes, families and future, the Lakota were so tenacious that by 1868 the United States had decided to sue for peace. An Oglala leader named Red Cloud spoke for all Lakota when he said to Federal representatives that, "The Great Spirit raised me in this land, and has raised you in another land. What I have said I mean. I mean to keep this land."

The United States agreed to abandon its forts along the Bozeman Trail and recognize Lakota ownership of their traditional homeland. The treaty that ended the hostilities stipulated that, "No white person or persons shall be permitted to settle upon or occupy any portion of the territory, or without the consent of the Indians to pass through the same."

Although young, Black Elk said that it was shortly after the war ended that he first heard voices emanating directly from God. "I was out playing alone," he remembered, "when I heard them. It was like somebody calling me, and I thought it was my mother, but there was nobody there." He later recognized this as a first step on his path toward becoming a holy man but at the time it "made me afraid."

A short time later, he spotted a bird that, to his astonishment, spoke to him. When he looked into the sky he saw two men descending from the heavens "headfirst like arrows slanting down." As they moved toward him they turned into geese and flew away. "Then they were gone, and the rain came with a big wind and a roaring." Unsure what the vision meant, he was confused, frightened, and told no one.

Over the next few years, "the voices would come back when I was out alone, like someone calling me." As a boy, however, he was more interested in learning to hunt and becoming a warrior so he tried pushing these spiritual experiences into the back of his mind. When messages are sent from the Great Spirit, however, they have a way of getting our attention.

At nine, he suddenly collapsed and couldn't walk. The next day, when his people moved camp, he had to be pulled atop a pony drag, his arms and face swollen. He drifted into a coma and for twelve days hovered near death, at times barely taking a breath. With family and friends huddled around him in worry, Black Elk experienced a sweeping vision that changed his life forever.

He was transported into the sky and taken to a place where "white clouds were piled like mountains on a wide blue plain, and in there thunder beings lived and leaped and flashed." He stood before six "Grandfathers" whom he recognized as "the Powers of the World." They had summoned him to impart sacred powers. The Grandfathers encouraged him to keep a strong heart, informing him that his "nation on the earth will have great troubles."

He was given visions of his people's future suffering. He knew intuitively they would die in large numbers. Many would lose hope. The bison would disappear and the Lakota nation would be driven from their homes by war and starvation. As he absorbed this grave message he could see that beyond the looming disaster would come a time of hope for all people. "I saw," he recalled, "that the sacred hoop of my people was one of many hoops that made one circle...and in the center grew one mighty flowering tree to shelter all the children of one mother and one father. And I saw that it was holy."

He awakened in his family's tepee. "I was sad," he said, "because my mother and my father didn't seem to know I had been so far away." In the days following, he felt awkward and preferred being alone. Whirlwind Chaser, a holy man, noticed his behavior and told Black Elk's father, "Your boy there is sitting in a sacred manner. I do not know what it is, but there is something special for him to do, for just as I came in I could see a power like a light all through his body."

Black Elk had experienced what the Lakota called *wakan*, "sacred and incomprehensible power," usually imparted through visions and dreams. For all Lakota, the partition between the visible and invisible worlds was thin and insubstantial. For those filled with *wakan* there was no partition. The spirit world infused everything.

The Grandfathers had told the truth about the suffering that awaited the Lakota. In 1874, the United States ignored its promises and sent a military force into the Black Hills under the pretense of conducting a survey but they were really looking for gold. When they found it, a frenzied herd of miners once again swept into Lakota country. Some, like Crazy Horse and Sitting Bull, wanted to fight the invaders. Others like Red Cloud counseled caution. Black Elk's family joined Crazy Horse.

By June 25, 1876, several thousand people from all the Lakota tribes, as well as friends among the Cheyenne and Arapahoe had gathered along the Little Bighorn River. Earlier that month, they'd defeated an army led by George Crook and most believed no other bluecoats would be foolish enough to attack such a large number of warriors. But Black Elk had premonitions of impending catastrophe. "I thought of my vision," he remembered later, "and suddenly I seemed to be lifted clear off the ground; and while I was that way, I knew more things than I could tell, and I felt sure something terrible was going to happen in a short time. I was frightened."

When George Custer happened upon this sprawling village of tepees he acted with his customary aggression, splitting his troops and attacking. Though some of the soldiers fighting under Marcus Reno and Frederick Benteen survived, all who went with Custer were killed.

In the aftermath of the Battle of Little Bighorn the army pursued the Lakota mercilessly. In the next months, as bone-freezing winter winds stung the plains, many surrendered. Amidst the chaos, Black Elk doubted his vision, "I wondered if maybe it was only a queer dream after all."

He may have had a direct experience of transcendent realms but it hadn't stopped things from falling apart. Like the splintered bones of the great bison herds beginning to litter the vast grasslands, death cast a shadow across his people. Eventually, even Crazy Horse surrendered but when he was murdered during a scuffle at Fort Robinson a small band of his followers, including Black Elk, broke away and headed toward Canada. By then Black Elk was a man, eager to help his people but uncertain if his growing spiritual power could make any difference.

Canada turned out to be a place of bitter exile. Although there were no bluecoats, there were conflicts with the Crow and Blackfeet. Winters were harsh and there were few buffalo. They missed their relatives and longed for the familiar hills, grasslands and rivers of their homeland. During these years, Black Elk continued to receive guidance from the Great Spirit. Far from the sacred Black Hills, he prayed for help from the Grandfathers.

In 1880 he returned to his homeland and surrendered. By then, he was openly pursuing the path of healer, learning the ways of medicine and mastering sacred rituals. His efforts focused on bringing peace to his people and sustaining them through their hardship. His connection with the spirit of storms and thunder was powerful medicine, giving him the ability to heal.

"All our people," Black Elk lamented, were now "scattered here and there across this hungry land, and around them the Wasichus had drawn a line to keep them in (a reservation)." Separated from the Black Hills, "The people were in despair. They seemed heavy to me, heavy and dark; so heavy that it seemed to me they could not be lifted; so dark that they could not be made to see anymore." Despite great sorrow, Black Elk continued to nurture the otherworldly thread connecting him to God.

Like other Indian nations, the Lakota had been driven from their homes and seen loved ones die from violence, disease or starvation. Their customs and rituals had been profaned by the degradations of reservation life. Their bison slaughtered, the white man's whiskey had devoured many despairing souls and steel bayonets had nearly severed the cords that bound them to their land. Their sacred places, the graves of their ancestors, had been overrun. In the bleak valley of their grief, many longed to return to a time before everything had changed, a time before things had gone so wrong.

In 1889, when word spread that a prophet had come speaking words for all Indians, many were eager to hear his message. This prophet's name was Wavoka. He was a Paiute living on a reservation in Nevada. When the Lakota sent a small party to hear his message they learned that Wavoka had received a vision. "I went up to heaven," he told them, "and saw the Great Spirit and all the people who had died a long time ago. The Great Spirit told me to come back and tell my people they must be good and love one another, and not fight, or steal, or lie. He gave me a dance to give to my people."

He said that if the people performed this ghost dance, it would herald the return of their dead relatives and the buffalo. Soldiers would disappear and the Indians' land and traditions would be restored.

To a people whose collective grief seemed as boundless as the sky, it was a compelling vision and soon Indians throughout the west were gathering to perform the ghost dance. On Lakota reservations, nervous white officials banned the practice but the Lakota danced anyway. Ominously, they added "ghost shirts" to the ritual which they believed would protect them from enemy bullets.

When reservation officials became alarmed that Sitting Bull might throw his influence behind the ghost dance, reservation police showed up at his cabin to arrest him. A fight broke out and Sitting Bull was killed. A wave of panic erupted. In December 1890, edgy troops massacred a band of peaceful Lakota camped along Wounded Knee Creek.

In many ways, the slaughter at Wounded Knee sounded the death knell for the traditional ways of the Lakota. The war for their homes and their way of life had ended in defeat. Looking back on it some forty years later Black Elk said:

> I did not know then how much was ended. When I look back now from this high hill of my old age, I can still see the butchered women and children lying heaped and scattered all along the crooked gulch as plain as when I saw them with eyes still young. And I can see that something else died there in the bloody mud, and was buried in the blizzard [that followed]. A people's dream died there.

Black Elk had seen his people's way of life destroyed. Expelled from their country, those who survived were confined on small, destitute reservations. Despite his efforts to help his people and hold fast to the power of the Great Spirit, he watched helplessly as loved ones died from diseases he could not cure. As many descended into depression, holding to his great vision was difficult. At times his energies waned. Although Black Elk never questioned the wisdom of the Great Spirit, he doubted himself. He wondered if he had really understood his great vision and the words God had spoken to him.

He continued praying for guidance, serving his people as best he could. He even tried to assimilate the spiritual teachings of white culture. When Jesuit missionaries arrived on the reservation he studied their religion and found that it contained some of the same wisdom of his traditional ways.

The merging of these two rivers of faith was not enough, however, to counter his sadness and grief. He wondered if he had failed to walk a path true to his early vision. As doubts came and went, he longed for affirmation and guidance. As he approached seventy, he lamented that he was "a pitiful old man who has done nothing, for the nation's hoop is broken and scattered. There is no center any longer, and the sacred tree is dead."

In 1931, after telling his story to writer, John Neihardt, Black Elk went with a small party into the Black Hills. On a clear day atop Harney Peak, he gave thanks to the Great Spirit. "Again, and maybe the last time on this earth," he said, "I recall the great vision you sent me. It may be that some little root of that sacred tree still lives. Nourish it then, that it may leaf and bloom and fill with singing birds." Neihardt recounted what happened then:

> We who listened now noted that thin clouds had gathered about us. A scant chill rain began to fall and there was low, muttering thunder without lightning. With tears running down his cheeks, the old man raised his voice to a thin high wail, and chanted: "In sorrow I am sending a feeble voice, O Six Powers of the World. Hear me in my sorrow, for I may never call again. O make my people live!"
>
> For some minutes the old man stood silent, with face uplifted, weeping in the drizzling rain.
>
> In a little while the sky was clear again.

*

There are times when the clamber and noise of events can drown out the voice of one's intuition or one's connection with the transcendent (God, higher self, inner wisdom, however one conceives it). For some, there are places we are apt to hear this inner voice more clearly. For Miguel it was in his homeland at his sacred place, for Black Elk it was in the Black Hills. For others it may be along the bank of a river or in the quiet of a summer morning. Others may hear this voice while holding a loved one's hand, listening to a familiar piece of music or acting with compassion. We are not dependent, however, on situations and places. No matter where we are or what we are facing, guidance is always available when we pause to listen closely.

Miguel felt kinship with Black Elk. Like the Oglala holy man he had become a doctor in order to serve others. Both had been healers, deeply connected to cultures that had come under pressure, both had been forced from their homes. Each had struggled with sadness and self-doubt. He speculated about the specific diseases the Lakota holy man had encountered. "I am sure his prayers for his patients were powerful," he said. "But without antibiotics, he must have felt deep pain. He could do nothing to stop the dying."

He asked questions about how the Indians were treated once in captivity, empathizing with the dehumanization and humiliation of being uprooted and treated unfairly. "When I was imprisoned by Pinochet they did things to me and my family that I was powerless to stop. I prayed to be given the strength to stop it, but I could not."

He looked at me solemnly, his eyes searching to make sure I understood that he was talking about something he'd tried hard to forget. I invited him to elaborate if he wished. He looked up at the ceiling as though it were drawing him back to an earlier time. "There were times in my cell when I wished I would die. The only reason I went on was because of the lives of my wife and daughter."

He paused. "It was also God's grace that saved me, but at the time I was sure God had abandoned me. Maybe I had just lost my ability to hear his voice."

"What did it mean to you, not being able to hear God's voice?"

"It meant that I," he searched for words, "had lost my path and would have to wander alone in a strange land."

"Are there any things that were not lost?"

"My family; spiritual faith."

168

"Did you discover anything through your suffering that was important?"

"I found much in my new life to cherish. But sadness surrounded me always like a shadow. Maybe I let sadness fill my heart so much that it drowned out God's call."

"What do you make of that scene of Black Elk on Harney Peak?" I asked.

He smiled. "He got a message that he'd been true to his vision despite his self-doubt."

"What about you Miguel? You asked the question on one of my visits. What became of that little boy in his sacred spot who has grown so old? Is he still in there?"

He nodded but didn't speak, reaching out his hand. When I reciprocated he squeezed my hand with a strength that seemed incongruously firm contrasted with his overall weakness. Tears watered the corners of his eye. I asked what he was thinking.

"You asked about that little boy. I thought he was gone. But I know now that he still lives inside me." He picked up the rock he'd shown me earlier and squeezed it.

I asked him how this awareness could make a difference as he died.

"I cannot go back to my home. But my home has come back to me. And I have come back to God."

When Black Elk met John Neihardt he'd never spoken about the details of his vision. Doing so might have diminished its power and perhaps even trivialized its sacredness. But in the fading light of old age he wanted to find a way to honor the traditions of his people and share some of the core truths of the Great Spirit.

By then he was nearly blind and images of the material world were being drawn into darkness. Long before, he had learned that the material world was not real anyway. He knew that there was a "world where there is nothing but the spirit of all things. That is the real world that is behind this one, and everything we see here is something like a shadow from that world." Many times he had doubted himself and questioned his actions, but always he had remembered what was real.

On Harney Peak, when he heard once more the responsive roll of thunder and felt the cleansing droplets of rain, he knew that he had been true to his vision. His connection with the Great Spirit was still strong, despite all the hardships and doubts.

"If I could stand on my sacred mountain again," Miguel mused, "I wouldn't ask for thunder and rain, I would ask for sunlight and the sound of the ocean birds."

His voice lifted and seemed to convey a sense of inner resolution. "One of the hardest things during all my years here was that I wondered if God had forgotten me. But I see that he is calling me again as I prepare to die."

As he thought about this, he smiled. His connection with the world of Spirit was still strong, far from the hills of his childhood.

As Black Elk neared the end of his life in 1950, he made it clear that he was ready to die. His daughter recalled that he told her "I am old, so don't take my death too hard. Do not mourn a long time, you know I will be happy. My suffering will be over, and I will have no more hurt. Pray for me as I taught you to pray in the early days."

During his long life, sudden changes or anomalies in the natural world had often been signs of the Great Spirit's presence. On the day Black Elk died, the evening sky became vibrant with the electric colors of the aurora borealis. William Siehr, a Jesuit missionary living on Pine Ridge Reservation, said that the night sky "was just one bright illumination. I never saw anything so magnificent. I've seen a number of flashes of the northern lights here in the early days, but I never saw anything quite so intense."

Section Five
What Lies Before Us
Moving On

*What lies behind us and
what lies before us are tiny matters,
compared to what lies within us.*

Ralph Waldo Emerson

The death of a loved one, while an end, is also a beginning. It begins a journey into grief and adapting to a world where our loved one is no longer physically present. Even when we have seen death approaching we cannot prepare ourselves entirely for this journey. Even though we may have used the time before death wisely, we will not escape moments of longing to have our loved one back so we can say "I love you" or "I will miss you" just one more time. Though we may have cried and grieved for weeks or months prior to death, we will have more tears to shed.

Grief and bereavement are individual enough that there are no foolproof road maps; much of the way ahead has to be discovered and navigated as it occurs. Family, friends, counselors, support groups and self-help books can all be important and helpful but the journey cannot be escaped. The final two chapters are about people navigating this part of life's path.

Chapter Thirteen
Canyon of Desolation
Trust

Gerta was worried about who would take care of Bill after she died. The fact that her health was good and Bill was dying was immaterial. She was convinced that she would die first. "I know what the doctors think," she said, "but they don't understand Bill. He would never leave me behind."

In her mind, Bill would fight his illness however long was necessary to spare her the pain of being left alone. Or, as she put it, he would never abandon her. After sixty years together, it was impossible for her to conceive of being without him; to the extent that she could, she was terrified. So she'd made up her mind that she would go first and that was that.

Given her certainty about this, I asked if she'd been having any thoughts about killing herself. Absolutely not, she said, she was "a survivor." To illustrate the point she offered a quick tour of her childhood as evidence. Born in Germany in 1928, by the time she was seventeen her parents were dead, her brother was missing and her older sister had turned to prostitution in an attempt to survive. Her voice was like tempered steel as she culled through memories of these years, salvaging the fragments of a life broken into ruin.

World War Two had wrecked her family. Driven by poverty and hunger, Gerta and a younger sister gathered whatever valuables they could find in their bombed-out city, piled them into canvas sacks and hiked out into the farmlands (which were not much better off) to barter for a few eggs and vegetables. "Everything I had was taken from me except my will to survive." She *was* a survivor. The one thing she was afraid she couldn't survive was Bill's death.

They'd met in 1945, when he'd been a soldier. Their connection was instantaneous and within a month they were married despite her sisters' objections to her marrying an American. As Gerta explained it, "You don't waste time when you've been through war. You learn to grab the good things when they come your way and hang on tight." Bill and Gerta moved to his hometown in North Carolina where he got a job installing air conditioners. She threw herself into learning English and discovering the customs of small town America. She began doing volunteer work, eventually becoming the director of a shelter for abandoned dogs. Her determination to find homes for these animals was so intense that people started calling her the rescue lady.

While Bill attended school to become an electrician she adopted many of the dogs the shelter would have had to euthanize. To accommodate her canine charges, Bill fenced in their backyard and built twelve doghouses. Later, he built six more. When he got sick Gerta toyed with cutting back but he'd encouraged her to continue taking the animals. "She thinks she's saving the dogs," he explained. "But when I'm dead, those dogs will save her."

When Gerta talked about her life she divided it into two parts: before she met Bill and after. Before Bill, her journey had been a chilling testimony to life's precariousness and suffering. In the span of five nightmarish years most of the people she'd loved had been killed, emotionally shattered or left homeless. Her country had been destroyed. Children she'd once played with had been sent to Nazi death camps along with their families and killed. At seventeen, she remembered, "My life was nothing but suffering and fear. I had no hope for anything except more suffering. If I had died then it would have been a relief."

When she met Bill her story became one of redemption and rebirth. She had vivid recollections of their first day in America – spotting the skyline of New York from the bow of a ship, passing small towns as they traveled south by train. With Bill, her life regained hope and purpose. As she saw it, he saved her life.

They had no children and had invested themselves in creating what Gerta called a "marriage of spirits." Every summer, for nearly forty years, they'd packed up their car and travelled west. Gerta loved recounting stories from their adventures, repeating her favorites whenever she had an audience. She especially liked to tell about the time she talked Bill into riding mules down to the Colorado River while visiting the Grand Canyon and how they'd had to extend their visit because "Bill's butt was so sore he couldn't drive."

It was easy to understand why she clung so tightly to her belief that Bill wouldn't go without her. Their relationship had been the foundation upon which she had rebuilt her life. The thought of being alone, of once more having that foundation crushed was too much to contemplate.

Initially Bill's response to illness had been to fight to survive at any cost. As the disease took a toll, though, he grew weary. Somewhere along the way Gerta's relentless insistence that he get better stopped feeling like encouragement and started feeling like pressure to do the impossible. The more he deteriorated, the more she demanded he fight. The harder she pushed, the more Bill pushed her away. Inadvertently, Gerta's single-minded insistence was driving a wedge between them at a time when what she most wanted was closeness.

"I can't talk to her," he said. "I'm going to die and instead of helping me she gets mad at me for being sick."

"Do you really think she's mad at you or is it something else?" I asked.

"I don't know about the psychological stuff. All I know is it feels like she's mad and blaming me for getting worse."

"Talk with her about it."

"I don't have the energy to get into an argument or try explaining things again. I don't think she'll listen."

I offered to facilitate such a conversation but he declined.

"What can you do about it then?" I asked.

He threw his hands up, "At this point I just don't give a damn."

"Is that really true?"

He shook his head, unsure, "Who knows?"

"You do," I looked him in the eye. "Do you really not give a damn or is that the frustration?"

"Frustration," his eyes watered. "She won't let me go."

I offered some thoughts on how fear and emotional pain can appear as unrealistic demands, anger or denial. "What do you think Gerta is *really* trying to say when she insists that you do the impossible?"

"I guess she's trying to say she loves me. She's terrified."

"Would it help to keep that in mind?"

"Yeah."

"How do you want to spend the time you have left?"

"I want her to stop pushing."

"I'm talking about in terms of what you can control. What can *you* do?"

"I can roll back my anger about this and make sure Gerta knows how much she means to me."

"How are you going to do that?"

He thought for a minute. "I guess I'll remind myself that she's scared and that I won't get another chance to do this. Once I'm gone, that's it, *hasta la vista.*"

If Gerta's unbending faith in Bill could have cured his pulmonary disease he'd have been restored to full vigor. But his illness was impervious to her hope. Throughout his last days Gerta remained convinced he would bounce back, refusing to speak about death. When he ebbed into a coma she pleaded with him to wake up. When friends from the shelter offered to spend the night she declined, assuring them there was no need since Bill was going to be fine.

When he died she was sitting by his bed. A friend was present and was surprised when Gerta seemed unfazed, calling the hospice nurse and matter-of-factly asking her to come by whenever she got a chance. When I arrived, Gerta's voice was flat, her eyes unfocused as though trying to awaken from the haze of a deep sleep. She talked about her dogs and the weather, seemingly unconcerned about Bill's death. Someone happening upon the scene might have assumed he was simply sleeping in the bed beside us.

Shock has many handmaidens, numbness and dissociation among them. When the people from the funeral home arrived, she discussed the details of the obituary and signed the release form as though in a trance. After they left, the psychic dam holding her pain suddenly broke. As she shook with sobs, she steadied herself by placing her hands on her knees. By sheer willpower, she composed herself and moved silently through a narrow hallway into the room where Bill had died and slammed the door. After the torrent of intense emotion had subsided, she returned to the family room, apologized for her "outburst," and offered to make coffee.

In the next few weeks she oscillated between numbness and waves of sadness, fear and anger. She searched for ways to escape the gravity of these painful emotions, distracting herself by keeping busy. She adopted another dog and lavished her with affection but the pain refused to subside. She tried giving herself "marching orders" about why she shouldn't feel what she was feeling. This didn't work either. Her experience was normal; chastising herself only created shame.

I saw her a month or so after the funeral. By then, anger was overshadowing everything. Every thought seemed leavened with rage. She was angry with Bill for "giving up." She was angry with God for "taking him from me," angry at hospice for "letting him die." Most of all she was angry with herself for letting him smoke all those years and not making him go to the doctor sooner.

As though rejecting reality, she'd packed all the photographs of Bill into the room where his hospital bed had been and locked the door, refusing to enter. It was like a vault into which she'd tried pushing her sadness, fear, and longing to have her beloved back, everything except her anger. To this she clung as though gripping an outcropping of rock above a precipice of despair. At times the energy of her rage and the distraction it provided seemed like the only thing keeping her from plunging into depression.

Beneath her angry exterior she missed him deeply. When she decided to unlock the door to his room and face her pain, she bolstered herself as though preparing for an exploration into a dangerous land. Then she spent the entire day going through his belongings, cleaning photographs and crying.

Once the door to her deeper feelings was opened, it nearly overwhelmed her. Anger had been less threatening than sadness and aloneness. Without its protective insulation she felt like she was "falling into a bottomless hole." By the time I visited again she had withdrawn from friends and appeared clinically depressed (something which can be difficult to tease out from normal grief, especially in its early stages). She was fixated on beliefs which were cutting into her like a tightly wound rope. Since Bill had left her alone he must not have really loved her. If he had loved her he would still be alive. If she had loved him more perfectly maybe he would still be here. These beliefs, however irrational, were resistant to my repeated attempts to help her see things from another perspective.

She was having trouble sleeping and had been having a recurrent dream in which she and Bill were climbing a hill. It was a warm day and the sun was comforting as they ascended a gentle slope covered with grass and wildflowers. As they climbed, the grade became steeper and a storm gathered. The ground changed from grass to rocks and they began losing their footing. Eventually the hill became so steep Bill had to hold Gerta's hand to help her move forward. After much exertion, their way was blocked by a vertical wall of rock. Bill searched for a toehold and finally found one on a small outcropping. He scaled the wall and lodged himself onto a ledge several feet above. He extended his hand down and she grasped it tightly. As he pulled, she struggled to propel herself upward by moving her feet against the wall. About halfway up, one of her feet became stuck in a rock. At the same time, Bill's hand became translucent and started "turning into jelly." She was unable to move forward because of her foot, but was losing her hold on Bill's hand as it became more ephemeral.

She squeezed with all her strength but her grip loosened and her feet slipped from the rocks. As Bill's hand dematerialized, she realized she was dangling above a bottomless canyon. She screamed in terror while Bill smiled at her calmly and lovingly. His body started to glow with a radiant light. In a gentle voice he said, "It's alright Gerta. It's time to let go." Her grip broke and she started falling. As things faded into darkness, she would awaken feeling agitated and afraid.

She knew it meant that she had to accept his death but was puzzled by how the dream ended. Bill's assurances that it would be alright seemed incongruous with her falling. Was he mistaken? Did he know something that she didn't? Given her distress, she was not inclined to trust that it would be alright.

"What might Bill know about you or your situation that tells him you'll be alright?" I asked.

She thought about it for a minute then tentatively suggested that "Maybe he knows I've fallen from cliffs before. I'm a survivor." She gave me an exaggeratedly menacing look, "I don't want to talk about this anymore."

Her dream reminded me of a story which called to mind the visit she and Bill had taken to the Grand Canyon. Maybe it would give her some insight or provide some helpful images. I asked if I could tell her about someone who found himself in a situation similar to the one in Gerta's dream: clinging to a sheer wall of rock, unable to move forward, afraid to let go.

*

John Wesley Powell was a survivor. He'd survived the boundless slaughter of the Civil War, a painful wound at the battle of Shiloh and the surgeon's blade that cut off his right arm. After Shiloh he returned to command his Illinois artillery battery and lived through three more years of terrible bloodshed. On returning to civilian life he had adjusted to the chronic, often agonizing pain emanating from his wound and the limitations of living with one arm. He was tough and, although he had seen how tenuous life could be, unflappably optimistic. In 1869 he was planning an expedition as dangerous as any Civil War battlefield, confident that, once again, he would live to tell the tale.

He intended to lead an expedition down the Green and Colorado Rivers to explore the Grand Canyon – a vast blank space on the American map that nobody had dared attempt to chart. Even John C. Fremont, whose wide-ranging explorations had earned him the nickname pathfinder, had recoiled at the prospect of such a journey. No one, Fremont said, could be found who was crazy enough "to undertake a voyage which has so certain a prospect of a fatal termination." Powell, along with the nine intrepid men who would accompany him, begged to differ.

The sum of what was known about the region was scant. Enough, however, was clear to make anyone think twice. Powell knew, for example, that the altitude of Green River Station (in present-day Wyoming, where he intended to begin) was 6,100 feet above sea level. The area along the Colorado where he planned to end his trip was only 700 feet. Somewhere in between, there was a decline in elevation of about 5,400 feet. For all he knew, he and his men might encounter plunges that dwarfed Niagara Falls. He knew there were places with towering cliffs surrounded by desert that would make escape by land impossible, where they would have no choice but to follow the river, whatever its perils. There were no settlements in the region where they could rest, resupply or gather information. They'd be entirely on their own.

The men accompanying Powell were a mix of out-of-work mountain men and ex-Union soldiers. One of them was his brother, Walter, who'd been an officer in the Union Army before being captured by Confederates and imprisoned. By many accounts the experience had wrecked him. When he returned from the war he'd vacillated between quick-tempered, sometimes violent fits of aggression and simmering withdrawal. Walter was along because his brother was going, the rest were motivated by a sense of adventure and the notoriety that goes with being the first to explore an uncharted region (not to mention the imagined prospect of beaver pelts).

On May 24 1869, they launched their boats into the cool waters of the Green River. The plan was to follow the Green south until it joined with the Grand River to form the Colorado. From there, they would follow the Colorado through the Grand Canyon. The group traveled in four boats specially built for the trip. Three were twenty-one feet, built of oak, reinforced for strength and durability. Powell described them as "staunch and firm." The fourth was lighter and built of pine. At sixteen feet, it was designed for speed and maneuverability and was used for travelling ahead to scout the terrain.

Although some of the men had experience on rivers, none had paddled through currents or taken on rapids as powerful as these. They spent their first few days running aground, losing oars, falling overboard and being spun about in whirlpools that formed between rocks. Billy Hawkins wrote in his journal that the men quickly realized that they "knew nothing about a boat." If they wanted to survive, they would have to learn fast.

On May 30, they approached the mountainous canyons of Flaming Gorge which marked a set of extremely dangerous rapids. The water churned into large waves as it crashed in all directions over boulders, some of which were submerged, others piercing the surface like stone teeth. As they approached the foaming tumult, Powell recalled that, "untried as we are with such waters, the moments are filled with intense anxiety."

As dangerous as these rapids were, they were benign compared to what lay ahead. Many, like the ones they saw two days later at Red Canyon, couldn't be taken head on and the boats had to be 'lined'. First the boats were unloaded of about 7,000 pounds of gear and supplies. Then, each was tied with rope and pushed into the river. As the men clung to the rope with all their strength, they worked their way down alongside the rapids to calmer waters. When the boats were safely downriver the supplies had to be hauled over slippery, rock-strewn earth and repacked. It was as nerve-wracking as it was strenuous. One slip on a wet rock or a foot caught in a crevice could mean a broken leg, cracked skull or worse.

As testimony to their endurance, when camp was set each afternoon, rather than rest, the men hunted, fished, repaired boats and wrote in journals. Powell usually climbed to the highest accessible point he could find to survey the river and do some exploring, determined to study everything from rock formations to plant life. He rarely left camp without one of his barometers or some other piece of scientific equipment with which to take readings or measurements. He may have lost an arm but his wiry body and unbending focus more than compensated as he scaled cliffs and balanced on ledges.

By June 8, the party had entered the gloomy Canyon of Lodore where walls reached over 2,000 feet. The river was a menacing cauldron of cascading chaos. In his journal, George Bradley described the stretch as "the wildest rapid yet seen." In spite of Bradley's misgivings, they decided to attempt the rapids by boat. Unfortunately, the water was too rough and one of the larger boats was smashed. Though the three-man crew managed to pull themselves onto a rocky sand bar, most of the boat's supplies, including hundreds of pounds of food, were lost.

The loss of so much food was a serious problem since the explorers were only two weeks into a journey they expected would take ten months. Just as frustrating, more stores were in danger of spoiling because of the constant soaking from waves spilling into the boats. George Bradley noted forebodingly that, "Our rations are getting very sour from constant wetting and exposure to a hot sun." Things were complicated by the fact that the hunters were coming back empty-handed. The problem, according to Jack Sumner, one of Powell's ablest men, was that "There is nothing in this part of the country but a few mountain sheep, and they stay where a squirrel could hardly climb."

Through June and early July they worked their way down the Green River. Every time they passed a creek or river emptying into the Green it meant more water pressed into the lean channels of the canyons ahead. To the world outside, it seemed like they had fallen into a hole and disappeared. Rumors circulated that they were dead. Articles appeared in newspapers like the Chicago *Tribune*, informing readers that the expedition had perished.

On the morning of July 8, the men were camped beneath cliffs and ledges so barren that Powell was "minded to call this the Canyon of Desolation." He and Bradley set out to ascend the heights carrying one of the barometers. The hike started well enough. "We start up a gulch," Powell wrote, "then pass to the left on a bench along the wall; then up again over broken rocks; then we reach more benches, along which we walk, until we find more broken rocks and crevices, by which we climb; still up, until we have ascended 600 or 800 feet, when we are met by a sheer precipice."

Most people would have turned back but not Powell. He handed the barometer to his friend and reached up to a rock with his only arm. He braced his feet into narrow crevices and pulled himself up a few feet. Once he was safely perched, Bradley handed him the barometer and climbed a few feet higher than Powell then turned to retrieve the barometer. In such a manner, they slowly made their way toward the summit, passing the barometer back and forth as they inched forward.

Well into their ascent, Powell got stuck when he jammed his feet into crevices and grabbed hold of an outcropping of the rock above his head. He found that he couldn't go forward or back. If he'd had his right arm he could have reached up while holding on with his left and found a way to extricate himself. But with only one arm all he could do was hang on. He couldn't move without releasing his grasp, but if he did so he would topple to his death.

Once Bradley understood Powell's plight, he made his way to a shelf of rock above. He looked for a tree or branch to lower to Powell but there was nothing. He thought about using the barometer case but realized it wouldn't work. All the while, Powell's strength was being taxed by the necessity of supporting his entire weight on the edge of the cliff-face. His legs began to quiver and burn, sweat poured from his forehead. Simply staying in place required all the strength he had. He couldn't remain pinned against the wall much longer before his hold broke. They had to do something or he was a dead man.

At that moment, Bradley had an idea. Like the rest of the crew, he was wearing only long underwear. Wet clothes weighed a man down enough to drown him in a fast moving river and they'd learned to dress light. In a scene that would have been comical were it not a matter of life-or-death, he removed his drawers and lowered them down. As they dangled just behind Powell's head, the expedition's commander was faced with another challenge. In order to reach the lifeline he would have to release his grip, trusting that he would be able to grab the line as he reached back. If he missed, he would plunge into the canyon. It was a pivotal moment and Powell's life hinged on it. Willingly or unwillingly, he had to let go.

Pulling himself as close to the cliff as he could, Powell released the rock and reached back. As his weight shifted he grasped the outstretched line and clung to it with renewed vigor, trusting in his connection with Bradley. The two men's fate merged as Powell slowly made his way forward. In the act of letting go, he was freed from the constraint of the wall and able to gain another foothold. Eventually he reached the top of the canyon.

*

Metaphorically, any of us can find ourselves dangling above our own Canyon of Desolation at one time or another. Clinging, as Gerta did, to anger or blame can sap our strength and lead to paralysis or despair. If we are to extricate ourselves, we have to find a way to loosen our grasp and reach toward something else. We must trust that, beyond the challenges and painful emotions, we will find our way.

Although Gerta had made progress through her grief, she was stuck on a cliff afraid to let go. As we discussed the story, she was particularly struck by the image of falling into the canyon. "I know what that feels like," she said, absorbed in thought.

She realized there were two things to which she was clinging: anger and fear. Her angry ruminations that Bill shouldn't have died had become an intractable belief, immobilizing her and making it hard to move forward. While anger made it difficult to accept that Bill was dead, fear made it difficult to trust that she could continue living without him. Fear also made it easy to justify withdrawing from people and the world around her. Anger and fear had pinned her against a precipice as real as any Powell encountered. "There's a big difference between me and Powell," she said. "He had something to grab hold of. I don't."

"Is there really nothing?" I asked. "Suppose you decided to reach out, what do you think you might find to hold onto?"

She was silent. Finally, she said, "Maybe I'd find my dogs."

It was a toehold. Once she found it, she thought of others, such as her community of friends, writing in her journal, the resilience of being a survivor.

As ominous and impassable as the rapids ahead looked to Gerta, she realized they felt familiar. As a young woman whose life was thrown into disarray by war, she had been in this place. After her town and family had been destroyed she'd felt intense anger and disbelief. "I just kept saying to myself, over and over, this should never have happened." There were days when she had longed for death to come and end the pain. She'd survived and gone on to live a meaningful life. She had done it before. She could do it again.

Gerta decided to make an appointment with a bereavement counselor. It was a step that affirmed life and openly acknowledged her separation from Bill. It was hard, but she was determined. Maybe if she let go of her grip on anger and reached out despite her fear, trusting she would find something to hold onto, she might not be destroyed by the pain of grief. When the visit with the counselor went well, she scheduled regular sessions to get help charting the rapids and whirlpools ahead.

As for John Wesley Powell, he and his band of explorers eventually made it through the Colorado River, braving hair-raising rapids, boulders the size of buildings and clumps of floating debris bigger than steam locomotives. They contended with hunger, anxiety, and longings to reach the end of their journey and be reunited with loved ones.

Three of his men became so disconsolate they left the expedition, choosing to scale the massive cliffs and take their chances in the surrounding desert rather than continue. Those who continued with Powell all made it back into charted territory. Those who chose to leave, the Howland brothers and Bill Dunn, were not so fortunate. They were killed attempting to pass through the desert. The identity of their assailants is still the subject of debate.

Chapter Fourteen
Standing at Lemhi Pass
When a Tough Journey Gets Tougher

"When I saw her that night the ice around my heart began to melt." Wes's voice rippled with emotion as he recalled how he and Shirley met. He remembered small details of that night: water pooling on patio tables under cold margarita glasses; the smell of insect repellent and the way Shirley's eyes radiated with vitality. He asked her to dance and they lost track of time gliding beneath the outdoor lights strung above a makeshift dance floor. By the end of the evening they were falling in love.

Three years earlier after his first wife died Wes had assumed that, except for the technicality of continuing to breathe, his life was over. Those years had been hard and he seldom spoke about them. When he did, he conveyed a sense of bleak anonymity as though straining alone against the relentless flow of an unfriendly river.

There was only one experience from this time that Wes discussed freely and enthusiastically – his trip retracing the expedition of Meriwether Lewis and William Clark. In the early nineteenth century Lewis and Clark had explored the American West all the way to the Pacific. Wes had long been captivated by their courage and determination, studying their travels and reading their voluminous journals. With the eloquence and imagery of a master storyteller, he spoke of his journey in their footsteps as though it were the needle of some existential compass pointing into his deepest self.

Amidst his grief he had followed their route west. It was something he'd dreamed of and, in the shadow of his painful loss, the idea of disappearing for a while was compelling. He began in Pittsburgh where, in 1803, Lewis had fitted out a large keelboat before heading down the Ohio River to a rendezvous with Clark. Wes followed their route down the Ohio, up the Mississippi, onto the Missouri River and all the way to the Rocky Mountains. Unlike Lewis and Clark's self-proclaimed Corps of Discovery, he didn't make it to the Pacific. He stopped at Lemhi Pass in present-day Idaho, a nondescript mountain passage that marks the continental divide where rivers begin running west instead of east. It was here Lewis and Clark first saw the formidable barrier of seemingly endless mountains that awaited them. Standing at Lemhi Pass, they realized their journey was going to be longer and harder than they had imagined.

Wes was vague about why he'd stopped. "I just couldn't go any further. That was far enough."

When he returned to New York City it no longer felt like home. The bustle and energy that had offered excitement when his wife had been alive now caused sadness. She seemed to peer out of every store window and arrive with each breeze, especially the ones carrying the familiar aromas of a bakery down the street where she used to buy croissants every Sunday. Even the muffled thunder of subway trains moving along the tracks conjured her memory out of their grimy steel and squealing brakes.

Acting decisively, he moved to a retirement community in Florida where he settled into a routine of solitary walks, working in his flower garden, reading mystery novels and writing poetry. He felt awkward being in the world without his wife and needed time to grieve. But as his inclination to socialize slowly returned he found himself among strangers far from the friends he'd left in his haste to escape New York. He forced himself to join activities and talk to neighbors. "If I hadn't done that," he said, "I'd never have been at the dance where I met Shirley."

Within a year they were married, inseparable and as happy as either had ever been. In contrast to the preceding years, Wes's reflections on this time drew a rich picture of vibrant, flowering life. Despite his metallic voice, he joined Shirley's choral group and learned to sing. Though she playfully chided him for his boyish romanticism, she began reading Lewis and Clark's journals. "We did everything together," he said, "from dentist appointments to grocery shopping."

They spent five years enjoying every moment before Shirley was diagnosed with Amyotrophic Lateral Sclerosis (ALS), a progressive neuromuscular disease usually known as Lou Gehrig's disease. Volcanic shock rocked them as they struggled to absorb this horrible news. Though they knew it was fatal they pursued treatments and therapies in the hope of extending her life. Nothing worked.

Both were in their eighties and had known from the start that their time together would be short, but accepting that it would end sooner than either had foreseen was difficult. As Wes put it, "We'd just found each other and then WHAM! Everything changed." They honed their focus down to each day as though it were a lifetime in itself, squeezing it hard for its full potential. As each day passed, they knew the time of separation was closer.

When Shirley began losing muscle control she and Wes moved to North Carolina to live with her son Patrick. It was a difficult decision but the impact of her disease made it necessary. Her physical limitations and growing need for assistance stood in contrast to her earlier life as a ballet dancer. Strength, flexibility and creative expression had been woven into the fabric of her identity; ALS left her incapable of voluntary movement.

Communication was reduced to eye blinks: one blink for yes; two for no. Her once subtle and expressive face was curtained behind a quiet flatness. Behind the curtain her mind was still sharp, her experience of emotion and ability to reflect on circumstances relatively unaffected. As Wes put it, she was trapped behind a wall that let her look out at but not participate in the world around her.

Wes found ways to stay connected. Sometimes he read her poetry or reminisced about their lives, at other times they simply napped side by side. As her condition deteriorated, Wes began speaking of death, using code words and euphemisms at first but eventually speaking more directly. She responded in blinks.

She was sleeping the day I first visited. Wes was thin and fit, conveying immense energy as we sat at the kitchen table discussing the time he and Shirley had spent together. The effects of Parkinson's disease were apparent in his slightly quivering hands but seemed of little concern to him as he explained the system he used to manage both Shirley's and his medications. When I noted that he was taking cardiac medicine in addition to those for Parkinson's he joked that he was racing her to the finish line.

When our conversation turned to death, however, it became clear he had no intention of crossing the finish line first. His eyes flashed with gentle intensity as he spoke of his determination to live long enough to accompany her to the end of her life. He attributed this determination to a long career as a firefighter during which he'd never left a building while someone was inside. It was an axiom: however perilous the flames, he stood by those in need until they were safe. The fact that he and Shirley were in love had distilled his determination into an essential and uncompromising potency.

This focus challenged him to think about what his life might be like after she died. He reckoned it would be a time of quiet reflection comforted by the knowledge that he had served Shirley devotedly. During our initial visit he made allusions to doing his "grieving in advance," expecting that when she was gone he'd feel relief at having done a difficult job well and that Shirley's suffering had finally ended. He envisioned the time after her death as a release from anguish and sadness, as though the terrain would suddenly become smooth and the winds favorable.

Fortifying this expectation was the fact that Shirley had made it clear she wanted to die. Once, her greatest challenge had been acceptance, now it was patience. Blinking eyes revealed a spirit that was tired and worn down. Haunted by thoughts that she was a burden to Wes, she struggled to find peace. Wes offered what reassurance he could, focusing on being with her in her pain and continuing to love her.

Although her last weeks were among the most difficult, she died peacefully. Her struggle with illness was over. The dull hum of the oxygen concentrator was finally quiet. Wes sat in this strange silence as two men from the funeral home removed a body that had once danced with life.

At such times, many have a tendency to move toward others and draw support and strength from close relationships. Some, like Wes, are drawn toward solitude. In the surreal and hectic days following Shirley's funeral, he decided to make a quick get-a-way to a remote cottage along the Atlantic Coast where he and Shirley had spent several weekends. In the days after her death it was a place of peaceful sanctuary.

I visited Wes about a month later as he was packing to go back to Florida. By then, grief had established an uneasy rhythm, never far away yet receding enough now and then to allow him to feel almost normal before hitting again with renewed intensity. We talked about Shirley and looked at some photographs from a vacation they'd taken on the Gulf of Mexico. He commented on her beatific smile and we laughed at his Bermuda shorts.

Despite his sadness, Lewis and Clark were never far from his mind. We spoke of their tenacity and recalled some of his favorite parts of their journey as though reminiscing about old friends. He seemed to gain strength as we did this and went searching for a large book buried under a stack of papers on a writing table. Soon we were studying maps of the Missouri River and paintings of Mandan Indians.

Our conversation moved between Shirley and the expedition until they melded like two tinctures forming a single color. He was surprised at the intensity of his sadness. He had believed that when she died the hardest part of the journey would be over and things would get easier but no easy passage had opened, and his grief was immense. The relief he'd anticipated was indeed present but so was the searing aloneness of separation. Although he'd prayed for her to be released from her struggle, he yearned to have her back. The two years of her illness that had seemed to move so slowly now seemed like a mere instant. Wrestling with sadness, Wes looked at the ground and shook his head.

"I just didn't expect to hurt this bad."

We both swallowed hard, allowing the silence to lengthen. I finally said, "You're standing at Lemhi Pass again Wes."

His eyes watered and he nodded in understanding. "Yep. That's it. I'm back at Lemhi Pass."

*

In 1803 the United States ended at the Mississippi River. The vast region from there to the Pacific Ocean was the subject of heated dispute. Much was claimed by European powers like France, Britain and Spain. Even Russia was eying parts of the Oregon Territory. Further complicating things was the fact that the land was already inhabited by Indian nations determined to protect their homes and families.

President Jefferson was eager to explore this territory and take it for his new nation. He'd secretly begun making arrangements to send out an expedition. His task was made easier when Napoleon Bonaparte of France agreed to sell the United States a huge swath claimed by France known as the Louisiana Territory, stretching from the western bank of the Mississippi River all the way to the Rockies.

One of Jefferson's priorities was to find a navigable water route connecting the Mississippi to the Pacific. For three centuries explorers had been searching for a waterway through or around the Americas in order to pursue trade and profit in the Orient. They called this imaginary shortcut the Northwest Passage. Preparing instructions for the expedition's leaders, Jefferson told them: "The object of your mission is to explore the Missouri river, and such principal streams of it, as, by its course and communications with the waters of the Pacific

Ocean may offer the most direct and practicable water communication across the continent for the purposes of commerce."

To head the venture he chose Meriwether Lewis, a twenty-eight-year-old fellow Virginian with plentiful experience as a woodsman. He was also Jefferson's personal secretary. For two years the President had been grooming him for this journey, giving him lessons in cartography, botany, geography, Indian diplomacy, and encouraging the young man's enthusiasm for the daunting task ahead.

With Jefferson's approval, Lewis offered joint command to William Clark, a tough, even-tempered woodsman with experience negotiating with Indians and a knack for leadership. The two had met while serving in the army and become close friends. Clark jumped at the chance to participate and the two made plans to rendezvous at Clarksville on the north bank of the Ohio River.

Despite knowing almost nothing about the territory they were about to enter, they expected to find the Northwest Passage. American ships had already charted the location of the Columbia River where it emptied into the Pacific in present-day Oregon. They were sure that the Columbia, when linked by a short portage from the headwaters of the Missouri, would provide the western flowing waterway to the ocean. The hardest part of the journey, or so they thought, would be moving against the onrushing currents of the Missouri River and ascending the mountains. After that, the westerly currents of the Columbia River would pull them effortlessly down what they expected would be a gentle mountain slope to the shores of the nearby Pacific. They had drawn a map in their mind as clear as any on paper, but it was based entirely on their imaginations.

By August of 1803 Lewis was in Pittsburgh about to guide a fifty-five foot keelboat manned by seven soldiers and a few recruits down the Ohio River. With the water level low, progress was slow. When the keelboat couldn't be rowed or poled, it had to be pulled with ropes or pushed by men standing in the water. Writer, Don Holm captures the experience, noting that it "was hot and humid that autumn. The thermometer in the cabin often reached the high eighties. Days were filled with strenuous exertions, dragging the boats over the shallow riffles and bars and rowing through water stagnant with scum and fallen leaves of buckeye, gum, and red sassafras. Frequent stops were made at river settlements, hiring and firing crew members, buying supplies, engaging teams of oxen from farmers. There was little time for sleep."

By October the group had muscled its way to Clarksville where they met up with Clark and selected nine more men from a pool of would-be volunteers. From there they headed to the confluence of the Ohio and the Mississippi, north on the Mississippi – moving boats against the current – all the way to Saint Louis. By then they realized the Herculean task they'd undertaken in challenging such powerful rivers and recruited additional hands from the military post at Kaskaskia.

Lewis and Clark set up winter camp outside Saint Louis, a city built where the Mississippi meets the mighty Missouri. They spent the next four months drilling the men into a crack team, leaving no doubt this would be a military expedition with unwavering discipline. When Lewis was not overseeing the men, buying supplies, surveying the surrounding country or writing reports, he was studying maps and speaking with those engaged in the fur trade, trying to get a picture of what lay ahead.

Saint Louis was the hub of the Missouri River trade so finding men who had traveled the river was not difficult. Few, however, had gone beyond the Platte River and none had made it to the Rockies. James Mckay had been as far as the Platte and he gave Lewis a hand drawn map of the Missouri all the way to the villages of the Mandan Indians in present-day North Dakota.

Between the Mandan villages and the Pacific was a vast unknown. But in Lewis's mind the way was clear. The Missouri continued on to the Rockies, which he believed was a single range of mountains no higher than the Alleghenies. From there, he thought, the party would find the Columbia nearby and it would take them to the Pacific, itself only a short distance, perhaps even visible from the crest of the mountains. With confidence in this map of the imagination, the explorers, now numbering forty, departed Saint Louis in the spring of 1804.

The swift current of the Missouri was fed by melting snow and they were fighting against it for every inch. Progress was slow and at times dangerous. Uprooted trees bore down on them like battering rams, combining into clumps to form floating walls that threatened to damage or capsize the boats. With the river's constant twists and turns, a day's labor often found them little distant from where they'd begun. Much time was spent in the water, pushing the keelboat and pulling on ropes. The mosquitoes were torturous; dysentery and painful boils plagued the men. Even walking along shore was dangerous as large chunks of earthen bank frequently crashed into the roiling water. Rattlesnakes were common. The heat was punishing and relented only to make way for fierce storms with blinding rain.

As if in some natural tendency toward balance, there was also an incredible abundance of plants and animals, some of which had never been seen by citizens of the United States. The crew's journals are replete with descriptions of seemingly endless flocks of birds and schools of fish. Elk, deer, antelope, and buffalo provided regular fare at meals, as did the berries, plums and cherries growing along the shore.

By August they had entered lands inhabited by the various tribes that lived along the northern plains. Jefferson had instructed Lewis and Clark to establish good relations with these nations since he hoped to gain control of the fur trade and ensure safe passage to future travelers. Beginning with the Ponca and Omaha, the expedition began holding councils as it traveled up the river. There was little variation in their methods or message. They typically began with greetings and then, with great solemnity, informed the surprised Indians that they were now on lands claimed by the United States. They impressed upon the tribes the importance and benefits of allying with the United States, handed out gifts, and provided some display meant to reflect America's military might such as firing off the cannon mounted on the keelboat.

By and large these meetings went well, although tensions almost led to bloodshed when they encountered the Teton Lakota, a powerful group of tribes closely allied with the traders of the British Northwest Company. Jefferson had singled them out as a people on whom "we wish most particularly to make a favorable impression." Though cooler heads prevailed and combat was avoided, the impression had not been favorable for either the Lakota or the expedition.

In late October, with winter coming on fast, the Corps of Discovery arrived at the Mandan villages. The Mandan, along with their friends the Hidatsa, were the pivot around which the northern fur trade revolved. They lived in two villages along the river. In summer months it was common to find traders from the British fur companies, French trappers from Canada, Spanish traders and Indians from many tribes gathered to exchange goods and supplies for pelts.

Winters were extremely harsh. The Corps built a stockade on the riverbank and for the next four months hunkered down beside the

Mandan praying for spring. As he had at Saint Louis, Lewis attempted to gain knowledge about the way ahead. Although the Mandan had never been to the Rocky Mountains, the Hidatsa had and they were happy to share what they knew. What they told Lewis fueled his hopes about a Northwest Passage. In his report to Jefferson, he wrote that the "Indians inform us that the country on the western side of this river consists of open and level plains" and that a river, which he assumed must be the Columbia was nearby and navigable to the horizon. Here, apparently, was proof that a water route to the Pacific existed.

By April the keelboat had been loaded with specimens of flora and fauna as well as maps and reports and sent back to Saint Louis with a detachment of soldiers. The main party was once again on the river, traveling west in two pirogues and six canoes dug out of cottonwood trees. Joining the group was a young Shoshone woman named Sacagewea and her infant son. As a child she'd been captured during a Hidatsa raid on her people. She was familiar with the western mountains and would act as a guide. The commanders also knew they would need horses to make the portage between the Missouri and the Columbia and that Sacagewea's people could provide them.

Without the cumbersome keelboat, the Corps made steady progress up the Missouri. In May, while scouting ahead, Lewis saw the outline of the distant Rockies, visible from hundreds of miles. Quickly his assumption that the Appalachians were the largest mountains on the continent was shattered. The Rockies rose like stone Titans, much larger than he'd imagined and he quickly realized "the difficulties which this snowy barrier would most probably throw in my way." For weeks these snow-covered behemoths would loom on the horizon, at once beckoning and foreboding.

By mid-summer the expedition was finally approaching the foot of the mountains. By then, they had struggled past the great falls of the Missouri in some of the most taxing and frustrating weeks any of them had ever experienced. When the Missouri had forked, they'd strained up the rising grade of the Jefferson River as its waters tumbled out of the hills, pushing them back at every stroke of the paddle. They'd also become uncomfortably familiar with the ferocity of enraged grizzly bears. Now they hoped they had to cross but a single chain of mountains; one last challenge before they reached the much-anticipated Columbia.

It had been over a year since they'd left Saint Louis and many of the men had expected to be on their way home by now. The impact of ongoing exertions and constant exposure to the elements was exacting a heavy toll. Lewis's medical skills, in demand for everything from eye infections to malaria, were pressed into service more than ever. Facing the great Rockies and needing every ounce of strength they could muster, the weary expedition resembled what historian Stephen Ambrose called a "walking hospital." They were sick and tired, and the Shoshone, on whose horses so much depended, were nowhere to be found.

On August 12, 1805, Lewis may have consoled himself with the thought that things would soon be easier. As he and three others scouted ahead, they were about to reach Lemhi Pass, a vantage along a mountain ridge from which they would finally be able to see westward toward the Pacific. Perhaps Lewis would even be able to see the waters of the ocean. It had been a hard trip – the arduous labor ascending the Missouri, enduring extremes of blistering heat and biting cold, the portages across rocky thickets of prickly cacti, sickness, fatigue, the relentless vigilance required in an unknown land far from home. As Lewis approached Lemhi Pass, he believed the worst was behind them. Soon the rivers would convey them forward, rather than work against them. The Pacific would emerge into view and before long they would be able to turn around and head home.

When Lewis reached the crest of the pass, however, he didn't see a sloping valley with a nearby river leading to the ocean. To his horror, as he later wrote in his journal, he saw "immense ranges of high mountains still to the west of us with their tops partially covered with snow." These were the Bitterroot Mountains, range after range stretching as far as they could see. Patrick Gass of the Corps remembered them as "the most terrible mountains I ever beheld."

There was no Northwest Passage. No river would carry them swiftly to the ocean. Winter would soon be upon them and they had no horses. The journey would be longer and harder than any had imagined.

*

There are times when the road we are on is hard and demanding. As our energies flag, we may long for a place of comfort and rest. If we can just get across the next river, scale the next summit, maybe our burdens will ease and we'll be able to cease our exertions. Though the summit may indeed bring relief, sometimes the terrain becomes more difficult. Wes's journey, like that of Lewis and Clark, would be longer and harder than he'd expected. There was no Northwest Passage through which he could quickly traverse the landscape of his grief.

"Maybe that's why I didn't go past Lemhi Pass after my first wife died," he said. "Those mountains were so damn high. It hurt just to look at them."

"But, by returning to New York, you *still* went on."

He looked at me as though his thoughts were impossible to articulate. "You know, a lot of people say Lewis had depression most of his life."

I nodded.

"I figured if he could keep going even after seeing the Bitterroots, I could go back to New York and find my way somehow."

"What about now?"

He smiled a sad smile. "Guess I'll go back to Florida."

"Find your way somehow?"

"Yeah."

"What do you think will help you do that?"

"Knowing Shirley is at peace. And that the Pacific is out there somewhere."

His return to Florida did not go well. The old routine of solitary walks and reading that had once helped him build strength and gain perspective no longer worked. He tried socializing but felt awkward. During one of our periodic telephone conversations he wondered if he was simply "running out of gas." In the listlessness of grief, he became lax about taking his medications and was eating only sporadically. He withdrew from friends and cut down on his walks. Although he'd scrupulously made sure Shirley never missed a dose of her medication, he failed to take care of himself.

About five months later I got a call from his daughter Trudy. Wes was in the hospital after a heart attack. "We're just camping out at the hospital," she said, "hoping he'll bounce back, but the doctors say he may not."

Lewis and Clark nearly died trying to find their way through the Bitterroots. Though they found the Shoshones and traded for horses, in the cold autumn shadows amid the rough snow-covered mountain terrain, game became scarce. The weakened men depleted their food

195

stores and were so hungry they killed and ate some of their precious horses. Morale plummeted along with the temperatures.

By the time they finally stumbled down into the western foothills, they were sick, battered, and near starvation. They would have perished if they hadn't met the Nez Perce Indians who protected them in their time of greatest need. Without the Nez Perce, Lewis and his men would have never been heard from again.

Several weeks after I talked with Trudy I got a phone call from Wes. He'd moved to Arizona and rented a small apartment about three miles from Trudy and her family. His voice was surprisingly strong and animated. He missed Shirley and thought about her often, but he was relieved that her suffering was over. Moreover, he was finding great joy being with his family. After taking care of Shirley for so long, he was in high demand with the great grandchildren as an "expert bath-giver." With winter descending and nearing the end of his life, he'd found safety with a friendly tribe, his tribe.

As for Lewis and Clark, after recuperating among the Nez Perce and caching some of their supplies for the return trip, they finally headed down the churning Columbia. By early November, Clark recorded in his journal, "Great joy in camp we are in view of the ocean, this great Pacific Ocean which we (have) been so long anxious to see."

Before the first pangs of another winter, the group built a stockade near the Clatsop Indians, not far from the Pacific Coast. As they ushered in the new year of 1806, many back east assumed the expedition wasn't coming back. Perhaps they had drowned, starved or frozen to death. Maybe they were killed by Indians or ambushed by French or Spanish marauders.

As soon as the Columbia was navigable that spring, the men (and Sacagewea and her child) wasted no time jumping into their canoes. Although the return trip was challenging, they knew the way, and this time the powerful Missouri River was at their backs. By autumn the Corps of Discovery was paddling in view of Saint Louis. To many, it seemed they had returned from the dead, wiser from their journeys, with many tales to tell.

Wes also had many tales to tell and he found a ready audience in his extended family. His grandchildren were fascinated by his life as a firefighter. They were also eager to learn about members of the family they would never know, like Shirley, whose stories he cherished and told with love and an eye for insightful and humorous detail. He and

Trudy even recorded a DVD in which she interviewed him about his experiences, preserving some of these stories for future generations. Like his longtime heroes, Wes had continued on from Lemhi Pass. Though the way was hard, his life had continued to hold meaning and his stories to inspire others.

The last time I heard from him was in the form of a card with a painting of a mountain swirling in green, yellow, purple and gray watercolors. The note inside was like a telegram from the other side of the mountain.

"Made it through the Bitterroots. Pacific Ocean was cold. Home at last."

The Cave You Fear to Enter

The cave you fear to enter holds the treasure that you seek.
Joseph Campbell

As humans we live in a vast sea of stories. As White and Epston put it, "Our lives are ceaselessly intertwined with narrative, with the stories we tell and hear told, those we dream or imagine or would like to tell, all of which are reworked in the story of our own lives that we narrate to ourselves."

Throughout time stories have been primary vehicles for the transmission of values, norms and ideas. Memory is preserved and spiritual traditions passed down using stories. They are foundational to our sense of individual and collective identity, inextricable with beliefs about how the world works, as well as what is and what is not possible.

The human family has a long tradition in which the telling of stories drawn from history has been a matter of cultural, communal, even sacred importance. In ancient Greece, for example, history was the subject of lyric poets who sang verse from Homer accompanied by the mystical sounds of their lyres. Though these tales were infused with myth and religion, they were taken as history and their function was to provide a moral and cultural blueprint for how to live in good times and bad. In ancient Gaelic culture bards known as the *Seanchaithe* wove history into stories intended to touch deep inner chords resonant with any in that culture and beyond. In the oral cultures of Native America, Osceola and Black Elk grew up hearing stories about their histories which introduced them to heroes, illuminated spirituality, cosmology and connected them to their ancestors.

Joseph Campbell, the well-known scholar of comparative mythology, spent his life studying myths, legends and sacred stories from the world's traditions. He found that these stories exhibit universal patterns and themes, what Jung called archetypes, such as redemption, birth and rebirth, facing death, overcoming fear or connecting with transcendent realms of experience.

Perhaps the most common pattern identified by Campbell is what he called the "hero's journey" in which a hero is invited, compelled, thrust or pushed beyond the threshold of normal experience onto a difficult and frightening journey of transformation. A journey often preceded or precipitated by a crisis of some sort. Along the way trials are faced, strengths revealed, power, perspective and wisdom acquired.

Though the world's stories and myths often paint such heroes in colors that are larger than life, Campbell's insight was that such a hero resides in every one of us. This journey across the threshold need not involve the literal facing of monsters, bringing back physical treasures or exhibiting supernatural powers. It may be an inward journey precipitated by a struggle with illness or the loss of a loved one. The monsters faced may be those of doubt or fear, the powers acquired may be inward peace, acceptance or the power of forgiveness.

Ultimately, Campbell tells us, the hero's journey is really about an inward shift, learning new ways of seeing the world, ourselves, and new ways of being. As he put it, the journey is about "transformations of consciousness."

For those facing their own mortality or the death of a loved one the outer world of events and inner world of subjective experience can shift suddenly and radically. This is what happened to Robert in Chapter One when he hurt his back, took disability leave from work then wound up serving as caregiver for his mother as she was dying. The experience shattered familiar routines, assumptions and expectations about the world, the future, and his sense of identity. It pushed him across the threshold of normal roles and events, requiring strengths he didn't know he had and changing his perspective in fundamental ways.

Gerta's world (Chapter Thirteen) shattered when Bill died and, as is so often the case, she was pushed across the threshold of normality against her will. The disorientation, anger and fear with which she struggled underscore how Campbell's use of the word "journey" should be understood. These are not winsome trips through a prosaic countryside and there are no assurances of an inevitable happily-ever-after. These journeys can unearth our deepest fears and, as with Paul in Chapter Six, penetrate our most entrenched defenses.

And things don't always go the way a hero hopes they will. Not every hero returns to tell the tale. In Chapter Ten, Hap's tremendous determination to live was, in the final analysis, no match for the ravages of AIDS. But it was those ravages which allowed him to shift from self-judgment to forgiveness and acceptance, and which helped him glimpse beyond his suffering into a larger unseen world before he died.

One of the most common images in this hero's journey involves descending, metaphorically, into the underworld – sometimes seen as the land of the dead, Hell or a dark place of danger – and returning changed by the experience.

Though there are multiple reasons such descents may occur when they appear in mythic stories (compulsion, seeking knowledge or information, to complete some task) it is often done to connect with, bring back or deliver a message to a loved one who has died or been taken into this underworld place. In Greek mythology for example, Orpheus descends into the land of Hades in order to retrieve his love Eurydice. In the mythic stories of India, Savitri follows her deceased husband to the underworld and confronts Yama, Lord of the Dead, in order to bring him back. Among the Iroquois, Sayadio goes to the land of the dead and retrieves his sister's spirit with the help of a magic rattle.

The reader might object that such stories are far too dramatic and fanciful to have anything to do with ordinary humans or the history stories we have considered. But the point of such stories and archetypes is that they speak metaphorically to the ways such things *are* a universal part of everyone's experience. Ordinary people map their way through the dark paths of the underworld every day.

Shaun, for example, had been a corpsman during the Vietnam War serving with a unit which saw much combat and suffered many deaths (a corpsman is what Marines call a Medic). When we met he was carrying a great deal of emotional and psychological pain. He also had undisclosed grief for buddies who had been killed. For decades he'd been haunted by what he called "the voices," intrusive memories of words, screams and other sounds friends had made just before dying.

He'd rarely spoken about these voices, fearing others wouldn't take him seriously to would think he was nuts. I asked if he wanted to talk about one or more of the voices. Maybe we could find a way to bring some peace. He wasn't sure.

His caution was understandable and realistic. In psychological terms he was experiencing effects of severe post-traumatic stress disorder with occasional states of emotional flooding (being overwhelmed by intense emotions) and acute anxiety. There was much to be said for backing off or, at very least, moving cautiously.

On the other hand, he was suffering. So I nudged him. By then he'd told me about his interest in the Underground Railroad, one of the hubs of which had been his hometown of Syracuse, New York. The "railroad" was a pre-Civil War network of safe houses, "conductors" and allies who assisted escaped slaves on their way north, either with an eye toward disappearing into one of the cities or getting across the border into Canada and freedom.

I reminded him about Harriet Tubman, who had escaped from slavery in 1849. Rather than remain in the North and attempt to hide, she chose to return to the South, the place of her deepest pain and trauma, in order to lead others to freedom. I suggested that sometimes, in order to become free from the bondage of one's deepest pain, one needs to descend into that pain.

The metaphor was springboard into an exploration of what it had been like for him to be a twenty-year-old corpsman in the middle of firefights where several buddies might be wounded simultaneously, often in unspeakably horrible ways. We spent time talking about each of the voices he'd been hearing (it turned out there were seven). He remembered each of his friends whose voices still haunted, told their story, gave thanks for their friendship, asked forgiveness for his inability to save them and told them he was sorry he'd returned home without them.

After the last voice had been summoned, its story told, Shaun reported a sense of peace. In the time remaining, although he still had vivid memories of each death, they no longer intruded or were triggered against his will. In an archetypal sense, he had gone into the underworld – in this case a literal land of the dead – and released these memories from the darkness, bringing them to the surface and freeing them. In so doing, he freed himself to begin grieving for the friends he had lost and for the savage brutality he had witnessed.

All of the stories recounted in the foregoing chapters have traces of this hero's journey. Many include moments descending into the underworld, acknowledging and facing fears, doubts or the past, then returning more whole, having gained a measure of peace and insight.

Moments pointing toward transformation are often subtle and less dramatic than Meriwether Lewis peering across the vistas at Lemhi Pass or the lifesavers at Pea Island rescuing travelers teetering on the brink of death. Transformation may be as simple and profound as Luke in Chapter Four shifting inwardly toward an affirmation of the life he had lived rather than its renunciation. There is a moment of transformation when Frances (Chapter Seven) decides to call her daughter Martha come what may. Such moments have the power to alter one's life (and death) in ways which are as profound as any mythic story or archetypal tale of trial and enchantment. And such accomplishments, in spiritual and psychological terms, surpass the accomplishment of Roebling's great bridge.

Of course there are other reasons to offer stories as we have seen. They may simply entertain, distract or bring a moment of joy. They may express care, cultivate insight, connect one to a place of inner strength or create a sense of warmth and connection between the one telling the story and the one listening. For those who grew up in families where stories were told, perhaps the proverbial bedtime story, listening again to stories when one is bedridden may conjure positive feelings, associations and memories.

In a larger sense though, stories, such as the ones we have drawn from American history, provide a bridge into the deep layers of consciousness. When they hit the right chord they can even change inner stories – the ones we constantly tell ourselves and which are often laced with unconscious assumptions and beliefs.

Indeed, it is upon this interior landscape that much of a person's last days may be spent. The grasping and allure of the outer world can quickly fade as roles and responsibilities are lost, energy fades and activities narrow. Big questions of a spiritual, moral and existential nature may arise. Life's deepest, sometimes simplest priorities may be discovered or remembered.

As we find ourselves distilled down to our inner voices, perhaps the voice of our deepest self, and as all things fade but love, memory, relationships, and the present moment, a good story can put us in the company of kindred spirits who accompany us as we trek across difficult and frightening terrain. "For," as Joseph Campbell reminds us, "we have not even to risk the adventure alone, for the heroes of all time have gone before us." It may be that in the hidden wisdom of a simple story we may connect with the hero within, face our dragons, affirm our relationships and find our way in times of adversity.

Bibliography

Ambrose, Stephen, *Undaunted Courage, Meriwether Lewis, Thomas Jefferson, and the Opening of the American West* (New York: Simon and Schuster, 1996).

Boyer, Paul and Stephen Nissenbaum, *Salem Possessed: The Social Origins of Witchcraft* (Cambridge: Harvard University Press, 1974).

Brach, Tara, *Radical Acceptance: Embracing Your Life with the Heart of a Buddha* (New York, Banton, 2003).

Brands, H. W., *The Age of Gold: The California Gold Rush and the New American Dream* (New York: Doubleday, 2002).

Brown, Dee, *Bury My Heart at Wounded Knee: An Indian History of the American West* (New York: Holt, Rinehart and Winston, 1972).

Brown, Dee, *The American West* (New York: Simon and Schuster, 1994).

Cabeza de Vaca, Alvar Nunez, (Enrique Pupo-Walker, ed.) *Castaways: The Narrative of Alvar Nunez Cabeza De Vaca* (Berkeley: University of California Press, 1993).

Calef, Robert, "Witchcraft in New England," in *America: Great Crises in Our History Told by its Makers, A Library of Original Sources*, vol. 2 (Chicago: Americanization Department, Veterans of Foreign Wars of the United States, 1925).

Campbell, Joseph, *The Power of Myth* (New York: Doubleday, 1988).

Cappon, Stanley (ed), *The Adams-Jefferson Letters: The Complete Correspondence Between Thomas Jefferson and Abigail and John Adams* (North Carolina: University of North Carolina Press, 1987).

Chase, Owen, *The Wreck of the Whaleship Essex* (New York: Harcourt, Brace, and Co., 1999).

Colton, Walter, "The Discovery of Gold in California" in *America: Great Crises In Our History Told by Its Makers, A library of Original Sources*, vol. 7 (Chicago: Americanization Department, Veterans of Foreign Wars of the United States, 1925).

Davidson, James and Mark Lytle, *After the Fact: The Art of Historic Detection*, vol. 1 (New York: Alfred Knopf, 1982).

Delaney, Frank, *Ireland* (New York: HarperCollins, 2005).

DeVoto, Bernard (ed.), *The Journals of Lewis and Clark* (Boston: Houghton Mifflin Company, 1953).

DeVoto, Bernard, *Across the Wide Missouri* (Boston: Houghton Mifflin Company, 1998).

Dolnick, Edward, *Down the Great Unknown: John Wesley Powell's 1869 Journey of Discovery and Tragedy Through the Grand Canyon* (New York: HarperCollins, 2001).

Duncan, David, *Hernando de Soto: A Savage Quest in the Americas* (Norman: University of Oklahoma Press, 1996).

Ehle, John, *The Trail of Tears: The Rise and Fall of the Cherokee Nation* (New York: Doubleday, 1988).

Ellis, Joseph, *Founding Brothers: The Revolutionary Generation* (New York: Random House, 2002).

Gilbert, Bil, *The Old West: The Trailblazers* (New York: Times-Life Books, 1973).

Gowans, Fred, *Rocky Mountain Rendezvous: A History of the Fur Trade Rendezvous, 1825-1840* (Utah: Peregrine Smith Books, 1985).

Hartley, William and Ellen Hartley, *Osceola: The Unconquered Indian* (New York: Hawthorn Books, 1973).

Hine, Robert and John Faragher, *The American West: A New Interpretive History* (Connecticut: Yale University Press, 2000).

Holliday, J. S., *The World Rushed in: The California Gold Rush Experience* (New York: Simon and Schuster, 1981).

Holm, Don, "Westward With Lewis and Clark: The Great American Adventure," in *Water Trails West: The Western Writers of America*, Donald Duke (ed.) (New York: Avon Books, 1978).

Jackson, Andrew, "Jackson's Defeat of the Creeks: His Official Report," in *America: Great Crises in Our History Told by its Makers, A Library of Original Sources*, vol. 5 (Chicago: Americanization Department, Veterans of Foreign Wars of the United States, 1925).

Jackson, Andrew, "After The Battle of the Horse Shoe General Jackson Made the Following Address to the Army, March 28, 1814," in *America: Great Crises in Our History Told by its Makers, A Library of Original Sources*, vol. 5 (Chicago: Americanization Department, Veterans of Foreign Wars of the United States, 1925).

Karlsen, Carol, *The Devil in the Shape of a Woman: Witchcraft in Colonial New England* (New York: Random House, 1987).

Koch, Adrienne and William Peden (eds), *The Life and Selected Writings of Thomas Jefferson* (New York: Random House, 1972).

Leckie, Robert, *George Washington's War: The Saga of the American Revolution* (New York: HarperCollins, 1992).

Leckie, Robert, *From Sea To Shining Sea: From the War of 1812 to the Mexican War, the Saga of America's Expansion* (New York: HarperCollins, 1993).

Levin, David (ed.), *What Happened in Salem?* (New York: Harcourt, Brace and World, Inc., 1960).

McCullough, David, *Mornings on Horseback: The Story of an Extraordinary Family, A Vanished Way of Life, and the Unique Child Who Became Theodore Roosevelt* (New York: Touchstone, 1981).

McCullough, David, *The Great Bridge: The Epic Story of the Building of the Brooklyn Bridge* (New York: Simon and Schuster, 1982).

McCullough, David, *John Adams* (New York: Simon and Schuster, 2001).

Neihardt, John (ed.), *Black Elk Speaks: Being the Life Story of a Holy Man of the Oglala Sioux* (New York: Simon and Schuster, 1972).

Norton, Mary B., *In The Devil's Snare: The Salem Witchcraft Crisis of 1692* (New York: Alfred Knopf, 2002).

Philbrick, Nathaniel, *In the Heart of the Sea: The Tragedy of the Whaleship Essex* (New York: Penguin Books, 2001).

Powell, John W., *The Exploration of the Colorado River and its Canyons* (New York: Dover Publications, 1961).

Schwartz, Richard, *Internal Family Systems Therapy* ((New York: Guilford Press, 1995).

Slocum, Joshua, *Sailing Alone Around the World* (New York: Barnes and Noble, Inc., 2000).

Spencer, Ann, *Alone at Sea: The Adventures of Joshua Slocum* (Buffalo, New York: Firefly Books, Ltd., 1999).

Steltenkamp, Michael, *Black Elk: Holy Man of the Oglala* (Oklahoma: University of Oklahoma Press, 1993).

Utley, Robert, *The Lance and The Shield: The Life and Times of Sitting Bull* (New York: Random House, 1993).

Ward, Geoffery, *The West: An Illustrated History* (New York: Little, Brown, and Company, 1996).

White, Michael and David Epston, *Narrative Means to Therapeutic Ends* (New York: Norton & Company, 1990):

Wright, David and David Zoby, *Fire on the Beach: Recovering the Lost Story of Richard Etheridge and the Pea Island Lifesavers* (New York: Scribner, 2,000).

Wright, Leitch, *Creeks and Seminoles* (Nebraska: University of Nebraska Press, 1986).

Zinn, Howard, *A People's History of the United States* (New York: HarperCollins, 1980).

Notes

Introduction
"The light has": McCullough, *Mornings on Horseback*, 287. Roosevelt's mother died from typhoid, his wife
    from Bright's disease: an acute inflammation of the kidneys.
"more than any": McCullough, *Mornings on Horseback*, 330.

Chapter One–Child of the Sun
"besides great fatigue": Cabeza de Vaca, 20.
"caulked with palmetto": Cabeza de Vaca, 29.
"Everywhere I went": Cabeza de Vaca, 52.
"all the people": Cabeza de Vaca, 108.
"They went on": Cabeza de Vaca, 110.
"we cured the": Cabeza de Vaca, 114.
"For the rest": Duncan, 218.

Chapter Two–Days of Forty-Nine
"the blacksmith dropped": Colton, 115.
"would make your": Holliday, 146.
"abundant and unmerciful": Holliday, 161.
"you will shed": Holliday, 291.
"without tents, many": Holliday, 313-14.
"traverse the same": Holliday, 361.

Chapter Three–Navigating the Strait
"sleep in the": Spencer, 92-93.
"drifting into loneliness": Slocum, 51.
"blowing a gale": Slocum, 95, 97.
"worth more than": Slocum, 99.
"compressed gales of": Slocum, 100.
"plunged into the": Slocum, 106.
"Any landsman seeing": Spencer, 128.
"than others that": Slocum, 132.

Chapter Four–Innocents on Witch's Hill
"foolish, ridiculous speeches": Norton, 20.
"Q. Sarah Good what": Levin, 4.
"her master did": Calef, 282.
"struck with consternation": Norton, 64.
"a very critical": Norton, 213.
"long train of": Norton, 213.
"persons of good": Norton, 216-17.
"I am no": Boyer and Nissenbaum, 7-8.
"Those who were": Davidson and Lytle, 33.
"he would not": Levin, 62.
"though the confessing": Calef, 285.
"it seemed to": Calef, 283.
"I petition your": Boyer and Nissenbaum, 8.
"several persons who": Karlsen, 41.

Chapter Five–Adrift in the Pacific
"came down upon": Chase, 11.
"tenfold fury and": Chase, 12.
"wandered around in": Chase, 20.
"it were possible": Philbrick, 103.
"violence of raving": Chase, 37.
"our suffering became": Philbrick, 125.

"Our suffering during": Chase, 49.
"Their physical torments": Philbrick, 133-34.
"Never have my": Philbrick, 135.
"Our bodies had": Chase, 56.
"either feed our": Chase, 71.
"were so feeble": Philbrick, 177.
"Our sufferings were": Chase, 78-79.

Chapter Six–Behind the Walls of Tohpeka
"vermilion war clubs": Ehle, 104.
"Determined to exterminate": Jackson, *Jackson's Defeat of the Creeks: His Official Report*, 238.
"It is difficult": Jackson, *Jackson's Defeat of the Creeks: His Official Report*, 237.
"Their walls became": Jackson, *After the Battle of the Horse Shoe General Jackson made the Following Address to the Army*, March 28, 1814, 240.
"Five hundred fifty": Ehle, 120.

Chapter Seven–Jefferson and Adams
"fighting fearlessly for": McCullough, *John Adams*, 135.
"hang together, or": Leckie, *George Washington's War*, 256.
"gives me great": Cappon, 13.
"appeared to me": McCullough, *John Adams*, 311.
"I shall part": McCullough, *John Adams*, 329.
"The departure of": Cappon, 23.
"one of the": Cappon, 177.
"in terms of": Ellis, 16.
"This letter": McCullough, *John Adams*, 600.
"not fail to": Ellis, 221.
"I have ardently": Cappon, 285.
"second [Rush's] efforts": Koch, 612.
"suspended for one": Cappon, 292.
"separation cannot be": McCullough, *John Adams*, 624.
"must expect that": Ellis, 226.
"Thomas Jefferson survives": McCullough, *John Adams*, 646.

Chapter Eight–Mountain Man Rendezvous
"make my living": Gilbert, 72.
"an anthill until": Morgan, 139.
"Why do you": DeVoto, *Across the Wide Missouri*, 159.
"a species of": Gowans, 156.
"solitude had given": DeVoto, *Across the Wide Missouri*, 44.
"the arrival of": Gowans, p. 30.

Chapter Nine–Rescue Line
"Robert Tolar discovered": Wright and Zoby, 227.
"From the moment": Wright and Zoby, 284.
"Although it seemed": Wright and Zoby, 294.
"Keeper Richard Ethridge": Wright and Zoby, 297.

Chapter Ten–Death of a Warrior
"This, you may": Wright, 275.
"I had not": Zinn, 143-44.
"the greater portion": Hine and Faragher, 180.
"seemed to be": Hartley and Hartley, 247.
"shook hands with": Hartley and Hartley, 247.
"He made a": Hartley and Hartley, 248.

Building the Brooklyn Bridge

"The completed work": McCullogh, *The Great Bridge*, 27.
"Before the accident": McCullough, *The Great Bridge*, 100.
"was of a": McCullough, *The Great Bridge*, 195.
"good enough to": McCullough, *The Great Bridge*, 316.
"could never have": McCullough, *The Great Bridge*, 329.
"At first I": McCullough, *The Great Bridge*, 452.
"I have carried": McCullough, *The Great Bridge*, 371.
"unsubstantial fabric of": McCullough, *The Great Bridge*, 486.
"has been for": McCullough, *The Great Bridge*, 492.
"Mrs. Roebling elevated": McCullough, *The Great Bridge*, 518.
"Long ago I": McCullough, *The Great Bridge*, 560.
"I don't know": McCullough, *The Great Bridge*, 519.

Chapter Twelve–The Nation's Hoop is Broken

"like some fearful": Neihardt, 7.
"every one was": Neihardt, 7.
"The Great Spirit": Hine and Faragher, 251.
"No white person": Brown, *Bury My heart at Wounded Knee*, 261.
"I was out": Neihardt, 15.
"headfirst like": Neihardt, 16.
"the voices would": Neihardt, 17.
"white clouds were": Neihardt, 19.
"the Powers of": Neihardt, 21.
"nation on the": Neihardt,. 25.
"I saw that": Neihardt, 36.
"I was sad": Neihardt,.39.
"Your boy there": Neihardt, 41.
"sacred and incomprehensible": Utley, 26.
"I thought of": Neihardt, 89-90.
"I stayed there": Neihardt, 92-93.
"I wondered": Neihardt, 116.
"All our people": Neidhardt, 181-82.
"I went up": Brown, *The American West*, 365.
"I did not": Neihardt, 230.
"a pitiful old": Neihardt, 230.
"Again, and maybe": Neihardt, 233.
"We who listened": Neihardt, 233.
"world where there": Neihardt, 71.
"I am old": Steltenkamp, 128.
"was just one": Steltenkamp, 132.

Chapter Thirteen–Canyon of Desolation

"bold enough": Dolnick, 51.
"staunch and firm": Powell, 119.
"We knew nothing": Dolnick, 24.
"untried as we": Powell, 134.
"the wildest rapid": Dolnick, 62
"Our rations are": Dolnick, 98.
"There is nothing": Dolnick, 98.
"minded to call": Powell, 191.
"We start up": Powell, 168. In his published account of this episode for *Scribner's* magazine, and in *The Exploration of the Colorado River and its Canyons*, Powell places this event at Steamboat Rock, rather than Desolation Canyon. Dolnick suggests this may have been to highlight the incident's drama.

Chapter Fourteen–Standing at Lemhi Pass

"The object of": Ward, 37.
"was hot and": Holm, 85.

"we wish most": Ambrose, 154.

"Indians inform us": Ambrose, 209.

"the difficulties which": DeVoto, *The Journals of Lewis and Clark*, 118.

"walking hospital": Ambrose, 261.

"immense ranges of": DeVoto, *The Journals of Lewis and Clark*, 189.

"the most terrible": Ambrose, 291.

"Great joy in": DeVoto, *The Journals of Lewis and Clark*, 279. It turned out that Clark was mistaken. He was actually seeing the vast sound that leads into the Pacific Ocean, rather than the ocean itself.

The Cave You Fear to Enter

"Our lives are": White and Epston, 19-80.

"transformations in consciousness": Campbell, 126.

"For we have": Campbell, 125.

Scott Janssen is a hospice counselor and educator with decades of experience serving people who are dying and their loved ones. He is also a historian who often weaves stories from America's past into his work with patients and families. His other books include the novel *Light Keepers*, a metaphysical adventure set along the North Carolina coast in the aftermath of the Civil War. For more on Scott's writing please visit: jscottjanssen.com.

Made in the USA
Columbia, SC
28 September 2017